I am so glad Maria Mies has written

T0294272

has been a courageous thinker and tl ...l
why. Maria has carried the village in her mind and heart, taking this other
imagination to an alienated and uprooted world. Her rootedness has given
her the conceptual clarity most academics lack. And it is this clarity
which is a gift to the world. It has definitely been a gift to me.

—Vandana Shiva, Winner Right Livelihood Award and Sydney
Peace Prize, author of *Staying Alive* and *Soil Not Oil*

A beautiful journey between two remote poles: The Self and the World.
The subtle connection between facts and fiction, autobiography and
novel, between the personal, the political, the economic, the historical,
the global and local. This book by Maria Mies is inspiring and creative.

—Nawal El Saadawi, Egyptian feminist and physician, author of
The Hidden Face of Eve and *A Daughter of Isis*

The Village and the World by Maria Mies, one of the world's great feminist
philosophers and visionary voices over the last four decades, offers us far
more than personal autobiography. This beautifully expressed work
delivers an inspiring personal and political odyssey across half a century's
geopolitical landscape. A wonderful book and I highly recommend it
to all students of these challenging times.

—Jerry Mander, Founder, International Forum on Globalization;
author, *In the Absence of the Sacred*, and *The Case Against the
Global Economy*, USA

Knowing Maria Mies, her crystal clear intelligence, her enormous
importance for and in social movements worldwide, I nevertheless was
astonished by the clarity of the thread running through her story:
Maria's story is a true love story of knowledge. Today, everybody can
see that capitalist patriarchy is obviously destroying the world instead
of developing it. Maria Mies has foreseen it. It is now time for us to act
immediately.

—Prof. Dr. Claudia von Werlhof, Department of Political Science,
University of Innsbruck, Austria, co-editor *There is an Alternative*

Readers will be gifted with a history of transformation of a woman – from a village girl to a student in town; a learner to a scholar; from social fieldwork to political activism and feminism. Maria's life is unique and she is indispensable for present and future generations of feminists.

    —Farida Akhter, FINRRAGE and UBINIG, author of
       Depopulating Bangladesh and *Seeds of Movements*

Maria Mies ties together her many years of experience, her life's work, into one, big, exciting, self-aware and humorous bow.

    —Richard Pestemer, *Tacheles Regional*, philosopher and
       journalist, Germany

An exciting book that doesn't just tell her life story, but also conveys an important point of time and women's history.

    —*Virginia* Germany

Maria Mies has written a personal story that will encourage others to fight for the 'good life'.

    —Barbara Linnenbrügger, *Beziehungsweise Weiterdenken*, author
       and activist, Germany

Maria Mies writes against forgetting and romanticising the past. She is a wonderful storyteller. Her memoir offers countless new perspectives. *The Village and the World* encourages social activism, a passion for down-to-earth research and comes to the conclusion that encouragement is the first step for change.

    —Elisabeth Loibl, Federation for Agricultural Concerns,
       Vienna/FemBio.org, Austria

MARIA MIES is a German feminist activist scholar who lives in Cologne. She is the author of numerous groundbreaking works on women and globalisation. She has worked at the Goethe Institute in India, conducted fieldwork in Andra Pradesh and was the founding director of the Masters in Women and Development at the Institute of Social Studies in The Hague in the Netherlands. She is Professor Emerita at the University of Applied Sciences (Fachhochschule) in Cologne.

She has always combined activism and scholarship and was central to establishing the first shelter for battered women in Cologne. Maria Mies has been involved in resistance to genetic engineering and reproductive technologies, the fight against the Multilateral Agreement on Investment (MAI), against the General Agreement on Trade in Services (GATS) and on issues of food security, all fundamental components of corporate globalisation. She is known around the world for the concept of 'housewifisation' and her writings on ecofeminism.

Other books by Maria Mies:

Indian Women and Patriarchy (1980)

Feminism in Europe: Liberal and Socialist Strategies 1789–1919 (1981)

The Lace Makers of Narsapur: Indian Housewives Produce for the World Market (1982)

National Liberation and Women's Liberation (1982, with Rhoda Reddock)

Fighting on Two Fronts. Women's Struggles and Research (1982)

Patriarchy and Accumulation on a World Scale: Women in the International Division of Labour (1986/1999)

Women: The Last Colony (1988, with Veronika Bennholdt-Thomsen and Claudia von Werlhof)

Ecofeminism (1993, with Vandana Shiva)

The Subsistence Perspective: Beyond the Globalised Economy (1999, with Veronika Bennholdt-Thomsen)

The Village and the World
My Life, Our Times

Maria Mies

Translated by Madeline Ferretti-Theilig

First published in English by Spinifex Press, Australia 2010
German edition first published by PapyRossa Verlag Köln, 2008

Spinifex Press Pty Ltd
504 Queensberry St
North Melbourne, Victoria 3051
Australia
women@spinifexpress.com.au
www.spinifexpress.com.au

© Maria Mies, 2010
© Translation: Spinifex Press, 2010

All rights reserved. Without limiting the rights under copyright reserved above, no part of this publication may be reproduced, stored in or introduced into a retrieval system, or transmitted, in any form or by any means (electronic, mechanical, photocopying, recording or otherwise) without prior written permission of both the copyright owner and the above publisher of the book.

Copying for educational purposes
Information in this book may be reproduced in whole or part for study or training purposes, subject to acknowledgement of the source and providing no commercial usage or sale of material occurs. Where copies of part or whole of the book are made under part VB of the Copyright Act, the law requires that prescribed procedures be followed. For information contact the Copyright Agency Limited.

Cover design by Deb Snibson, MAPG
Typset in Fairfield Light by Claire Warren
Printed by McPherson's Printing Group

National Library of Australia Cataloguing-in-Publication entry (pbk)

Author: Mies, Maria.

Title: The village and the world : my life, our times / Maria Mies.

ISBN: 9781876756826 (pbk.)
ISBN: 9781742193878 (DXReader)

Notes: Includes bibliographical references and index.

Subjects: Mies, Maria.
Feminists—Germany—Biography.
Sociologists—Germany—Biography.
Women sociologists—Biography.
Women social reformers—Germany—Biography.
Women political activists—Germany—Biography.
Ecofeminism—Developing countries.

Dewey Number: 305.42092

PEFC
PEFC/21-31-16

Contents

Preface

Tabo Didi, a fellow who did not conform to the norms of our village, once said, "It isn't easy being human!" I have never forgotten this philosophical adage.

It is not easy to pack seventy-seven years of my life between the two covers of a book, especially when this life was lived between two such remote poles as the *village* and the *world*. Tabo Didi said, "I have seen the whole world! I have been to the district of Prüm. I have been to the district of Daun and I have even been to Neuerburg Castle!" This was the world for him. Likewise, for my mother, the world was our village that she left only occasionally, mostly when she was expecting another baby.

However, this small world was not enough for me. Throughout my life, I felt drawn to the *big wide world*, despite my perennial homesickness.

During the writing of this book one of my friends asked me, "Why are you writing the story of your life yourself? Couldn't someone else do it? And do it later, when you are dead? Why now? And what for? Isn't it narcissistic and nostalgic?"

"No," I replied, "I have to tell and write the story of my life and my times myself." Only I know how it was all interconnected and interrelated: the village and the world. What's in the book is not the whole of my story, nor does it necessarily follow a chronological order. These are *stories* that particularly matter to me. Stories in which my life took a new direction, when something special happened to me. Stories about when I, mostly with others, was able to get something to happen, or make a difference. These are stories about times when

I gained new experiences, acquired new knowledge – and changed myself.

But these are also stories from a time when the world changed so rapidly and so profoundly as perhaps never before.

I am telling these stories myself because I do not want anyone else to write them down. Others know only fragments and would interpret them according to their own understanding and their own liking. That's not what I want to happen. In my opinion, there is no such thing as an 'objective' historical record. Years ago, with my students, I coined the phrase, "We write our history while we are making it."

We followed this principle when we fought for the first autonomous women's shelter for battered women in Cologne. We documented the history of our movement and published reports every year. I also followed this advice in Holland, with my women students from the so-called Third World, when we established the 'Women and Development' programme. I continued to follow this important principle throughout my practical and theoretical work, as well as in my teaching.

I do not want our struggles, our successes and our failures to be totally forgotten. But I also wrote these stories down for all those people who fought with us against violence, oppression and exploitation in general.

But why today, or at all?

I write against oblivion

It has never been more imperative to maintain a *vital connectedness* between yesterday, today, and tomorrow in the minds and hearts of every individual. Today, all memory of the existence of the people before us who made history is being destroyed. Not only in Europe, but all over the world. My life stories are not the stories of those who rule, nor of uninvolved spectators. They are stories about myself and other people whom I met during the course of my life, even if they have long since died. I hope they are useful stories and will continue to help myself and others to fight for the 'good life'.

These stories occur within a real geographical, political, and historical context. They are not *virtual* stories to be looked at on computer screens: seen today, forgotten tomorrow.

I belong to a generation who personally experienced how the Nazi era began, how World War II started, how the nightmare of the 'Third Reich' collapsed miserably and pulled millions of people down into its abyss. We also experienced the reconstruction after the war. Our mothers were the 'rubble women' who cleared the layers of debris and enabled 'life to carry on'.

I myself experienced the time after World War II as a new beginning, hoping for a really new and better world. The time between 1945 and the founding of the Federal Republic was an interim period. It was a fantastic time. Everything was at its beginning, everything seemed possible. I left my village during these years and went out into the 'world'. It was fortunate that I, a village girl, had the chance to enjoy higher education, that we had teachers who had confidence in us and filled us with enthusiasm. In every respect, they stimulated our creativity. Learning was not about competition and individual effort. We were taught about intellectual freedom, collectivity, international understanding, critical thinking. I discovered the world, love, and myself during these years. It felt like a miracle to me. I could do what I had always wanted to do. I wanted to become an artist. My teachers supported me in this ambition.

Today, such a school is hard to imagine

I wish all young people could today experience such a school and such inspired, and inspiring, teachers. But the twenty-first century is different. During the course of my life, I had to learn that what is possible at a certain time may no longer be possible later on. The important thing is to do what is possible and feels right at a specific point in time. *Carpe diem* was our motto in those days.

Of course, as in every life, there were not only 'high points': there were low points and 'grey times' that had to be endured. But consciously – unconsciously, I have followed a certain *Leitmotif* throughout my life. Naturally, I could not achieve all I set out to do. But this central theme has led me to many places, to many people, and provided many experiences, struggles, victories as well as defeats, that I could never have dreamed of when I started out. In retrospect, my life appears to me like a meandering river which started out as a small stream in the mountains of the volcanic Eifel. The stream eventually collected more waters, grew broader and broader, and branched out into a huge network that now encompasses the whole world. This river did not always flow straight ahead. It followed curves and bends, and sometimes appeared to flow backwards or to stop completely, like a stagnant pool. At every watershed, at every bend, the river had to decide where to go next.

The title of my book *The Village and the World* expresses the general direction of this river, the tension between the here and there, between home and the world, the unknown and the familiar. Often, this tension was a balancing act that cost much strength and energy. But at the same time it was an extraordinary opportunity to see and understand the world from at least two different sides. It created the necessary distance to discover the self in what is foreign, and what is foreign in one's self. This was an exhilarating experience. It has given me the courage to repeatedly start out to new shores, reach for new horizons, and gather new experiences. I could not have experienced this life if I had remained settled in one place. Oscillating between the two worlds provided me with the opportunity to realise that what happened in one country was not the whole story. From this vantage point I could put into perspective many things, especially self-centered nationalism and patriotism. Whoever can see the internal from the outside, and the external from the inside, can no longer take many things so seriously.

Narcissism?

Yes indeed, I confess that I do like myself and think that my life has been – and is – really interesting. I have never known feelings of guilt or fear. As well as that, as a farmer's child, I have never had an inferiority complex. I owe this to my parents who never put pressure on us children to obtain outstanding marks at school, or to 'catch up with the Joneses'. They were, in fact, not even interested in our school reports. We were good enough for them as we were. They never thought that we should be something 'better' later on. They were just peasants, not upwardly mobile. I am eternally grateful to them that they did not have any ambitions for us.

During my youth, my fantastic teachers promoted this self-confidence and opened my eyes to what existed outside my village: the world, literature, foreign languages, philosophy, and politics. But what made me set out into the far away world was the love for a foreigner, a sailor from Pakistan. I have learned almost all I know today from this love story.

This love story was the reason that I became an internationalist very early on, and then discovered Marxism. The eleventh thesis on Feuerbach from *The German Ideology*, "the philosophers have only interpreted the world in various ways; the point is to change it", has remained my motto to this day. Love taught me that the other/the others are not 'hell' as Sartre thought. On the contrary, I believe they represent the diversity and abundance of life. However, I also learned about the barriers that very old power systems have set up: the patriarchal domination of men over women, of capitalists over the working classes, of the colonialists over the colonised, and, finally, of humans over nature.

The advice, "the point is to change it" was the impulse not only to *analyse* and *describe* these barriers, but to fight them as an *activist scholar*.

Despite all my travels around the world, I have never forgotten where I came from: from a peasant family in a small village. This not only helped me keep my feet on the ground, but also protected me from excessive romanticism and quixotic idealism. I know that food doesn't come from the supermarket but from the soil. My origins have made me immune to the promises of industrial society and capitalism. Nowhere have these promises managed to provide the 'good life', neither in the globalised village nor in the globalised world. My life has taught me that *subsistence* in the village and in the world probably provides the only hope to maintain life on this planet nowadays and into the future.

Nostalgia?

Yes, nostalgia has also made me write this book. Nostalgia does not mean glorifying the past. Instead it is the recollection that life was once better than it is today, despite all the progress and the abundance of goods in the supermarkets. Today, many children do not have a happy childhood, many adolescents have no prospects for the future, many adults know only anxiety and stress, and many pensioners only illness and loneliness.

I also know that another world is possible, because I know that a better world has existed in the past, and another world has already begun.

For this reason, I do not just look back at the past with nostalgia, but also into the future with anger.

Finally, I hope for myself and all of humankind that we can say at the end of our lives what my mother said, when she looked back on her life, "Wasn't that a good life? It was a lot of work, but then I enjoyed working."

1

Home

The Region

The notion of 'home'[1] provokes different feelings and memories in different people. When I think of 'home' I do not just, or primarily, think of my family or our house but of the area in which our village lies, of the volcanic hills in the Eifel region of Germany, of its broad horizon and its forests.

Auel, our village, is situated on the western fringe of the Volcanic Eifel about halfway between the cities of Trier and Cologne, approximately thirty kilometres from the Belgian border. The village lies in a beautiful floodplain. It is surrounded by gently rising slopes of meadows, fields and small forests. Geologists say that the valley was once a volcanic crater. The name 'Auel' means roughly 'low-lying meadows'.

Extinct volcanoes are the most important characteristic of our region. To the north of our village lies the Kyllenberg,[2] used by the Romans to quarry volcanic tuff, the material with which the houses in our region were traditionally built until not too long ago.

---

1 The German term for home, 'Heimat', cannot be comprehensively translated into English. It comprises a whole range of feelings, experiences, memories, longings, culture and history, as well as our local dialect. In essence, 'Heimat' defines who I am.
2 The term 'Kyll' is Celtic in origin – the proto-language of this region – and means 'beech tree'.

Kyllenberg was our stomping ground. We spent almost every Sunday on this mountain, built mini-landscape gardens, climbed around the volcanic gorges and crawled into the cave in which the famous robber Schinderhannes hid himself – or so the story goes. And above all, a flat promontory jutting out from a steep cliff was our declared sports field. This was where we carried out all sorts of self-invented games and daring feats.

Kyllenberg attracted as much adventure in winter as in summer. If you lay down in one of the many little hollows filled with bushes of marjoram and thyme on the side facing the village, you could see the village, our farm, and most of all, the beautiful baroque church with its steeple so untypical for our region. Its onion tower is more reminiscent of church steeples in Bavaria or Austria – but I did not know that as a child yet.

From Kyllenberg you have an expansive view in every direction. Towards the east, one volcano chain follows the other, inviting the eye to explore new horizons. Towards the north you have Steinbeuel in the forefront – a little woodgrove where we would find wild cherries. We later took possession of this little grove in our imagination and in our play. In good weather you could also see the northern Eifel mountains, the Nürburgring and the Hohe Acht, the Eifel's highest peak. Towards the west lay Steffelberg. Its volcanic cone-shaped peak was the most beautiful in the entire region, a natural historic monument. It looked like a wild boar's head and was overgrown with old beech trees.

Steffelberg was not only geologically but also historically interesting. In Roman times charcoal was produced in burning kilns here with which the iron smelting furnaces in the vicinity were fired. A Roman bypass allegedly went past Steffelberg. Our mother told us about the 'seven chambers' existing in the mountain – probably caves that were created at a time when grinding stones were quarried from it. During the Thirty Years' War (1618–1648) people fled with their livestock to seek refuge there. A 'St. Mark's cross' stood at the top of this mountain, and in spring a 'St. Mark's procession' was made to this cross to pray for a good harvest.

The procession and cross do not really have anything to do with St. Mark, but stem from pagan tradition. As early as in Roman times, processions were held in the fields to appease the 'stem rust demon'.

The destruction of Steffelberg began in the early 1960s as part of a modernisation programme that primarily sought to develop rural areas by building better roads. One of the projects planned was the construction of the freeway ('Autobahn') from Cologne to Trier, which has still not been completed.

The lava sand that made up a great part of the mountain was particularly sought after by Autobahn construction companies for building roads. The Steffelberg had been a 'Commons' since time immemorial – now it was to be enclosed and privatised. In 1963–1964 a company bought the mountain from the village council and began excavating the lava sand. Prior to this, the mayor and district council succeeded in striking this unique mountain off the nature conservation list. Yet even the higher authorities and the Land Rheinland-Pfalz did not seem to think it a problem, since our villages as well as the Land was ruled by the CDU (Christian Democratic Party). At that time, environmental movements did not yet exist and the mayor was pretty well able to rule unchallenged. The village mayor at the time worked hand-in-hand with the district authorities.

The citizens did not even oppose the destruction of their beautiful mountain. As always with such projects, the operators and authorities promised great advantages to the community: jobs, higher income for the municipality through the sale of sand, compensation for those owning land on Steffelberg, and income through the sale of beech wood from the mountain.

However, once the lava sand began to be quarried it soon became clear that all these promises were empty words. From 1964 to 1980, only eight to ten people were employed at the lava site, most of them not even locals. When the contract was closed, the mining company was obliged to recultivate the mountain as soon as the sand had been completely extracted. In the end, the community had to pay 20,000 DM extra for this 'recultivation'.

The impact on the environment and the climate has been negative. The plant and animal diversity that existed earlier on the mountain has disappeared. Clouds now pass over the village where they once stopped to drop their rain.

What is left is a huge hole that by means of 'recultivation' has been artificially transformed into a 'volcanic garden'. Instead of the real volcanic sand mountain there is now a tiny imitation volcanic sandhill. Where once geological field studies were carried out, there is now something resembling a laboratory nature trail. And the steep walls of the atrocious hole created by the ruthless exploitation of volcanic tuff have now been polished smooth, as smooth as a gravestone.

Every time I enter this 'volcanic garden' I am reminded of Claudia von Werlhof who quoted 'environmentalist' Lucius Burckhardt (1987), "Only once man has destroyed nature does a landscape become beautiful ... Tahiti was not peaceful because the lion grazed with the sheep, but because 'man' had turned it into a battleground."[3]

'Wild' Steffelberg was unprofitable – not so today's 'volcanic garden' for tourists.

In spring, we would discover the first anemones on Steffelberg, and in May, the first lilies of the valley and sweet woodruff. A small brook called Oosbach flowed past Steffelberg, and this brook had many little pools. My older brothers went there often and caught trout with their bare hands.

Steffelberg marked, so to speak, the end of my world to the west. As a child I imagined that behind it there was one more brook and after that the world ended. Later, I heard my mother say that there

---

3 See Claudia von Werlhof (1991, p. 165). In her article, von Werlhof criticises Burckhardt's concept that only a man-made landscape – after beating nature into submission by machinery and technology – could be beautiful and hence peaceful.

was indeed one more brook to the west, but it was not the 'Oos' that flowed past Steffelberg, but the 'Rossbach'.[4] My mother then added, "Children, never cross the Rossbach!" – a saying she heard from her grandmother.

Why was the Rossbach such a dangerous boundary?

First of all, the warning was directed to all young people of marriageable age. Because back then you did not marry just 'for love'. A suitable partner for marriage was someone who was considered to have enough 'to stand on', as the German saying goes. This meant that on the western side of the Rossbach the terrain began to climb and the climate became colder, the soil less fertile and the people poorer than in the valley meadows of Steffeln and Auel in the east. It was therefore not very advantageous to marry towards the other side of the Rossbach.

Moreover, whoever crossed the Rossbach and continued about thirty kilometres further westward, through forests which in earlier times were probably demarcation zones, finally arrived in Belgium.

Before and after World War I, smugglers from our villages went across the Rossbach and into Belgium to buy cheaper goods. This was always a very dangerous thing to do. My father also went over once during the depression in 1930. But he was not a very experienced smuggler and did not return home with much. And our mother was completely terrified when he went away smuggling.

In addition, the Rossbach was, although not the border between Germany and Belgium itself, near enough to it, and various wars were fought over it. In the northwest lay the hard-fought-over cities of Eupen and Malmedy. After the Franco-Prussian War of 1870–1871, the German Empire annexed these areas.

After the Treaty of Versailles in 1919, Eupen and Malmedy were returned to Belgium. During World War II, our region was used, as in many of the wars before, to deploy armies for the Western Front.

---

4 In the Rhineland and in many parts of Germany, the names of rivers and brooks are feminine. This is so because they were named after goddesses who protected the land.

The 'Siegfried Line' began just beyond the Rossbach. It was therefore a dangerous boundary in the opinion of our old folks. Which brings me to the topic of war, but more on that later.

Today, when I take a walk through this region, when my sister picks me up from the train station in Jünkerath, and when I reach the heights behind the village of Lissendorf and get a first view to the east and west over the volcanic landscape, I know, "now I'm home. Now I'm free, now I can go wherever I want to, despite any fences or ownership titles. This is our land, my land. Common land. Home."

This region is not just beautiful at any time of the day or season. Every hill, every roadside cross, every brook carries a story. Not only stories from earlier days, but also from our childhood, of world history and stories from today as well.

Our parents never tired of telling us such stories. In the evening and after work. Or during work, for instance while cooking or peeling potatoes, or while taking Sunday afternoon walks through the fields and the woods.

The Old House

The 'Kellish House'

To me, however, home also means our old house, the 'Keller's House', called 'Kellish' in Low German.[5]

---

5 The names of houses in the villages of the Eifel are not identical with the family names of those living in them. House names are retained even if the residents change. Our house, the Kellish House, was built in the seventeenth century by my father's great-grandfather, Bartholomäus Keller. The house kept this name even when his daughter Katharina married Paul Baur from Scheuern. The oldest son from this marriage was named Michael Baur. The Baur line in the Kellish House died out when both of my father's uncles died childless, and their sister Katharina Baur married a Johann Peter Mies from Stadtkyll who was my father's father. Yet when my father inherited the old Kellish House from his childless godfather Johann Baur, it was not renamed. It continued to be called Kellish. In our village we were never called the Mies children, but rather the Kellish children. That is how it still is today. Only recently have the villages begun to differentiate between house and family names. Many houses have been sold to people

Our house was a large old farmhouse built in 1750. Its exterior walls were eighty centimetres thick. The windows in the lower rooms were secured with rod iron grills to prevent robbers from entering the house. When I was a child, the house was considered old-fashioned. The iron grills embarrassed us a little. Later, when one of my brothers married a woman who grew up in a town house, he had the grills taken out.

The house did not have a front hall. From the front door you stepped directly into the 'kitchen', which consisted of a large room with an open hearth under a huge funnel. Bacon, ham and sausages were cured here. Sixteenth century cast iron plates with reliefs of saints or heroes hung behind the hearth. Made in iron foundries of the area, they not only protected the wall from fire but also warmed the room behind the kitchen, used for special festivities. Above the hearth hung an iron blade with teeth and gears, called 'Hohl', from which a large cast iron pot hung, which according to necessity could be moved up or down through the 'Hohl'. However, when we were young, this kitchen was no longer in use.

In addition, our old, big baking oven stood in the kitchen. It was fired with brushwood and kindling. The wood was stacked on top of the oven and was therefore always dry, while ashes from the oven were collected beneath it. In earlier times ashes were used to wash clothes. In my childhood we used it as fertiliser. To the right of the oven stood a big sandstone trough in which we stored bran for our cattle and pigs.

The kitchen also had a water pipe and a sink. A well, called 'Puetz', once stood next to the front door, from which water was

---

from outside'. We are now witnessing a process identified by Otto Brunner in his studies of eighteenth and nineteenth century Germany. At this time the idea of the 'entire household', which encompassed a life-long production and living community and included in most cases three generations of family, domestics and farmhands, began to be transformed. With industrialisation, the term 'family' was introduced, replacing the old term 'entire household'. An increasingly smaller group began to be identified with the term family, which ultimately included only one male, his wife and their biological children – the so-called nuclear family (see Otto Brunner, 1966, pp. 23–56).

pumped for household use. Before there were community water pipes, every household had to have such a 'Puetz'.

This expansive kitchen was an all-purpose space for people and animals.

In my early childhood we did not yet have electricity in all rooms. In autumn and winter, the kitchen became our ideal adventure playground. We made up our own game, for instance, of hide-and-seek where we would crawl into the various corners and hollows that the old, dark kitchen offered us. The most exciting thing about this game was that you had to make as little noise as possible, otherwise it would give you away. Playing this winter game in the dark was for me the epitome of the mysterious.

From the kitchen you could enter four other rooms: the room we used for special festivities, a pantry, and a room that later served as a kitchen-living room. This is where our entire family life took place. And next to that there was a 'workshop' containing a work bench, all kinds of tools, and miscellaneous old stuff. In one corner of this room we stored small potatoes, called 'pig potatoes', which were considered too small for use, and those sorted as 'seed potatoes' for the next season. In the kitchen stood a large wood-fired cooking cauldron in which the 'pig potatoes' – which we fed to the swine – were cooked. Later, an equally large washing cauldron stood next to it which was wood-fired as well. The smoke from these two cauldrons drifted into the open funnel.

A door on the right side of the old kitchen led to the cowshed and barn. People and animals were united under one roof, as in most of the old houses in the Eifel. At night you could hear the cows mooing or being fidgety. Hearing them became particularly important when a cow was ready to calve. This was when our father and mother had to be there to help her. Humans and animals were not really separated.

Our toilet was also in the cowshed, right above our liquid manure pit. This was very practical. Unlike most others, we did not have to cross the farmyard to reach the outhouse – a wooden hut often built over the dungheap that was dark at night, and cold and draughty in winter.

The fact that our barn was directly accessible from the house was also of great advantage to my mother. She could take her small children and hold them up so that they could go to the loo without much ado. All of them wore little skirts, even the little boys. Mother was very proud of the fact that all her children were 'dry' – or toilet-trained – by the time they were two, and that they never had nappy rashes.

From the old kitchen a wide set of oak stairs with a most beautiful baroque banister led up to the second floor.

The massive funnel took up most of the space here. You had to walk to the left around it in order to reach our parents' bedroom, and behind it, the 'boys' room'. Other rooms were to be found to the right of the funnel: a small bedroom for our oldest sister and next to it an 'empty room'. It had never been renovated. The flooring was broken, the plaster was flaking off the walls, there was stuff everywhere. Later, I often wondered why our father never refurbished this room despite the great number of children, so that we little girls could at least have had a room for ourselves. OK. We had no money. But he and the older boys could have done much themselves. Why not?

But these kind of repairs were not up father's alley. The house was in a pretty run-down condition when he moved there after marrying my mother in 1920. And it remained in this state until after World War II. It was good enough for my father. My mother was always vexed by it.

How did father come to possess this house? It happens to be a long story.

History: Michael Baur (1707–1779)
The house was first built by Johann Michael Baur (1707–1779). Above the choir in the Auel church a square gravestone is fixed onto

the wall. Two crossed hands are depicted hovering over a rose. The one hand holds a banner with a rose on it, the other holds a sword. Above this is a chalice and on each side of it a skull. In one of the upper corners a heart with three nails is depicted. An inscription runs along the edges of the gravestone and reads, '1779.9.May obiit A.R.D. MichEL BAUR MILES MARITUS SACERdOS FUNDATOR IN AUEL. R.I.P.' [On 9 May, 1779, the venerable Michael Baur died, soldier, husband, priest, founder in Auel. Rest in peace.]

According to an *Eiflia Illustrata* report, Michael Baur was born on 7 February, 1707 in Keller's House in Auel:

He began his studies to acquire the profession of a minister, to which he felt particularly inclined. However, when his father died, leaving his family in a poor condition, Baur was forced to give up his studies. He then went to Luxembourg and entered the Austrian military as a volunteer. He was soon promoted to officer and accompanied General Superi, a Hungarian, as adjutant in the war against the Turks ... When Superi was killed in combat, Baur took command and was responsible for contributing to the favourable outcome of the battle. Count Superi's widow offered the colonel her hand and, although he refused to be raised to nobility, moved with him to Temesvar, where she deceased six months later, after naming Baur heir to her vast estate (see Gehendges, Ed, *Eiflia Illustrata*, 1982, pp. 120–121).

Baur sold the estate and returned "with donkey carts full of gold" – so the legend goes. He placed his money "in a capital account with the Duke of Aremberg." Then he went to Cologne, entered the Seminary and was soon ordained priest. After returning to Auel, where he enlarged the existing small Chapel of the Virgin Mary – a pilgrimage chapel – in the baroque style he had become familiar with in Austria, he 'modernised' the church by installing new altars in the popular rural baroque style of the time. A very beautiful and large statue of the Virgin and Child rests on the main altar: Celestial Mother. She is more 'elegant' than the other figures on the side altars and was purportedly taken from Himmerod monastery, a Cistercian monastery founded under the auspices of Bernard of Clairvaux near Manderscheid in the Eifel.

Baur then commissioned a parsonage to be built, since up to that time Auel did not have its own pastor. He also completely refurbished his parental house, the Keller House. He made it bigger, more solid and comfortable than before. This is the house I spent my childhood in.

In addition, in 1778 he established a scholarship entailing "an annual stipend of 70 Thalers for a scholar ..." This scholarship was initially intended for his relatives, particularly those from his parental household. "... if, however, no one of qualification exists, one who was born in Auel, or even if lacking this, an outsider ..." The candidate for scholarship – who, naturally, should become a priest – was to enjoy the scholarship during the time of his studies without any other obligation than to daily recite the 'offizium parvum immaculatae conceptionis B.M.V.' – the Minor Divine Office in honour of the Virgin Mary's Immaculate Conception.

After many wars and political changes had passed over our village and over the Eifel since Michael Baur lived in the eighteenth century, the scholarship had depreciated in value to such an extent that, by World War II, only 120 Marks were left over. This money was divided between the only two Baur heirs left who, after 1946, were eligible to attend secondary school: a distant male kin, and myself from Baur's 'parental house'. I was the first girl from Auel to have ever attended and graduated from a secondary school.

Books

In our house we had quite a few books. Some originated from Michael Baur. These included a few bibles, the Old and New Testaments, and a book of sermons from the sixteenth century for every Sunday of the year. In this book, sermon samples were collected, allowing pastors to do nothing more than learn them by heart and give their parish a real talking-to without having to exert much energy in putting together a 'good' sermon.

In winter, we sometimes read passages from the sermon book and laughed our heads off at its strange, old-fashioned language, especially at the extreme and graphic descriptions of the kind of hell-fire agonies that sinners were to expect after death. It was obvious that the object of these sermons was to put the sinner into a state of terror. A compilation of the legends of the saints was also among the religious books in our house. And there were books on politics and the natural sciences, for instance a collection of newspapers published during the French Occupation, before 1815, in which the new Napoleonic laws were explained. There was a book that probably came from the 'Wiesenbaumeister' Johann Peter Baur, a comprehensive geometry book, and a fat *Brehm's Life of Animals* with wonderful copper etchings of all the animals, especially of the exotic ones. In addition, there was a multi-volume *Conversation Lexicon* from the nineteenth century. We heard that this lexicon was bequeathed to us by a relative from Hillesheim who had died.

But how did this old house come into the possession of my father, Johann Mies? This is how it happened: Father's mother, Katharina Baur, was born in the Kellish House, a multi-family or kind of joint family house called 'Stockhaus'.[6] She had two brothers: Johann

---

6 The Kellish House was probably a 'Stockhaus', or 'stem-family' dwelling. Peasants who sought to keep their estate together built houses that would allow their children to continue to live at home as adults. Once children left to marry or move elsewhere, Rhineland law prescribed peasants to pay out their inheritance in real assets, meaning also in land. This led to an increasing segmentation of peasants' landed estates and often

Peter Baur and Johann Baur. The younger of the two studied, but died without having married. He carried the title of 'Wiesenbaumeister zu Auel'. He was probably employed by the Prussian government which ruled the Rhineland at that time and which carried out an amelioration programme to improve the region's agriculture. In our area the programme primarily involved draining marshes, laying drains and drying up the ancient volcanic lake near Duppach. Today we know that this drainage policy was an ecological catastrophe, but in this way new meadows and farmlands were created for the poorer regions of the Eifel.

The other male heir, Johann Baur, 'Uncle Jannes', married and had one child. This child, however, drowned in the brook that ran behind our house. His wife was so grief-stricken that she sickened and died as well. Johann Baur did not marry again, but bequeathed his property, his parental house and his portion of the landed estate to his godson Johann Mies, our father.

Father's father, Johann Peter Mies, came from Stadtkyll. After his marriage to Katharina Baur he built a small, one-storey house next to the large Keller's House. When father returned from World War I in 1918, he found everything in a decrepit state: his brother was sick, the work horses were gone, only a few cows were left, and the house was dilapidated. And, most importantly, there was no woman in the house!

For an Eifel peasant it was impossible to run a farm without a wife. That is why the first thing father did was to look for a bride. When he married in 1920, he was already thirty-five years old.

---

enough resulted in the ruin of the peasant economy.

It was therefore not unusual for a daughter or son to remain living in their family's 'Stockhaus', where they had the life-long right to live and subsist, and where they would work on the farm together with the farm's heir. Unmarried siblings would also often leave their portion of the inheritance undivided as part of the whole 'Stockhaus' unit, which over time became wealthier as a result. In the nineteenth century, of the twenty-two houses in Auel, eleven were stem-family, 'Stockhaus' units. These units also sought to increase their wealth by advocating the privatisation of common land in order to acquire it for themselves. The communities, however, resisted the privatisation, went to court and finally won. Today, only a few pockets of common land are left (woodland, fallow lands, brooks, field paths and roads).

My Family

My Parents

Back then it was not very easy for an older bachelor to find a bride. Certain unspoken rules had to be observed. Mother often told us how our father went about winning her hand in marriage after World War I. He once visited her house in the neighbouring village of Steffeln. Steffeln is only one kilometre away from Auel. One of mother's brothers was in charge of the local Raiffeisen Bank.[7] This bank also sold shoe grease and other important articles for peasants. My father went to Steffeln under the pretence of buying shoe grease. In reality he was looking out for a 'good housemaid', so he wrote in his memoirs. In the *Schiffering's House* lived a few young women of marriageable age. When mother's sister Agnes saw 'Kellish's Jannes' approaching them through the meadow valley between Auel and Steffeln she said, "I'm not staying here". She did not want to keep company with the 'man from Auel'. Mother, called 'Trout' (from Gertrude), was less shy and stayed. The 'man from Auel' took the first opportunity to ask her if she would accompany him to the war veterans' festival to be held on the following Sunday. She was hesitant at first, which was proper for her to be, and did not answer with 'no' or 'yes' explicitly, but said she had already received an invitation to Auel.

On the following Sunday, mother put on her good dress and tied an apron over it. She did not want to give the impression she had been waiting for the 'man from Auel'. When he came to pick her up, she agreed to go with him to the festival. This was in the spring

---

7   Friedrich Wilhelm Raiffeisen (1818–1888) was the founder of small, rural cooperative banks. The goal of these banks was to overcome the extensive poverty of the peasants, particularly after the year of the great famine (1846–1847).

of 1919. "How the Auel villagers stared when they saw old Jannes with this young girl!" mother said.

After that, the two did not see each other the entire summer until autumn, when the 'man from Auel' showed up at the Steffeln fair; after that he came every Sunday. Now he came to truly 'court' my mother. 'Courting' meant that a man wanted to marry a woman. This was subject to very strict rules. The suitor was obliged to visit the girl's family and hold conversations with the old folks, in most cases with the father. He had little opportunity to be alone with his chosen one. She was allowed to serve him refreshments and demonstrate how good she was at being a housewife, and what a healthy and strong woman she was. During this period of 'wooing', the suitor was allowed to take his girl out to dance and bring her back home punctually. Intimacies were practically impossible.

It was customary for children to work in other farm houses. They herded cows and performed other light jobs. In return they received their meals and a few pennies. Mother told us often how she had worked in other houses since the time she was six years old. Just before she married, she worked in a house where some bachelors lived. The news went around very quickly that Mies Jannes from Auel was wooing Schifferings' Trout, that he wanted to marry her. One of the bachelors mentioned above said to her, "Trout, you have to hold on to that man from Auel. He's from a good family." Father's parental house, the Kellish House in Auel, may have been dilapidated, but the 'House', meaning the family itself, still had a very high reputation. Mother had to tell us this story over and over again.

The wedding ceremony took place on 12 February, 1920, in the Auel church. Father picked up his bride in an old carriage that had been standing around somewhere, a left-over from the Kellish House's 'good-old-days'.

In February of the following year a little boy was born. He was followed by a girl and then four more boys. After that a girl was born, 'little Marie', who died a few months later. Then I came. I was followed by five more children, two girls and three boys.

My Father

Throughout his life, our father was conscious of having come from 'a good house'. He was a proud man. A part of him, however, held the 'masters', whoever they were, in contempt.

Father did not only derive his self-confidence from the fact that he was the descendant of a respected family. He knew that on his twelve-hectare farm, he and his wife and children were capable of producing everything they would need in life themselves. Great wealth was not to be expected, but we always had enough to eat, a roof over our head and we were warm in winter. Wood was readily available in the forest Commons. Admittedly, we did need money for shoes and clothing. Money was always lacking, as was the case for all peasant families. Some money came in when we sold a few of our livestock, our cows, swine or little pigs. We also received money for our milk which, back then, was delivered to a cooperative dairy for further processing. In autumn, if we produced more grain and potatoes than we needed, we also sold these to local merchants. Most of the money went towards buying fertilisers in the spring. Oftentimes not much money was left over from that to pay the cobbler and seamstress, who came into the house to make our shoes and clothes. The more children were born, the more money had to be spent. And, like many of the peasants, we were in debt and had to pay interest on a regular basis.[8]

Yet father lived in the consciousness that 'the Lord will provide'. He was not a businessman, but rather a peasant who did not want to be dependent on anyone. In fact, our economic situation was no worse than that of most families in the village. We were also not the

---

8 Our family's debt was partly incurred by loans that our father received for alterations and renovations to the old Kellish House, partly by paying his deceased brother's children their share of the inheritance, and partly by the loss of my father's share in the Steffeln cooperative credit bank when it went bankrupt.

only ones to have so many children. We were not the wealthiest but not the poorest either. In my childhood I never had the feeling of being 'poor'. I have never had any feelings of inferiority because of my background as one of the many children of a peasant. Perhaps this had something to do with the pride and self-confidence that my father, and also my mother, had. It was the self-confidence of peasants who were capable of feeding and taking care of themselves without having to be completely dependent on the market. It was the self-confidence of subsistence peasants.

Father was also something of a 'peasant-philosopher'. On Sundays, after Mass in Steffeln, he would get together with his brother-in-law, the communal forester, and the pastor of Steffeln to philosophise and talk politics. He liked reading books the pastor lent him. When he was younger he once wrote a long romantic prose poem that was full of pathos. The history of our house and our forefathers inspired him a great deal, and he told us stories about them again and again.

Father was not very big, just about 1.64 metres tall. Back then, this was the normal size for most men. He had thin, red-blonde hair, a moustache and a long nose. Besides his nose, the most striking feature of his face were his big, blue eyes. These eyes sparkled and widened when he was telling something exciting, and they would also flash when he got angry. Which happened often. He was quite the hot-tempered patriarch. He could not tolerate it when someone did not obey, or when someone tried to talk back to him. Our older brothers and my sister in particular, as well as our mother, could tell a story or two about his hot temper. For example, he expected the older boys to clean out the cowshed and bring down the hay from the hayloft by the time he came back from the fields. Yet the boys were very playful and did not start until they saw father coming in with the harnessed team of oxen. Mother helped them in the cowshed because they all feared father's temper. Including my mother. But she was still the stronger of the two. He often put her on the same level as us children – she was 12 years younger – and in his eyes she was therefore still a 'child'. "You're just as bad as the children!", he would say to her when he came into the kitchen-living room and saw mother playing with us while she worked – despite all our commotion.

However, if they did get into a serious fight with each other, she would glare at him with her dark eyes – she was dark, had dark hair, brown eyes – and would fall silent. Then he would leave. And she would remain silent. That was her way of punishing him. "Your father could not bear it," my mother would later explain. "I was never the first one to give in. He was always the first to make peace, I was the stubborn one." This was because he loved her. And he was sentimental, plaintive and in need of affection and love, as choleric people often are.

He also loved us children. I can remember him taking me with him to work when I was about three years old, and putting me down on the edge of the field. It was common for the men to take their small children to the fields. In this way children were not only introduced to nature but also to work before they were old enough to work themselves. And then, when his day's work was finished, he would set me before him on his horse and in this manner we would ride home together. This is the earliest and most beautiful memory I have from childhood. I held tight onto the horse's mane, and my father sat behind me. Sometimes he would sing. What ever in the world had I to fear?

Father could not sing very well, yet he sang with us when we took our walks through the fields on Sundays. He taught us how to identify bird calls and plants. And when my mother cleaned on Saturdays he would sit down with us young children on the big kitchen table and sing old soldier songs, making terrible faces in the process. I particularly remember the song, 'When the Romans got cheeky'. At dinner he always had one of the small ones on his lap.

And most importantly, he was a tireless storyteller. We often pressed him to tell us stories from 'the old days'. Many of his stories dealt with his experiences in World War I when he was an officer's coachman. We also heard a lot about the village, the people who lived in it earlier, and many tales about general history. It often began like this, "When the French were here ...",[9] or, "when Napoleon marched on Russia ..." or, "when wolves still roamed our area ..."

When the number of children increased, neither he nor my mother considered this to be a burden. One of father's sayings was, "Gibt Gott ein Häslein, gibt er auch ein Gräslein." Which means something like "If God makes a bunny, he also makes grass to feed it." Having many children also meant prosperity to subsistence peasants. They represented working hands. While still young, they all helped on the farm. When older, they were trained in some trade and became craftsmen or peasants. The young women worked as housemaids and farm servants until they married. All of them supported their family financially. There was no fear of having to be poor in old age.

Even after World War II, when my five older brothers returned safely from the war, and although they had not yet learned a trade, my father thought they could all stay home and live in the village. "Our forefathers had always been able to find an income here," he said. But this was no longer true, as we know now.

Since the middle of the nineteenth century, the Eifel has witnessed various waves of emigration, where young peasants' sons and daughters moved to the Ruhr area, Germany's industrial heartland, and most importantly to North America and later South America.[10]

---

9 After the French Revolution, France occupied the Rhineland from 1794 to 1815.
10 These emigration waves were not only caused by poverty and a desire for adventure. In a chronicle on the series of emigrations to the United States from the Daun region in the year 1850 one reads that not only men left their home to seek their fortune in the 'land of unlimited opportunities', but women also. Often these women had 'illegitimate' children who were discriminated against by all. No male wanted to marry such a woman. When women left their Eifel villages for the larger cities such as Cologne, Bonn, or the Ruhr area, they often went as housemaids. They 'worked' until they found a husband.

Even my father's eldest brother, as well as two of my mother's brothers moved to the Ruhr region. During the world economic crash in the early 1930s, all of the children of my father's eldest brother emigrated to Brazil.

Indeed, many of our peasants' children did not follow their fathers' footsteps to become small farmers and craftsmen in the villages of their birth. Michael Baur's example has already shown us that two impulses have always existed which have motivated the Eifel peasants' children to go out into the world: adversity is one; a longing to travel (the search for adventure) is the other. Sometimes just one is the crucial factor, at other times both of them play an important role. The fact is, although the Eifel may have been a relatively poor area, its children have for many years gone out into the world, and their descendants are to be found on every continent. After World War II, this, of course, was also to become our fate.

Father, however, did not want to know anything of that at all. He wanted us all to be around him.

My Mother

Mother was a totally different person from my father. She was just slightly smaller than him, had broad shoulders and a wide, round back capable of carrying heavy loads. She proudly told us that when she was young, she could carry home from the fields a hundredweight sack of potatoes on her back. Like all women in our family, she had 'childbearing hips', as my sister the midwife would say. In later years she would sometimes point to her tummy and say, "All of you were in here once!"

She also had a completely different temperament than my father. She was more realistic, cheerful, had more courage to face life, and was less emotional. There was no problem she would not take on and solve with willpower and creativity. "Where there's a will, there's a way!" was one of her favourite wisdoms. Father was not quite convinced that this was true. He was not optimistic enough to believe that you could overcome all hurdles in life with willpower. He tended to give up.

Mother's optimism and will to life was based on a very concrete physical fact: she was healthy in body and soul, and even if we never had enough money when I was a child, she was never pessimistic. When I think of her, I am reminded of a realisation that came to Dorothee Sölle from her experience in the slums of South America, "The poor cannot afford to be pessimistic. Pessimism is a luxury of the wealthy."

Like the poor in developing countries, my mother had to solve a series of problems day in and day out that would constantly pop up again and again. Whether it was about putting something to eat on the table, or taking care of a broken arm or collarbone, or dealing with one of her children suddenly becoming sick, or making a new piece of clothing from an old one – mother always had good, practical solutions for taking what she had at her disposal to accomplish whatever had to be done. She was a genius in improvisation.

This creative ability 'to make something out of everything' was particularly important during the war, when staples such as sugar and other foodstuffs were rationed. She sent her five sons 'at war' regular army-post packages filled with sausages from home slaughtering, so-called war cakes invented by her, and clothing she knitted herself.

Despite all of this, she was not a 'proper' housewife whose primary ambition was to establish a perfectly organised, i.e. bourgeois, household as is the case today. She often told us that as a child she much preferred working outside than in the house: she liked being in the fields, in the garden, the cowshed and the woods.

One of my favourite memories is of outings with my mother to the woods as children which took place between the hay and wheat harvests. This was during our school holidays. In the country, these holidays were not meant for recreation. Rather, children were supposed to help the farmers in their important work during the summer months. Our outings to the woods were therefore not just about having fun but about doing work. Blueberries had to be picked first, then wild raspberries and later blackberries. Even today, wild raspberry jam is my favourite. In between, we also collected kindling with our mother and strung them together in bundles, called 'Schanzen'. This was the most important material we used to fire our huge baking oven. Of course, we needed a huge amount of wood because every two weeks we would bake bread. The oven was big enough to hold twelve large, round loaves of rye bread.

Our outings into the woods were an adventure, because we were discovering wilderness. The woods were Commons and whatever one found there did not have to be bought. The ancient hunter-gatherer instinct resurfaced in many of us during our summers in the woods. To this day, I miss this wilderness in our automobile-dominated cities, in our machine civilisation.

My mother did not raise pigs in order just to stock up our household cash. This was women's work and women's income no matter where you went. Mother often did not have enough money to buy sugar and other goods that were not produced in the country. She would give us a few eggs with which to pay our account at the 'colonial goods' shop in the village.[11] Back then, it was still common to pay for necessities by trading goods.

The fact that children were also sent to 'other houses' to work is to be understood within the context of 'mutual help', rather than within the context of 'child labour'. The principle of mutual help was one of the necessary conditions for survival in a rural agricultural economy.

---

11 The 'colonial goods' shops were grocery stores all in women's hands. Apart from goods produced in Germany, such as salt, soap, sugar and vinegar, exotic goods such as spices (cinnamon, pepper, cloves) as well as rice, coffee, and cocoa imported from the colonies were sold here and had to be paid for in cash. Eggs would not do for imported foods.

Mother was the ideal subsistence peasant's wife. Our father could not have found a better one. It was a matter of course for peasants' wives – and their children – to help out with any work that needed to be done on the farm, in the fields, in the cowshed and barn and in the woods. A woman who was 'just a housewife' was of no use.

However, there was a certain division of labour between the sexes. Men were responsible for the heavy physical labour involved in using draught-animals (oxen, cows and horses) and machines. Other specific tasks were always women's work, such as taking care of the chickens and swine, milking the cows and raising pigs, as well as to a great extent working in the garden. Goods produced by this 'women's economy' were also marketed by the women themselves. Women thus had access to income, and although they spent it primarily to support the family, it was their *own income*.

It made sense for women to take care of small livestock and milk the cows. Their own physical experience had taught them how the animals 'felt' when they had offspring: when a cow calved or a sow gave birth to her litter. Mother was against having the men try to pull the calf out of a cow by force. "You have to work with nature, you can't force it," she used to say to them.

When a sow gave birth to a litter, Mother often spent entire nights in the pig stall to make sure that the sow did not get nervous and in her excitement squash or even attack one of her precious piglets. She sold the young pigs at the pig market in Hillesheim, and this was a very important source of income for her. But her care of the animals was not based on material or financial concerns; it derived from her deep love for, and empathy with, all living things.

I once asked her what time of the year she liked most. "Spring. That's when all life begins again. You not only have new plants and flowers but also new chicks, rabbits, calves, pigs and even new babies." Most of us were born in either February or March.

Not until later, when I was involved in the environment movement, did I realise that mother's connectedness to all living things, that her sense of continuity between animals and humans, and between humans and humans, was the basis for her philosophy of life.

This world view and perspective on life also determined how she behaved towards other people, particularly those who were less well off than we were. "You always have to look below you, not above you," was one of her principles. She was known and well-liked among all the beggars and gypsies who used to go from door to door during my childhood years. She could not give these people money, because she did not have much herself. But she gave them bread, or a piece of bacon, or she invited them to stay for dinner. Something a gypsy once said has remained in my memory, "You'll have lots of luck with all your children."

Before mother died she looked back at her life. She said, "Wasn't that a good life?"

My oldest sister, Agnes, who knew mother still in her younger years, was of the opinion that, in retrospect, mother wanted to make her life seem better than it was. She, Agnes, knew how hard it was for mother to give birth to a new baby almost every year, to always keep washing nappies, to cook on the woodstove, make oatmeal, breast-feed her baby and soothe it with all kinds of rhymes and songs. Although the older children were increasingly able to take care of the small ones, the main burden and care still lay on her shoulders. But I believe what she said; that she had had 'a happy life'.

This 'happy life' not only consisted of the many Sundays and holidays that gave structure to the farming year when I was a child, but there were also periods of rest that were dictated by nature, by the working rhythm and working 'tools' – including the animals. In these periods of rest we pressed our parents to tell us about the old days. We wanted to know how life was when they were still children, who our relatives were and the experiences they had had. In this way we developed, from early on, a very keen sense of history, at first with respect to the history of our family and village, and then with respect to the 'greater' world history.

My Birth

On 6 February, 1931, my mother gave birth to me in the hospital of the Franciscan sisters in Hillesheim, a little market town eight kilometres away from where we lived. I was the first child in our family to have been born in a hospital.

As mother told me later, it was a difficult birth. It took a long time before I saw the light of day, and my mother was so exhausted by her contractions that she fainted. "That was her last breath," she heard a sister saying, "Poor man, poor children!" Mother told us this story a thousand times. And she told us how the sister then took her bottle of 'Kölnischwasser' – a very precious eau de toilette at that time – and poured it over her face, whereby she slowly came to herself.

I, too, did not seem to really want to live. Although I had left mother's protective womb, I did not breathe, or at least not enough. They plunged me into a tub of cold water and gave me a smack on my bum. "They beat me into life," I sometimes told myself later.

The winter of 1931 was a hard one. Father walked on foot to visit mother – and me – in the hospital. The snow was piled up metres high. And public transportation such as automobiles or buses just did not exist back then. "I never walked through snow as fast as then!" my father reported.

Why did mother have to go to the hospital to give birth to me? The midwife had already brought seven children into the world before I came. The seventh one, 'little Marie', was born a year before myself, but died a few weeks later. After that, mother had complications giving birth. Our family doctor told father that home births were dangerous because mother always lost too much blood. That is why father brought his pregnant wife to the women's clinic in Bonn to give birth to every child born after me, which involved taking longish train trips. After a while mother would come back with a new baby. She would bring hand-knitted socks and gloves for us children as presents. Sometimes even a few oranges and rubber dolls. This was all she could afford to buy. We divided the oranges amongst us all. There would be one or two slices for each.

The winter of 1931 took place in the middle of the world economic depression. There was massive unemployment everywhere. The Eifel peasants had also become impoverished and were in debt. To repay their debts, they were forced to sell the draught animals and milk cows that were so important to their families. These were the poorest times my family had ever experienced.

And yet, I believe I was a 'wanted child'. Before me, five brothers and a sister had been born. After all those boys mother wanted a girl she could call Maria. Because in every Catholic household you had to have a girl named Maria. When 'little Marie' died, mother was very sad. And when I came, mother and father were happy I was a girl, because both honoured Maria, the Mother of God, very much. It was therefore a matter of course to name me Maria.

My Brothers and Sisters

I was number seven in a series of twelve children: eight brothers, four sisters. The older six, a sister, Agnes (the second eldest), and five brothers, Klaus, Michael, Mathias, Eberhard, and Franz, in a sense formed their own, separate generation.

This generational divide became particularly apparent in 1939 when each of my five brothers had to go to war one after the other. Even my older sister Agnes – who had always been a second mother to us – decided to go away voluntarily. She first went into the 'Voluntary Labour Service'[12] and then became trained as a nurse.

---

12 The 'Voluntary Labour Service' (Freiwilliger Arbeitsdienst) was introduced by Hitler. Every young person, male and female, had to join this labour service. Peasants' children, however, were exempt from it.

She just wanted to get out of our village. Between 1939 and 1945, and in the years after as well, those siblings living at home were the six smaller children. First there were the three girls: Maria, Katrin and Trudel. Then came the three smaller boys: Johannes, Hermann and Gottfried. Gottfried was born in 1940, almost twenty years after the eldest was born.

In the early years of my childhood, between 1931 and 1939, my five brothers played a very protective role for us in our village and during any conflicts that took place in our one-classroom village school. And they were a great help in solving all sorts of practical problems. They were good at repairing broken things. Even though my father was less talented, my brothers taught themselves everything they needed to know about 'being practical'. They repaired everything: bicycles and electrical circuits, school satchels and chains, shovel handles and sleds. Something was always broken. This did not bother father much, but it would aggravate mother who would say, "Can't somebody please fix the wooden crate somehow?" And sometimes one of the older brothers would fix it, just to please her.

Not because they were particularly fond of working or were particularly eager to be industrious. All of us, of course, tried to dodge the constant work that needed to be done, whether it was about chopping wood, carrying wood into the house during winter, bringing in potatoes for the pigs and cooking them in the big old cauldron, cleaning the cowsheds, throwing down the hay from the hayloft and spreading it out for the livestock in the shed, taking out turnips from the frozen storage clamp on the field in winter and cutting them up to feed to the livestock. We often had fights about who was supposed to do this or that job. And we were good at explaining why it was not our particular responsibility, "I got the wood yesterday, it's Franz's job today!"

Mother's directions were often very vague. Instead of saying, "Franz, it's your turn to get wood!" she would say, "There's no more wood left in the crate again! Can't one of you go and get wood for me?" Of course, none of us felt directly responsible for getting the wood. In short, there were always all sorts of fights between us about who was supposed to do which job.

As with the adults, there was a specifically defined division of labour between boys and girls. Washing, cleaning, sweeping, tidying up, helping mother to cook, peeling potatoes, getting salad and vegetables from the garden and cleaning them, washing clothes and laying them out on the grass behind the house to bleach in the sun, hanging up clothes and ironing them – all this was girls' work. Darning, mending, knitting, crocheting, sewing – all so-called needlework – was done exclusively by the women and girls.

At school there was a woman from the village who came to teach the girls needlework in 'knitting class', as it was called. In this class we primarily learned how to knit, because knitting was important: all the socks, all the sweaters, shawls, waistcoats and gloves were handmade. Almost nothing was bought.

During the war everybody took out their old spinning wheels again. We had also bought a milk sheep – 'Lottchen' was her name – and her wool was wonderfully soft. Back then, individual peasants did not keep sheep because all the land they had was needed to raise crops and pasture their cows. But there were shepherds in the Eifel villages who had the right to pasture everywhere and would drive their large flocks of sheep across the countryside every autumn and spring. From Michaelmas on (29 September), all private landownership was virtually suspended until spring (Candlemas, 14 February), during which the ancient Commons law took hold. This meant that not only sheep, but also cows could pasture everywhere; all meadows and fields were open to them as of this date. This was always an exciting time for the children who herded their family's livestock. In the morning at school they would make arrangements to meet at a particular place within the Auel village limits where they would drive their herds to pasture. At their meeting place they would make a fire and pass their time with wild games. Their cows would graze wherever they wanted.

Mother took little Lottchen's wool and spun yarn out of it. I did not learn to spin myself, although my younger sisters did. I helped with shearing the sheep, hackling, combing the wool and winding the spun wool into balls. Each of these tasks required special tools.

I only learned how to knit, darn and carry out a few basic sewing techniques, such as how to put a patch on ripped trousers and how to cut an old bed sheet down the middle and sew the edges together again.

I did not like going to knitting class. What did make it a little more interesting was the fact that the woman who gave us instructions also taught us numerous songs, so-called kitchen songs, that were popular among the women at that time. Songs like, 'Little Marie sat crying in the garden', or 'Why are you crying, fine young gardener woman?' or 'There once were two royal children', or 'Tired is the wanderer on his way home . . .' These were all long ballads full of romance and sentimentality, with innuendoes and associations I only half understood. They did, however, fire my imagination. Of course we also sang them at home when we washed the dishes or peeled the potatoes.

Later I learned that all these songs were 'kitsch' or excessively sentimental. As of 1933, Nazi songs were dominant in public and in school: songs like 'Rotten bones are shaking', the 'Horst Wessel Song' – which was the official National Socialist Party song – and others. But the women remained true to their old ballads.

Work and Play

During work, the adults and children would sing. But as children we also tried whenever possible to include all sorts of games and funny inventions while carrying out our onerous and often hard work. For example, during the grain harvest we had to bind the reaped stalks of grain into sheaves which was a nasty job because thistles would often grow between the stalks and scratch our arms and legs. When the field had been completely reaped, the sheaves would be vertically arranged into small pyramid-shaped structures called 'stacks'. This was done to dry the grain in the fields and protect it from rain. We would play hide-and-seek in and among these stacks. When the grain was dry, it was brought home into the barn. In winter the grain was threshed, when I was young by hand on the floor of the barn. Later in my childhood, threshing was done by a machine. The threshed grain had to be carried in sacks by strong men up into the loft. There it was stored through the winter until the next grain harvest. We not only used the grain to make bread but we kept some as seed for the next planting.

In spring we had to help plant potatoes, not only on our own fields but in the neighbours' as well. The same was the case when the turnip seedlings had to be planted into the field, and the area had to be weeded. Weeding was tough on your back because you had to do it in a stooped position. To distract us from its harshness we would divide the rows amongst us and compete with each other about who would be the first to complete all of his or her rows. We did, however, also help each other during these competitions.

In summer, which was the 'hay season', everybody had to share the necessary work of making hay for the cows in winter.

I remember experiencing very direct sensuous pleasure from working in the freshly tilled soil with my hands. Whether it was in spring while planting potatoes, or in autumn during the potato harvest when we had to pick up and gather the lovely new potatoes – all of this work was not only a burden but also a joy.

This work was *necessary*. It was indeed not alienated work as you would do in a factory. We learned about the entire working process, and the product of our work belonged to us. Without doubt this work was the very basis upon which our existence rested. Our work, then, had meaning.

This very immediate insight into the necessity of our work – without which we would have nothing to eat – helped us to carry it out without too much protest. Maintaining, as well as re-establishing, a concept of work representing both a burden and a joy is still a major political goal for me.

Even before they went off to war, our five 'big brothers' did not like having us smaller girls around them during their wild games in our village and in the surrounding fields and meadows. We were particularly unwanted when they played war games between Auel and the neighbouring village of Steffeln.

From very early on I noticed that certain games and customs were reserved only for the boys. One example of this was *Kleppern*, a practice carried out on the three holy days before Easter. Tradition had it that during the three days of Jesus's entombment the bells would not ring because they had gone on pilgrimage to Rome. Yet bells had to be rung for peasants once in the morning, once at midday, and once in the evening so that they could keep track of time while they were out on the fields. Therefore, to replace the bells, school boys would walk through the village from Good Friday on and make lots of noise with rattles and wooden flappers. While doing this they would also sing. At the end of the three days, the boys would go through the village and collect eggs as their reward.

I, too, wanted to go with the 'Klepper boys', but mother said that girls were not allowed to go. When I asked what we were allowed to do, she replied, "Well, girls have to help with cleaning and baking to prepare for Easter."

This made me angry and sad. I believe sentences such as these made me become a feminist, although back then I did not know what that was.

Female Trinity

I was the oldest in the group of six smaller children. Of all my siblings, this group of six was my most important peer group. It gave me the feeling of never being alone. I was followed by two more girls and then three little brothers. I was closest to my sisters Katrin and Trudel. We did almost everything together. We played, worked, learned for school and life together. When one of us had to go to another village, at least one sister or even a little brother would accompany us. We were never alone. The contemporary ideal of individual and isolated activity did not exist then. We were always *we*.

This constellation of three women also had a visible counterpart in our village church. On the left side, the 'women's side', a side altar depicted the three Holy Helpers, St. Barbara, St. Apollonia, and St. Catherine. We learned the saying, "These are three holy girls: Barbara and her tower" (patron saint of fire and burning), "Apollonia and her teeth" (patron saint against toothaches), "Catherine and her wheel" (patron saint of wheel-makers).[13]

We were anything but holy. But people said we looked like the Auel saints with their round cheeks, sturdy figures and broad shoulders. Our church also had a statue of the holy female trinity of St. Anne with the Madonna and Child. St. Anne, seated with the Holy Virgin on her lap, holds a book in her hand. The book stands for Jesus.[14] I, myself had for years thought that Jesus was a girl. A picture of the Holy Family hung above our kitchen table with Jesus, in a pink dress, between Mary and Joseph. Whoever wears a dress

---

13 Peasant religion is materialistic. There is little interest in purely spiritual or transcendental subject matter among peasants. Therefore, all of the saints in our village church had a practical function: St. Bridget was responsible for the cows, St. Wendolin for the sheep, St. Eligius for the farrier, St. Anthony for the swine. If one of our cows was about to give birth, my mother would pray to St. Anthony. These were all 'ancient' saints whose names and legends were derived from pre-Christian and early Christian times.

14 At that time I did not know that this female trinity was the continuation of a pre-Christian, Rhineland tradition of the Three Matrons: an old woman, representing old age, autumn and dying; a mother at the height of her fertility, symbolising summer; and a young woman representing a new life cycle and spring. In the iconography of the St. Anne statue, it is St. Anne, the mother of the Virgin, who is depicted as the largest figure, and is thus the most important patron saint of the group. Jesus, then, has without much ado been added to this female genealogy and cosmic cycle of time.

is a girl. Later, when I learned that Jesus was a boy I was completely shocked.

This female trinity model has unconsciously been with me throughout my entire life. In secondary school and during my training as a teacher (see Chapter Two) I had two girlfriends with whom I am still close. Later, when I studied sociology at the university, I again had two girlfriends. Together we lived through the beginning of the women's movement and developed the basis for our collective practice and theory. To this day we have continued practising collective actions, reflections and analyses. These friendships have always been very helpful and inspiring to me.

My parents' goal – and that of all people in our village – was not to raise isolated, independent individuals who were to carry all responsibility alone. Their goal was set on the group as a whole, on the community: the family and village community.

I was not particularly industrious. My two younger sisters were especially exasperated by this. "Maria lets us do the dishes and then she tells us a story and we don't even notice that she's not doing anything," they would say. Sometimes they would cite the New Testament, in particular the story of Martha and Mary, Jesus's female friends. When Jesus came to visit them, Martha, the older one, did all the chores to serve him properly. She worked, ran back and forth, the ideal housewife. Mary, however, sat down at Jesus's feet and listened to his words. Finally, Martha could not stand it any more and said something like this to Jesus, "Can't you tell my sister to help me do the work? Don't you see how hard I'm working?" Jesus answered, "Martha, Martha. You're doing so much! But Mary has chosen the better part."

In the Christian tradition, Martha stood for the active life, Mary for the contemplative one. Yet all of my siblings, not only my sisters, did not think much of Jesus's words. For them, Mary was just plain lazy, and the sentence, "Mary has chosen the better part," was used to express their critique of me.

The whole village was our playground, especially the meadow and brook behind our house. The boys would catch trout and tadpoles. And then there were the rocks near the mill where wild strawberries would grow. We would hunt for them everywhere in June, because back then strawberries were not grown in our gardens. We would look for them in the lanes and the woods. Our particular technique for transporting them back home consisted of stringing them onto a long stem of grass like a row of pearls. We called this a 'schmilm'. Sometimes our father would make us such a schmilm. And it was quite a special pleasure to use our mouths to pick off those ripe strawberries from the schmilm.

And then there was the 'red sand' on the way to Duppach, where we would always get sand to 'bake cakes'. How many small pails of sand did we carry home to make 'cake' and distribute them to everyone!

All of these games and adventures meant we also had to walk great distances and trudge up and down the hilly landscape. We probably covered at least five kilometres a day in this manner.

My little brothers are allowed to play with us

We three bigger sisters were the leaders of the games we played. It was a matter of course for our brothers to play with us. Whether it was about creating gardens on Kyllenberg, or furnishing a 'house' where we would welcome visitors, or about declaring a rocky plateau our sports field where we would play sports and practise climbing – our brothers were always with us.

One of the biggest attractions were my play performances. One time I made up a story called 'The Snow Queen'. I had painted figures for this story on cardboard with watercolours an 'uncle' had given to me. I then cut them out. I had to invent something to make the figures stand. At the footend of each figure I left about a one and a half centimetre edge of cardboard which I then cut at the centre. I bent one flap forwards and the other flap backwards. The figures stood. I used these figures to perform the entire story for my smaller siblings on the kitchen table. I sat on one side of the table, they sat on the other side, and I moved my figures back and forth while telling my story. And whatever was missing as a backdrop, our imaginations provided.

I experienced my first moments of happiness and success when the little ones on the other side of the table – particularly my brothers – began to cry with emotion.

I loved my little brothers. First there was little Johannes. He had the cutest blonde curls you could imagine. He was always beaming with joy. When my mother returned from visiting her sisters in Steffeln he would run to her with his arms wide open and call, "Motter, Motter!"

And then there was little Hermann. He was born in 1938. Hermann, too, had light blonde curls, even lighter than Johannes's. I envied his beautiful hair, because I did not have a single curl. Little Hermann got very sick once when he was two. We all worried about him. We went to church and prayed for him. And he got well again.

And finally there was little Gottfried. He had chestnut red hair and a perennially runny nose. I sewed a doll for him during the war. This little doll-boy was made of manchester cloth taken from an old pair of trousers and was filled with bran. We did not have anything else. Gottfried loved his 'Fritz' dearly, and if anyone took it and threw it into a corner he would cry and get angry. Later, a hungry mouse chewed a hole in Fritz to get at the bran.

From my childhood days on I tried to show my small siblings that there was a wider horizon beyond the village which offered enticing new experiences and adventures. I wanted to pass on to them the things that attracted and inspired me.

I wanted to make life interesting for them and trigger their imagination. Some followed my encouragement, others did not. I am sure that Hermann and Johannes received some of their longing for 'the far away' from me then, a longing that later played a great role in my and Hermann's life.[15]

15 My brother Hermann, after having completed his apprenticeship as a mechanic, rode his bicycle around the whole Mediterranean, from Morocco, via Egypt, Palestine, Turkey and Greece. When he arrived in Greece he bought himself a donkey and rode 'Korfi' all the way home. Later on he went to Chile with a development NGO, fell in love there, got married, started a small mechanical workshop, 'Centro Mechanico', which later became a medium-sized factory. Even now, he still suffers from homesickness.

2

My Village

Auel – A Subsistence Village

When I was a child, our village of Auel was to a great extent self-sufficient. Although it only consisted of thirty-one houses and 300 residents, it still offered everything we needed to survive. Even during long, hard winters, when all roads to and from the village were blocked by snow, no one had to die of hunger or cold.

Of course, agriculture formed the basis of our subsistence economy. All the families living in the village owned land – some more, some less. Even the village tradesmen often owned land. And those who did not have enough, leased additional land from the church which of course owned a great deal of land and woods as it did everywhere else. Or they would lease it from the community which opened communal property such as fields and paths for pasturing cows and goats. It was therefore possible for almost every family to have a few cows, goats and one or two pigs. Most of the village residents also had enough land to be able to grow rye and make their own bread.

The craftsworkers were often paid in kind – in grain or potatoes. This was convenient not only for peasants who were always lacking cash, but also for the tradesmen who in this way made sure that their families had basic foodstuffs in the house.

A further source of self-sufficiency was the tradition of 'mutual help'. Certain seasonal field work, such as planting and harvesting potatoes, threshing grain in winter, required more workers than a single family could provide. For example, a neighbour always helped our family to plant potatoes and other vegetables. The same happened when harvesting rye and potatoes. Work like this was never paid in money but in natural produce. One could also alternatively exchange services, "If your children will help me to plant potatoes or other plants (in May), we'll help you to harvest your rye." When I was ten and eleven years old, for instance, I myself helped a neighbouring family to plant their turnips.

The principle of mutual help functioned whenever someone needed help, such as when building a house or when a cow was giving birth to a calf, or when weddings, baptisms or funeral festivities needed to be planned. Basically, neighbours shared whatever tasks a single family could not manage.

In addition, there were *communal tasks* in the village which required one able adult – whether male or female – from every household to co-operate in completing those tasks. These tasks were: clearing snow from the village roads; repairing municipal roads – which included making gravel by crushing basalt stones with a hammer; and clearing the ditches. Another task was planting new trees in the communal forests. As already mentioned, not only certain parcels of land but also most woods existed as Commons. In these woods, each family had the right to gather firewood for their private use.

I would also like to note here that these *communal tasks* which were directly linked to *common property*, or *Commons*, were not in any way considered to be primarily burdensome and compulsory, and they were not carried out by each family for their individual and personal advantage only, as Garrett Hardin argues.[1] Communal

---

1   Garrett Hardin (1968) writes in his article "The Tragedy of the Commons" that due to competition, self-interest and private property, all Commons would eventually be destroyed, hence would end in tragedy. But even today there are still Commons in our villages, such as communal forests, hills and fallow land.

work, such as planting trees in the commons forest, may have been hard work when I was a child, but for the people it was also fun – something like a party which would be the source of lasting memories and stories.

Our craftsworkers

In 1986, my sister Trudel wrote down all the trades- and craftspeople she could remember which still existed after World War II until the 1960s. The following is based on her observations.

Our village had a farrier (who was also a wagon-maker), a carpenter, a shoemaker, a painter, a tailor, a tanner, a sexton, a family butcher, and a miller. We also had three healers and faith healers who would not only 'pray away' sicknesses for our livestock, but also for people, especially when they had skin diseases such as psoriasis. It often worked back then – as it does today. These healers were peasants like the rest of us.

Back then the village had a school. This fine, two-storey sandstone building was taller than all the other houses in the village. Teaching took place in one big room. Sometimes fifty children from first to eighth grade were taught by one teacher. Two linden trees, which were rather rare in our region, stood in the schoolyard.

Almost anything that was not made in our village itself could be bought in the 'colonial goods' store: coffee, oil, sugar, salt, raisins, herring, rice, spices and other foods. People usually paid with eggs, because they often did not have cash. For instance, you could buy one herring for an egg (but no imported goods). We also had a post office with a telephone, and a village announcer. The announcer had the task of making public all official and ministerial information that was relevant to the village citizens. Swinging a large bell he would go through the village and call out his announcements. People were not informed individually. He was also responsible for announcing all the important decisions made by the village council.

Our village had an inn with a dancing and meeting hall. The inn must have been a thriving business once. Trudel writes, "During the pilgrim processions (in the eighteenth century) there were three inns in Auel."

From Trudel's report we know that our village's subsistence economy slowly began to disappear in the 1960s. "Families had more money." Where did this money come from?

The younger sons and daughters who had left the village to live in the city initially supported their families by sending them money. But after World War II, important new agricultural policies were implemented. Before I go into this in detail I have to say something about the social and economic differences that existed in our village. Although you could definitely speak of a village community that included everyone whilst I was a child, differences between families did exist.

Poor and rich

The poorer families were those of trades- and craftspeople, especially the families of the grinder, shoemaker, tailor and painter. Although they also cultivated land, they were dependent upon cash income – and were often short of cash because people tended to pay belatedly or in kind. Because of this, they tried to find additional sources of income. Our tailor was also our paramedic, our grinder was also a disinfector, our painter was also the sexton.

In the 1920s and 1930s, workers employed at the factory in Jünkerath, which was owned by Demag (German Machine Building Co.) at that time, were also from poorer families. During the world economic crash between 1929 and 1933, most of these men lost their jobs and 'hung around'. Our father, like many of the farmers still do today, thought they could find another job somewhere else if only they wanted to.

Belonging to the poor were also men who seemed to have come to Auel after World War I and who worked as casual labourers for the peasants. There was, for instance, a man they called Blefka – he was either Polish or Czech. He did not live long enough for me to know him, but I heard a lot of stories about him, such as:

If Blefka has a flea on his hip,
then he gets himself an insurance slip.
If Blefka has a bug or a sore,
then he gets himself to a hospital ward.

A further mocking rhyme was:

If on *Peter and Paul* there's no work to do,
(Saints' feast day, 29 June)
why should we work on the feast of *Mary's Visitation* too?
(Feast day of the 'Visitation', 31 May)

Such verses expressed the kind of derision for the 'lazy foreigners' who, although unable to speak German, were still able to take advantage of Germany's social benefits as they existed in the Weimar Republic of the 1920s. But they were just as much part of the village as other 'different' individuals who did not conform to the peasants' and tradespeople's expectations. This group also included younger siblings living in the village's 'Stockhäuser', or stem houses. They remained in their parental house, their land was not divided up. They did not marry, and thus had the right to stay in their parental home. They helped out on the farm as 'Ühm' (uncle) or 'Jött' (godmother) and did every kind of work, often as unpaid servants.

Tabo Didi

As children we used to mock such people; Tabo Didi was one of them. He was the younger brother of the tanner who came from a wealthy Stockhaus. He only worked occasionally. In the summer he would gather berries and brushwood, and at times he would help out in the fields. You could find him sleeping in a ditch. My brothers said his bedroom was full of books and clocks and many other gadgets. He supposedly could repair clocks. He would also boast of being able to speak several languages, including French. When they asked him what his name 'Johann' meant in French he would respond, "Tabo Didi." Ever since then, the entire village called him Tabo Didi. As little girls we used to imitate his waddling gait. In autumn, Tabo Didi also helped to thresh grain when many workers were needed. We would feed all of them in our house. While eating their meal they would always tell great stories and jokes, and we would listen to them intently. I remember a story by Tabo Didi. I do not remember what the story was about any more, but I do remember his philosophical conclusion, spoken in the Eifel dialect, "Et oss net liecht en Mensch ze senn." ("It isn't easy being human.")

Later, when at secondary school we were asked to write essays, I chose this sentence as my title and wrote about Tabo Didi and his philosophy of life, which was based on only working as much as was absolutely necessary. My German teacher was so enthusiastic about my essay that he would carry it around with him and often cite Tabo Didi's statement, "It isn't easy being human."

Cultural life in the village

As described above, our village was a subsistence village. This not only included material things but also cultural aspects such as festivals, conventions and customs, choirs, musical and theatre groups. We had one school and a church. The village teachers also often directed the choir and theatre association. An old neighbour of ours told my sister that a men's choir had been founded in Auel in 1875, which existed until 1938.

Moreover, the village had a very strong neighbourly tradition. In the summer, people would sit together after work, tell stories and sing. In the winter, they would visit each other at home. They would call this "ze Huurte john".[2] During these visits all sorts of work

---

2 This term is explained in the next paragraph.

would be done: the women would spin, knit, crochet; the men would make baskets or brooms. And while doing all this, they told stories and jokes and sang songs. The people had a good time together. Radio and television did not yet exist.

I do not know where the term "ze Huurte john" came from, which means "to go to huurt." A 'huurt' was a protective screen made of wood and straw that was erected on the fields in the cold months of autumn to shield the workers from wind and rain. People would huddle closely together behind such 'huurts' and keep each other warm.

Twice a year, most often in winter, the theatre association performed a play in one of the inn's meeting halls, mostly a comedy. I remember one play in which my older brothers also acted. It was a Christmas play directed by the village teacher. It was a wonderful experience. The play was the subject of discussion for weeks before and after the performance. And the Christmas nativity plays, usually performed in the church at midnight on Christmas Eve, also greatly inspired me.

And Christmas and St. Nicholas on 6 December! I do not know how my mother was able to make a present for every one of us. Most of the time we received knitted gloves, socks and shawls; sometimes even a pullover. She had to do all of this work after supper when we little ones were in bed, because we still believed the 'Kristkind', or Christ Child, brought all those beautiful new things. The Kristkind also baked all those plates of cookies. That is why mother had to bake her wonderful cookies at night. Sometimes, two or three cookies would be lying on the windowsill in the morning. We could smell them when we woke up and we knew the Kristkind had brought them.[3]

---

3 The belief in the Kristkind (today it is Santa Claus) was for us children the first dogma of our faith in something supernatural. According to this belief system, all good things came from heaven. 'Good children' were given goodies. Bad children were punished. When I found out that the Kristkind did not really exist, that mother had baked all these cookies, I began to lose my faith in the supernatural.

In the weeks before Christmas, our brothers built a nativity scene and cut our Christmas tree in the woods. As long as the Christmas tree stood in the 'good room' the whole family would gather around the tree, light the candles and sing Advent and Christmas songs. We did this until the feast of Epiphany on 6 January. Our father would even interrupt his work to come and sing with us. One of his favourite songs was "Es ist ein Ros' entsprungen" (Lo, How a Rose E'er Blooming), the words and melody of which deeply moved him. Actually, he seemed to be even more pleased than us children when he saw the table on Christmas morning with all those presents. Every single one of us received a full plate of gifts.

The magic of the Christmas season stayed with me for a very long time even after my childhood.

For years I did not know whether I liked winter or summer better. I leaned more toward winter because there was so much mystery and adventure involved. And so much fun and snow. Back then winters were often long and very snowy.

Despite the cold we spent most of our time outside skating and sledding. Father had a long sled made for us by the village carpenter that would fit eight children. He also opened the barbed wire fence behind our house so that we could have the longest possible slide when we dashed down the hill on our sled.

But in the evening we would come back with frozen hands and feet, and when we lay in bed at night chilblains on our feet would bother us and itch terribly. For years we tried different remedies to get rid of the itch, such as running through the snow with bare feet, sticking our feet in a bath of elm bark, or making a footbath with onion skins. The main reason we got frostbite was because we had grown, and the shoes handed down to us from our brothers or sister had become too small.

I was a very playful child. I played and fantasised wherever I was, whether at work, after work, in school and in church. When I was thirteen I could not imagine I would ever stop playing.

Politics and Contemporary History

Peasants and 'Häre' (Masters)

Our father, as described earlier, had a particular interest in history. He often told us what had happened in our village during the 'time of the French', that is, after the French Revolution, and particularly after 1794, when the French occupied the Rhineland. He also spoke of Napoleon who despotically imposed the principles and laws of the French Revolution on our villages, and then was forced to withdraw after his ignominious defeat in the 'Russian winter'. Father told us that after that defeat, lice-ridden and hungry French soldiers marched through our area on their way westward.

The French government tried to forcibly establish its revolutionary principles of liberté, egalité and fraternité (liberty, equality, fraternity) among the Eifel peasants. French administration was introduced, the region was divided into *departements* and *mairies* (municipalities), a costly bureaucracy was installed, and the peasants were burdened with new taxes. Monasteries were secularised, priests were forced to swear an oath of loyalty to the Republic, general compulsory education was introduced and priests were appointed as 'inspectors' of the schools. 'Freedom trees' were planted in the villages, decorated in the Republic's colours: 'bleu, blanc, rouge'. The months and weekdays were renamed according to the Roman model and religious holidays were abolished.

My father presumably knew about these new regulations from a book in the old Kellish House, in which all the ordinances from Paris for the 'Mairie' responsible for our region were compiled. The book was a collection of newspapers and probably came from father's uncle. The peasants hated the French and their new laws. And the French despised the uneducated, backward and noncompliant peasants.

As in other regions, peasants in the Eifel began to rebel against French domination. Michael Bornemann who was a pastor and school inspector in Daleiden, reported in 1841 that the peasants of Arzfeld and its surroundings (an area near Prüm), had literally instigated an uprising against the French (Bornemann, 1841). They marched with swords, scythes, pitchforks and cudgels against the highly equipped 'modern' French army. They began to cut down the 'Freedom Trees' in their villages and set out to plunder the parsonages first, because the pastors – still called 'de Häre' (from 'die Herren', or masters) in our region today – co-operated closely with the French. In this way, a few villages were 'liberated'. Bombarded by cannon fire, the peasants' revolt against the French failed and they were massacred by the thousands.

Karl Marx and Friedrich Engels, enlightened sons of the bourgeoisie, shared the modern Frenchmen's contempt for the dumb, backward peasants. In one of his writings on the German peasantry and the 'glorious revolution of 1813–14' Friedrich Engels stated,

> True, there was great enthusiasm then, but who were these enthusiasts? Firstly, the peasantry, the most stupid set of people in existence, who, clinging to feudal prejudices, burst forth in masses, ready to die rather than cease to obey those whom they, their fathers and grandfathers, had called their masters; and submitted to be trampled on and horse-whipped (Marx and Engels, 1846).

Engels may indeed have been referring to the rioting Eifel peasants here.

Karl Marx, in *The Eighteenth Brumaire of Louis Bonaparte* (1852), compared the French peasantry with a 'sack of potatoes'. Because, according to him, each is individually and purely concerned with his subsistence, and

... insofar as there is merely a local interconnection among these small-holding peasants, and the identity of their interests forms no community, no national bond, and no political organization among them, they do not constitute a class (Marx, 1852).

I have come from such a 'class', or rather 'non-class' of 'potatoes in a sack'.

Our father was still very angry with the French. He also despised any kind of master, no matter what form they took. The masters, the 'Häre' of his time, not only included the traditional feudal lords but also the new masters established by the French and later, after 1815, by the Prussian state. These were primarily civil servants, head officials, tax collectors, forest officials, teachers, and in particular pastors, as representatives of the Catholic Church, who functioned as inspectors of the schools all over the country. It is the latter who still are called 'de Häre' in our dialect today.

Although the peasants had to obey and pay taxes to these masters as representatives of the state, they would nevertheless make fun of them in many ways. Mother and father would tell us jokes and true stories about the 'Häre'. One of father's favourite sayings was, "Wenn der Bour net wär, verreckte de Här", which means, "without the peasant, the master would die."

The fact that everyone in the village could make a living and all were connected to each other, either by tradition or blood relationships and through mutual help, did not mean that there were no conflicts and animosities that could ruin the entire village's atmosphere. Often such conflicts arose when parents had died and their children had to divide the property. But also political issues divided the village.

Nazi era and the war

This was the case in the early 1930s when National Socialism found its way into our village and politics divided individual families. I was too small to understand what was happening. I only heard what mother and father and the other older siblings were saying. Mother told us, for instance, that she was always afraid for my father when he went to the church council meetings in Duppach, our parish village. She was afraid 'they' would beat or kill him on his way home at night. I didn't know who 'they' were.

I also saw how at school my older siblings were picked on and insulted with the name 'nose kings', which would put them in a rage and get them into terrible fights. 'Nose king' was a word one of my father's enemies used to insult him because of his long nose. This name promptly stuck like pitch onto our entire family and was even transferred to the next generation. Father suffered from the name-calling. He turned to a cousin who had gone to university to ask him what long noses meant. He wrote back, "Long noses are a sign of intelligence. Goethe and Frederick the Great had long noses." This put father's mind at rest.

Today, I wonder what the real reason was behind the animosities. Was it envy? Was it because we were so many children? But we were not wealthier than most of the other peasants. In 1933, there were already eight of us – and like many small peasant families, we were in debt (see above). Or were personal conflicts involved? Father was a proud and often hot-tempered man who did not mince his words. Yet he never went and stood around with the others for long at the pub. We did not have enough money for that. But he was conscious, as already mentioned, about coming from 'a good family'. The sense of being special probably did not make him very popular in the village. Incidentally, I and a few of my siblings also inherited this feeling, even though we were doing very poorly during the global depression in the early 1930s and therefore there was no visible reason for this pride.

Or were political differences the cause? Auel was one of the first villages in the Daun district with a National Socialist German Workers' Party (NSDAP) unit. There is a photograph of a rather large fire brigade procession where a swastika flag was being brandished. There is also a school photograph from the year 1934 which shows the older boys wearing swastika armbands. My oldest sister is in the picture. She is carrying me on her arm. I was three years old.

The members of the National Socialist Party and Nazi stormtroop (SA) were primarily unemployed workers. These young men would often march through the village singing and waving flags. Father despised them. For him they were 'layabouts'. Mother hated them. In particular, she hated the party's arrogant location group leader. In the 1930s, being the loyal Catholic he was, father sympathised with the Centre Party.

Perhaps it was political differences like these that were behind the village's animosities. In any event, I never again experienced such a politically charged atmosphere in our village as in the early years of my childhood.

War

Our village teacher was a member of the NSDAP and it was his duty to indoctrinate us children with the Nazi ideology, particularly with the attitude that Germany was the greatest country in the world. This indoctrination was done mainly by singing Nazi songs and by marching through the village as far as the sports ground which was very close to the school.

Josef Goebbels, the Minister of Propaganda under Hitler's rule, knew very well how best to spread Nazi ideology throughout the country: you have to implant it into the minds of children and the youth. Boys were the particular target of this indoctrination. They

learned how to march: left-right, left-right. And all of us learned the
most famous Nazi songs such as the 'Horst Wessel Lied':[4]

> ... wenn alles in Scherben fällt. Denn heute gehört uns
> Deutschland. Und morgen die ganze Welt (... when everything
> falls apart. Because today Germany belongs to us. And
> tomorrow the whole world).

From early on I realised that Germany was getting ready for war,
even if only in play. War was considered heroic and adventurous. I
entered school in 1937. In school we would play a kind of war game:
we would draw a circle on the floor and divide it up into slices as we
would do with a cake, each slice being a particular country, i.e.
Germany, France, Russia, England, and so on. One child would
begin and call, "Oh, you dumb, very dumb France," for example. All
would run away. The child who called out the war provocation
would try to catch the 'French' child. If successful, she could take
a piece of the 'French territory' and add it to her own.

We children would emulate in play what we had learned in class:
that after World War I, Elsass-Lothringa was given to France,
Eupen-Malmedy was given to Belgium. Before that, these regions
belonged to Germany.

The boys were not content to play such harmless games. The Auel
boys planned a real war against the Steffeln boys. Between the two
villages a certain rivalry had always existed.

---

4 Horst Wessel was a young enthusiastic follower of Hitler. He was a member of the
stormtroop (SA). He was shot by a communist and became the martyr and hero for the
Nazis. The 'Horst Wessel Song' became something of a Nazi anthem. One of the verses
described how he was shot by the 'Red Front and Reaction'. I did not know what 'Red
Front' and 'Reaction' meant, but like the others I learned this song. We were of course
proud of our great country. During my later school years in Gerolstein and Prüm there was
less of this triumphalism. Probably because Germany no longer went from victory to
victory. Particularly in our border area it became clear that this war would end in a disaster.

Steffeln was somewhat wealthier and larger than Auel. Despite the rivalry, the two villages had always been connected by marriages between its residents – our mother came from Steffeln. They are only one kilometre away from each other; together they now form one municipality.

But in the political climate before 1939, Steffeln was seen as the 'natural enemy' by the Auel boys. And they prepared their war with strategic military precision: they collected 'weapons' and blank cartridges, made wooden swords, searched for old World War I weapons and 'ammunition' from the last manoeuvres of the past years. Kyllenberg, the mountain between Steffeln and Auel, was chosen as the theatre of war. A day was also scheduled for the war to begin.

My five older brothers hid their weapons in the 'dark cubbyhole' of our house, a tiny windowless cubicle next to the chimney. As we often visited our uncles and aunts in Steffeln, I once boasted about my brothers' huge weapons arsenal and how they would surely defeat the Steffeln boys. When my brothers heard of this, they were angry with me and called me a traitor.

I do not know how the war between Steffeln and Auel ended, but my older brothers are still enthusiastic about recounting the heroic deeds they accomplished back then against their Steffeln adversaries.

The game gets serious

It was not long after the children's war that their play turned into serious war: in 1939, the German Wehrmacht marched into Poland. It was clear to everyone that there would soon be war. First there were the men who built the Siegfried Line, or 'Westwall' as it is called in Germany, and the access roads to the western border which was only thirty kilometres away. All of these workers on the 'Westwall' were quartered in our villages. They came from Saxony,

Bavaria, Berlin and various other places in Germany. They camped out in our barns.

After 1939, we always had soldiers in our village and barn. At first they were infantrymen, then other army units came. Toward the end in the autumn of 1944, SS-men came.

The soldiers were simple men who suffered from homesickness. They always sought contact with the village people and often spent time in our living room-kitchen. By then we had acquired a radio which stood in our kitchen, the only room that stayed warm in winter. That is where they gathered to listen to either the news or music.

My smaller sisters and brothers were always hanging around somewhere near the soldiers who would sometimes give them army pan loaf or something from the 'field kitchen'. And the soldiers would play with them.

The same happened after the war when the Americans entered our village. They parked a huge tank in front of our house. Behind the house they set up their army tent. They gave us chocolate which was something we hardly knew.

For us children, the games we played and the stories we heard from the soldiers served to conceal the terrors of war behind a smoke screen of adventure, although the horrors of war were indeed very real.

My five older brothers were recruited one by one to go to war and, as part of Germany's standing army, they were deployed somewhere on the Eastern Front. The youngest, Franz, was just 15 years old when he was recruited from school to serve as an anti-aircraft auxiliary. His unit was stationed near Leipzig.

We prayed for our brothers at the front. Mother baked 'war cakes' according to a special recipe where she used molasses instead of sugar which was rationed. She knitted socks and gloves and put together packages for her sons on the Eastern Front. Of course we knew that soldiers were killed in the war. But somehow I lived, we lived, in the belief that this would not happen to our brothers. My parents' unswerving faith in the particular protection of the Holy Virgin, Mother of God, probably contributed to this belief.

Even when in the autumn of 1944 the National Socialist Party location group leader came to break the news that our brother Michael had 'fallen on the field of honour' and that we should be very proud of him, I could not believe it. Mother cried and was at the same time angry at the location group leader for his Nazi talk. It then seemed like a miracle when Michael showed up a day later on our doorstep, alive and healthy. He had been wounded in Hungary, had lain in a military hospital and was now returning on home leave.

The horrors of war crept ever closer to us. Hitler's wonder weapon, the V-1 rocket, almost never reached enemy lines in the west, but came down on our meadows and fields, tearing up huge craters in the process. Since the beginning of the war we also gave shelter to refugees who had been evacuated from villages near the Western Front. They, too, lived in our overcrowded house. We also heard and read about bombings in the big cities, the hunger and destruction that was taking place there.

All of this was without doubt terrible. But for us children, this terror was also connected with a great deal of adventure. The war was still not a direct experience for me.

Not until I once saw a large troop of forced labourers who had to pull a huge wagon as big as a railcar. They were being driven on by German SS-soldiers with whips and sticks. At the last house one of them stepped out of line and wanted to drink water. He was brutally bashed for it.

I had another similar experience of horror toward the end of the war. While retreating eastward, the defeated German troops destroyed everything so that the 'enemy' could not get their hands on it. For example, they killed army horses, skinned them (their hide was still useful), and dragged their skinned corpses through the village and dumped them into the craters left by V-1 rockets on fields. After the war, in the wonderfully warm spring of 1945, the dead corpses polluted the entire blossoming landscape with their stinking smell of rot. This was one of the worst atrocities of the war I personally experienced.

However, I was not afraid of 'war'. It had become a part of our daily life. Although a lot of the food was rationed, and despite the taxes we had to pay to the government, we as subsistence peasants still had enough to eat: enough bread, potatoes, milk and butter. We were also able to slaughter a pig and make do with its meat for the entire year. Hunger was unfamiliar to us – in comparison to many other children in the cities. We also had enough wood from the communal forest to heat our kitchen. The Western Front was never close enough as to fear grenades and bombings. This changed shortly before the end of the war when the Americans advanced with their tanks into Germany after their invasion of France. This was when Auel also came under fire and we had to seek shelter at night in a neighbour's cellar. My father did not want to leave our house. He said, "I live here, and if it pleases God, I will die here." He went to bed and slept quietly, despite the cannon thunder and grenade explosions. It was too boring for me and my youngest sister Trudel in our neighbour's cellar. In the middle of the night we got up and ran home. Shell splinters whizzed past our heads. At home, we lay next to father and felt secure. His faith in God, or more accurately, his trust in the Mother of God, protected us.

I was also not afraid when I had to take my brother Franz, the anti-aircraft auxiliary, on my bike to the train station in Gerolstein twelve kilometres away after his short Christmas home leave in 1944. Had the fifteen-year-old not returned to his troop he would have been considered a deserter and would have been shot. When I biked home it was already dark. The light on my bicycle was not working, neither were the brakes, and there were soldiers lying everywhere in the woods. But I was not afraid. I had never heard of rape.

The war ended in May 1945. During the course of the spring and summer of 1945, my brothers returned from the war and prison camps; the youngest came first. He trudged back from Leipzig on foot. Because he was so young, the Americans let him cross the Rhine bridge at Remagen, the only bridge not destroyed during the war. They thought he was a child. The last of the five, however, was a prisoner of war in Russia and was not released until 1949. He finally returned, gaunt but healthy. My parents attributed the fact that all of their sons had returned safely from prison camps and the war to the particular protection by the Holy Mother of God. They certainly could not explain why other families, who had lost their sons, were not as lucky. In the opinion of many, the Holy Mary was also responsible for protecting our villages from destruction. The pastor of Steffeln erected a small chapel in her honour on a mountain in the vicinity. Since then it has become a place of pilgrimage.

Although I left the Catholic Church later on, I know that my parents' absolute faith in God, their conscious awareness that all of us were under the particular protection of Holy Mary, most probably formed the basis for my trust in life. Deep within I believe that nothing bad will happen to me. Even if this belief was not always – and will not always – be confirmed by real events, it did save me from fear, despondency and depression. Without this courage to live I would not have so unhesitatingly thrown myself into life, I would not have undertaken such bold projects as I did.

As already mentioned, my mother was the more optimistic of my two parents, even though she had more than enough cause for worry and fear. The following story shows the kind of courage she had. It took place toward the end of the war. Later, when I was theoretically working with the issue of subsistence, I remembered this story.

Researching the history of subsistence inevitably brought me to the deeper insight of how one's own life story is intricately interwoven with contemporary history. When I asked myself where I should begin the review of my childhood, my mother came to mind. I would like to recount this story in her honour.

My mother and the sow: Life must go on

It was in February or March of 1945. The war was coming to an end. Our village was near the Western Front. Around this time defeated German soldiers, tattered and verminous, were retreating from the west and seeking warmth and a little food from the peasants in the Eifel. Every evening, mother cooked a pot of milk soup and a pot of potatoes. She said, "I hope that some other woman somewhere is doing something like this for our boys, too." Every evening, soldiers sat with us at the dinner table.

Many people had given up hope. Most of the peasants had slaughtered their cows and pigs, they were not thinking of cultivating and sowing their fields. Everyone was waiting for the end of the war without thinking beyond it. At this time my mother brought her sow to a boar. Peasants in the Eifel all had a few pigs, sows or mother animals capable of giving birth to little piglets. Male pigs were usually castrated. Our little village did not have a boar. This would have been a waste. And boar meat did not taste well. Our boar was in Steffeln, in a kind of cave quarried out of volcanic rock.

Usually our older brothers were responsible for driving our sow in heat from our village to Steffeln which was often an adventurous undertaking, as the animals were very excitable in that state. Our brothers had to stay by the 'Bier', which in our Eifel dialect means 'boar'. When the sow got covered, they had to make sure the sow 'stood'. Otherwise, impregnation would not result. And it only happened if the sow wanted it. Raping does not work, neither with pigs nor with cows. Of course, now they are artificially impregnated by force.

It was boys' work to drive the sow to the 'Bier'. They learned quite a few things about sexuality and impregnation. However, during the war all the boys were gone and mother had to drive the sow herself to the 'Bier'. Our neighbour laughed at her and said she would be better off slaughtering her pig. Did she not realise everything was coming to an end? My mother answered, *"Life goes on!"* Perhaps she also said, *"Life has to go on!"*

She brought her sow to the boar. And her sow 'stood'. At the end of May, when the war was over, the sow gave birth to twelve little pigs. No one had piglets, calves or foals at this time. And because money was not worth anything any more, mother exchanged her piglets for shoes, trousers, shirts and jackets for her five sons who, one after the other, returned from the war. Life went on.

But did it go on by itself? My mother did not just sit down and say to herself, "Life will go on somehow." Neither did she say as a Christian peasant's wife, "The Lord will provide somehow!" She knew she had to do something; she had to work with nature in order for life to continue. Life had to go on. That was her wish, her passion, her philosophy, this is what gave her courage and a zest for life.

My mother was not a feminist, and the word ecology was not familiar to her. But she did recognise something that has meanwhile become as essential as our daily bread: she realised that we have to take responsibility for life if we want it to continue. Today we know that life will not just simply continue 'naturally'. Increasing ecological catastrophes are showing us that our modern industrial society, rooted in its chase for constant growth in goods and capital, is progressively destroying nature's ability to renew herself to the point where it no longer can. This applies to human nature, especially to women and children, as well as to the rest of nature.

Up until now it was women, women like my mother, who in their daily lives – particularly also after wars and other catastrophes – took responsibility for life to continue for their daughters, sons, husbands and for nature. When wars are carried out by men against nature and foreign peoples, it is the women who clean up afterward. Yet we must not only make sure that life continues after a patriarchal war, we have to fight that such wars no longer take place at all.

3

The World Opens Its Doors
– *Happy Coincidences*

"I am an artist"

From very early on I knew who I was and what I wanted. From the time I was little it was clear to me that I was an artist. I could draw and paint well. Whenever I found a piece of paper and pencil I drew something. I loved to draw imaginative shapes the most. When herding our cattle, I would take clay from the brook to make little figures. By chance I also later received coloured pencils. An 'uncle', who always visited a neighbouring family in the summer, gave me a watercolour set and later two small sketch books. They contain some of my very first works.

When I was six, I entered our single-class village school. Back then, fifty children from the village still went to our school. They all sat on long wooden benches in a room about ten by six metres. There was only a small aisle on the right side of the room for our teacher (who was initially a man; later during the war a woman taught us). The first-graders sat in the front; in the back were the older, eighth-grade pupils. Teaching a class of so many different ages demanded particular teaching skills. While the teacher instructed the older ones in calculating interest, the little ones had to be employed with writing, arithmetic, handwriting or memorising the multiplication tables. Sometimes the teacher asked one of the older children to take the first- and second-graders outside into the hall where they sat on the steps and read out loud to the 'assistant schoolmaster'. The principle of 'each one teach one', as practised everywhere in Maoist China, was something I learned in my early childhood.

This principle was not only important in school but more so at home, where the older brothers and sisters would help the younger ones with their homework. Despite the didactic attempts of the teacher to keep the class occupied, I still had enough time left over to draw, think up stories, or play games with my neighbours on our slate boards.

I was not particularly good at arithmetic. I was not interested in numbers. My sister Katrin was much better at it. She could recite the multiplication tables forwards and backwards – like our mother. But I could read very well, write essays, recite poems, and of course paint! I was an artist, remember?

In 1942, the Nazis opened a 'Hauptschule', a kind of middle school, in the town of Gerolstein, twelve kilometres away, to promote talented children from the country. Our teacher recommended to my parents that I attend this school. I was eleven years old. This middle school had only a two-year programme.

This meant I had to travel by train to Gerolstein. Yet Auel was five kilometres away from the next train station in Oberbettingen near Hillesheim. It was therefore not possible for me to make daily trips from home to Gerolstein and back. There were no buses and I could only reach the train station by foot.

My father knew a postal officer who lived in a twin house in Gerolstein. This man spoke to his neighbour, a widow, who lived in the other half of the house. They agreed that I would live with her and eat my meals with the postal officer's wife. This worked wonderfully. I do not know whether the cost for my board and lodging was paid by my family or by the state. Probably the latter, because the government had an interest in promoting talented country children. We did have to pay for the cost of travelling between Gerolstein and Oberbettingen ourselves, but it was only a few Marks.

On the weekends I went home and walked on foot westward from Oberbettingen to Auel. This was always a great joy for me. When I reached the top of the hill just above my home I could see our beautiful village spread out before me, nestled in its wide valley, with the tiny baroque church at its centre. Then I was home. I had returned from the 'east', from 'the world outside'.

'At home' I once again was a child like all the others and had to help, but I also played a lot. However, the youngest, Gottfried, felt I did not quite belong 'to us', that I was a stranger. Because I was not 'there' most of the time. That is why he did not want me to bathe him in our zinc bathtub in the kitchen on Saturdays. We all took baths in that bathtub. Bathrooms were unknown.

When the weekend was over, I had to get up very early in the morning to walk the five kilometres to the train. In the winter it was still very dark. This was when one of my older brothers would sometimes take me on his bicycle to Oberbettingen. I sat sideways on the middle bar; my baggage was strapped to the rack on the back.

Going to this school marked the beginning of an education career totally untypical for young country girls back then. It was not a very special school. We may have had a little bit more German, history, and geography than in our school in Auel. We also had local history and geography lessons – which was a particularly interesting subject in Gerolstein because it was my first contact with the prehistory of the volcanic region I call home. Its diverse geology was visible wherever one went. From the limestone crags of Munterlay and Auberg mountains west of the Kyll – that tiny river which cuts its way through the Eifel mountains to reach the Mosel river – springs the famous Gerolstein sparkling mineral water. This spring is still the most important employer of the region and city today. Today, the *Gerolsteiner Corporation* has become a 'global player'.

There are many such 'sparkling springs' of mineral and iron rich water all over the region. We call such springs 'drees'. Many villages have their own 'drees'. I was very interested in all of this and more, such as the 'Buchenloch,' or birch hole, which was an ice age cave on Munterlay mountain where traces of ice age humans and animals were found. Earth history and human history, both tangibly present and visible, were taught at our school.

In addition we learned *English*. This was later to become a very important factor in my life. I was not conscious of it then. I did notice, however, that I enjoyed foreign languages and was able to learn them quickly.

In 1944, after two years, I had to leave this school which actually should have also meant the end of my school career. But I wanted to continue learning. Then something came to my help, something which continued to happen throughout my life: *A happy coincidence occurred*. It became possible for me to finish my school education at the Regino-Gymnasium[1] in Prüm, until then a practically impossible achievement for any girl who did not come from Prüm itself. This was because once more, there were no buses and the next train station on the line between Gerolstein and Prüm, Müllenborn, was ten kilometres away from us. It was therefore much more difficult to get to the station than it was during my school years in Gerolstein.

In addition, there were no boarding homes for girls in Prüm, although there had already been one for boys for many years in the form of an episcopal boarding home. This was because the Bishops of Trier were particularly interested in attracting intelligent boys from the purely agricultural and Catholic Eifel region to become priests. The classical gymnasium in Prüm served to provide these boys with the necessary education for the profession, in particular

---

1 The gymnasium in Prüm, a preparatory school for university, goes back to Princess Betrada of Mürlenbach (mother of Charlemagne), who founded a Benedictine monastery on her estate of Prüm in 720 B.C.E. The Benedictine monks opened a cloister school, which later became a humanist gymnasium (see Friedrich Gehendges, *Eiflia Illustrata*, 1982, vol. 3, pp. 324).

with knowledge of Latin and Greek. The gymnasium also accepted boys who did not intend to become priests. A few of my cousins who were sons of the forester, attended the school in this way.

The National Socialists broke the church's monopoly on the 'human capital' of this region. They opened the boarding school for all boys and built a further boarding home as an extension to the old monastery in Niederprüm. Two of my older brothers were able to attend the Regino-Gymnasium in Prüm because of this.

My parents did not have to pay anything for this school. As is the case still today, no fees are required for state schools, and the costs for room and board were paid by the government for families who had many children.

When I came to Prüm in April of 1944, the Nazis had also opened a National Socialist girls' boarding home. This gave girls from the surrounding villages a first-time opportunity to attend a gymnasium.

My attendance at this school, however, only lasted from April until September 1944. It was war time and Prüm is situated near the Belgian border. The Western Front was only a few kilometres away. We had to haul sand and fill sandbags which were intended to protect us against the cannon fire, the thunder of which seemed to get closer over the months. It was a silly activity. All of the schools near the front had to do this. By September 1944, it had become too dangerous to continue normal school activity. The school was closed.

No one was happier about this abrupt ending than I. Never in my life, neither before nor after, have I ever suffered from *homesickness* as much as I did during those five-and-a-half months in Prüm.

Homesickness

When I left school and returned to the girls' boarding home, I escaped to the church and cried. When we had to haul sand, I dashed into the bushes, threw myself on the ground, and cried. At night I cried myself to sleep. Auel, my village, was only twenty kilometres away and I could take the train home every two weeks. When I had to return to Prüm on Sunday evening that miserable feeling of being cast out would begin. My mother often accompanied me with the five younger ones to the train station in Müllenborn. On the way, I would already begin to cry and my mother and the others cried with me. It was terrible.

I was envious of the most stupid boy in the village. He was allowed to stay home, eat fried potatoes with his brothers and sisters in the evening, and drive the family's cattle to the meadow.

And the cows! How I missed the cows and their smell! All of this was home to me. When I came home on my weekend visits I did not go through the front door of the house, but through the cowshed. Here I was met by the smell of milk, cow dung and our cows' breath. I was home then. In the cowshed we had our mother to ourselves. After her day's work she still had to do the milking. For this she would sit on her three-legged stool and the warm milk would squirt into the pail between her legs. Sometimes we drank the milk fresh from the cow. My mother would squirt the milk directly from the cow's udder into our mouths.

We could ask her things while she was milking in the evening that, in the noise of work and our children's squabbles, often would not find an attentive ear. Mother said milking was her recreation.

I missed all of this in the girls' boarding home in Prüm. *The theme of my life appeared with its terrible homesickness: the tension between a longing for the faraway, for the world, and a longing for home.* This issue is still with me today.

I have often wondered why this homesickness hit me so powerfully in Prüm of all places. It was not the first time I had been away from home. When I was eight I was chosen to go with my brother Franz to take part in a 'children's country recreation' program. I was a lanky, small girl with skinny legs and thin braids. We were 'sent' to Lake Constance. I was homesick there, too, because my brother Franz was placed in a different family. I did not know where he was, and he did not try to find out where I was either. I cried all the time and did not want to eat.

But the homesickness I had in Prüm was different. It was deeper and touched that very rift which has continued to run through my life. What exactly triggered that homesickness? It was not only the fact that, if I wanted to continue my education (which I did), I would no longer be able to stay at home.

I think it was experiencing the kind of *institutionalised discipline* as was practised at this boarding home. We were allowed to wear only slippers inside. But I had no slippers. We were at war and there was no money for things like slippers. We also had to observe 'silentium' in the afternoons – which meant we were not allowed to speak when we did our homework. There were specific times for getting up, eating, going to bed. The kind of freedom and play I had known until then was now restricted. Unconsciously I think I rebelled against this discipline, but felt alone and helpless at the same time. I just wanted to leave this *exile*. The end of the war was my salvation.

Schools after the war

I still wanted to attend higher education. It was clear to me that if I wanted to become an 'artist', my primary education in Auel would not suffice. The end of the war, however, put an end to these dreams. All secondary schools were closed. There were not even enough teachers available who could teach in the elementary schools. Like my younger siblings, I stayed at home and helped in the house and on the fields.

When I was fifteen, my mother said the time had finally come for me to go to Cologne and work as a servant-girl in a household. Because that was the normal career for girls in the Eifel villages. They went to the city to work as maidservants, learned how a bourgeois household functioned, and waited until they met a man who would marry them.

I knew I did not want *that*. Because all my dreams and plans would come to an end if I married. But what was the alternative? One after the other, my brothers began to return from being prisoners of war. Thank God all were healthy, but none had become trained in any skill. All concern was directed toward helping them get a job or an apprenticeship somewhere. It was clear to my parents that I would marry, as all girls do.

In this seemingly hopeless situation I again was aided by a few *happy coincidences*. A man with some money had opened a 'lamp factory' in an old inn in Steffeln. In this 'factory', unemployed war veterans carved lamp stands for lamp shades made of oiled paper. Because I could paint well, I got my first job: I drew deer, stags, trees and fairytale figures on the lamp shades as decoration. The work was fun. It was a 'real' job where I could work as an 'artist' and earn some money. Unfortunately, the factory – which was a true small industry – had to close after just a few months. With it my career as a worker and artist was put to an end for the time being.

Everything seemed pretty hopeless again. I absolutely did not want to take the usual path taken by girls back then and become a maid-servant.

Once again, a *happy coincidence* helped me. We were hacking turnips on the field when our teacher came by. She said, "Maria, the French are opening a new school in Trier. If you take the entrance examination now and pass, in four years you can take the final examination. After that you can study at an institute of education and become a public school teacher. Are you interested?" Of course I was!

The 'Paedagogium' in Trier and Wittlich

I went to Trier. I passed the entrance exam and in April of 1947, at the age of sixteen, I once again became a student. I attended the 'Paedagogium', which is how the French occupation government, who ruled the French Zone, called this pedagogical institute.

In 1947, miserable conditions existed in all cities for carrying out regular school activities – even in Trier. We used the Friedrich Wilhelm Gymnasium building which had not been destroyed during the war,[2] and went to class in shifts. We had to share this school with other pupils and had to keep moving back and forth. We received our meals in the Kolping Association building and in private households which was paid for by the French government. Our teachers were retired gymnasium and public school teachers chosen by the French: all were open-minded and wanted to promote international understanding.

The goal of the French was twofold. The first was to train as many new public school teachers as possible, since, all over the country, schools were in a real state of emergency. Teacher training, as practiced before which involved going through gymnasium and proper teacher seminars, would have taken much too long. Moreover, there were not enough gymnasium teachers left to teach. Many of them had died in the war. However, the training concept developed by the French gave both young men and women the opportunity to become public teachers after four years of attending the pedagogical institute, followed by two years in an academy of education.

The second goal of the French was a political one. The new teacher training was established according to the French *École Normale* system. The French occupation government tried to more firmly embed French culture and its school system in Germany; in a sense it sought to re-educate the Germans. The French occupation government selected the schools' teachers. Most importantly, our first foreign language was French, and teachers from France taught us the language.

The French also carried all of the costs related to the training, not only for the pedagogical institute, but also later, for the teachers' academy. Their only condition, however, was that all public school

---

2 Karl Marx received his Abitur, or matriculation, there which I was not aware of at that time. I had never heard of Karl Marx.

teachers passing the teachers' examination agreed to remain and teach for the next five years in the French zone, later the Land of Rheinland-Pfalz.

I was excited about this school from the start, especially with regard to our director, Karl Kaiser. He was a painter and admirer of French art and culture. It was his desire to stimulate our creativity and interest in foreign cultures. But most importantly, he opened our eyes and our senses to the beauty of art and nature.

A first Impressionist exhibition was organised in Trier at that time. During the Nazi era, this would have been impossible. Our director took us to the exhibition and explained the pictures and colour effects. Afterwards, we wrote essays on what we experienced. Excerpts of my essay were published in the *Trierische Volksfreund*, which was, and still is, the local newspaper. My first public success!

I do not remember exactly what we were taught at this school in Trier. But I do remember the excursions 'der Kaiser', as we called him, organised for us to the city and surrounding forests. On these excursions, he showed us that the woods were not just green, but brought our attention to the blue-green light shining through the trees. In the city, he sharpened our awareness for architectural beauty, even if what we were looking at were Roman ruins. He introduced us to the history and art history of this old city.

I painted and drew as much as I could and 'der Kaiser' praised my first attempts. He taught me how to create wonderful artwork with carbon black and water. Because at that time we did not yet have water colours or oil colours.

The spring and summer of 1947 stays in my memory as one of the happiest, if not even *the happiest*, times of my life. Every morning I woke up happy and looked forward to going to school. I was glad that I could learn about and do things in the vocation I had planned for myself. My homesickness had disappeared, once and for all.

It was a warm and sunny spring. I was enthusiastic about everything I heard and saw. Whether it was the ivy climbing its way up the old sandstone ruins of St. Maximin Church, or my school classes in the old Friedrich Wilhelm Gymnasium, or the meagre meals we got in a church building, I was just thrilled. Despite the difficult and, according to today's standards, very poor circumstances, I was happy. I felt I had arrived where I had longed to go.

The major source of my enthusiasm of course was 'der Kaiser'. He was not only a teacher who could enthuse (in my opinion, a teacher's most important quality), but he was also an 'attractive man'. He was tall and handsome with steel-blue eyes and brown hair. No wonder we sixteen-year-olds – and especially I – adored him; we were all in love with him. But being in love with him remained restricted to the daily joy of being able to see him, hear him and be with him.

Unfortunately, this time did not last very long. The entire school was transferred to Wittlich at the end of 1947. There the old Cusanus Gymnasium was rebuilt as a boarding school to house the Pedagogical Institute for Girls. A huge sleeping hall was installed on the top floor. The kitchen and dining rooms were on the ground floor, the classes were arranged on the second and third floors. They also functioned as our recreation rooms.

A woman became our director. Our old director, 'der Kaiser', was replaced, because he was 'only' a public school teacher. The new director tried to turn the school into a 'normal boarding school for girls', which we all rejected. Luckily, she did not stay long. She was replaced by Dr Hans Wink whom the Nazis had suspended from teaching because of his progressive ideas on education. His new job as director of the Pedagogical Institute for Girls in Wittlich was his first employment after the Nazi era.[3]

---

3 He never said whether his suspension was connected with socialist or even communist ideas. He did tell me much later that he was disappointed because the Social Democrats never rehabilitated him.

He immediately began to restructure the school according to the progressive educational ideals of the 1920s. He first brought together a team of like-minded colleagues who would back his concept. Then he rearranged the rooms. The sleeping hall was transformed into small rooms shared by four pupils each. The classrooms were divested of their long benches. Tables were installed, each seating four pupils who could freely choose to sit and learn together. The classroom looked like a coffee house. Because these classrooms were also our recreation rooms, we had cupboards painted in red and blue where we could keep our things. An L-shaped bench and table stood in one corner where larger groups could get together – with our teachers as well – and engage in discussions.

The goal of all of this restructuring was evident: instead of achievement, individual learning and individual competition, as is the case today, cooperation and mutual help within the group was promoted. Trust and freedom, instead of control, were the most important pedagogical goals. Our rooms were to be arranged in an appealing design in order to make us feel comfortable and where we could develop our diverse talents.

This new concept was not only manifested in the school's spatial design, but also in a number of pedagogical innovations which were unusual at that time.

For instance, every week we held a general assembly or student parliament in which we criticised our teachers – who were also present – very sharply. The director often held speeches in the hallway in front of the dining hall to keep us up to date on the most important political developments, and we learned how to discuss them.

We did not have regular political instruction. That subject did not exist yet. Yet we became so politicised by our teachers that we were all against the Federal Government's decision to re-arm Germany, and we held intense debates about it. I remember suggesting we organise a kind of boycott against the re-armament.

German and History classes were the subjects in which we primarily became politicised. We read, of course, the classics in these courses: Schiller, Goethe, Kleist, and also modern authors such as Borchert (*The Man Outside*) or Anouilh (*Antigone*).

Our Teachers

Our school director was able to put together a team of teachers who in some way or another shared his progressive ideas – in those days this was still possible. Some of them were not much older than ourselves. Our male teachers had just returned from the war and were inspired by the idea of promoting international understanding and peace. The French occupation government also supported these ideas. French was our first foreign language, and our French teachers were, of course, French.

Together with our German instructor and class teacher, Heinrich Holkenbrink, or 'der Holkenbrink', we read Schiller's *The Robbers*, *Don Carlos*, and *Wallenstein*. We then read Schiller's *Aesthetic Letters* which induced intense debates on Schiller's essay on the 'naïve' and 'sentimental' concept of nature. We read Kleist's *Marionette Theatre* as well as his *Penthesilea*. And of course we also read and discussed Goethe's *Faust I* and *II*.

The teacher's aim was not only to promote our knowledge of language and literature, but also to stir and strengthen our interest in the deeper philosophical questions addressed by this literature. Our teachers were just as enthusiastic as we were, and often overextended their teaching beyond the scheduled end of the class.

They also furthered our independence and creativity wherever they could. Dr Wink, for example, encouraged me to put together an exhibition on baroque art and install the show in the school hallway. For this, I also had to prepare a paper. I gathered illustrations from old newspapers and illustrated books and explained the baroque style to my class. Armed with an old projector, I presented my essay and projected photographs of baroque buildings onto the wall.

In the German class, we were invited to write papers on themes we were interested in ourselves. The kind of freedom we enjoyed is illustrated in the following story. It also shows what good relationships existed between us and our teachers.

I was enthusiastic about Kleist, especially with regard to his tragedy about the Amazon queen *Penthesilea*. I wrote my essay on *Penthesilea* and publicly announced the date of my presentation. However, when the time came, 'der Holkenbrink', our German teacher, did not stop in time but continued to lecture, as he habitually did. The same happened the next week and the week after. I was fed up. I told my fellow classmates I would no longer present my paper. Our teacher's behaviour injured my dignity.

Who would have thought: the next time we had our German class, 'der Holkenbrink' finished earlier and said, "Well, we still have Maria's paper on Kleist's *Penthesilea*." I gathered all my courage and replied, "I no longer see any point in reading my paper!" Our teacher turned chalk white and rushed out of the classroom. My classmates rebuked me. How could I be so rude? How could I insult our beloved and honoured teacher in such a way? But I had to.

For weeks I did not speak to him. After a long time, I could no longer bear it and told him I had to do it out of self-respect. He understood. Everything was fine again.

As a young woman I was enthusiastic about literature, philosophy, art and the concept of international understanding. I began to become interested in politics. When a local chapter of the Junge Union (Young Christian Democrats) was established in Wittlich (any other party would have been unthinkable in the Catholic Rhine-Mosel region at that time), we all went to join in the discussions. We debated Germany's re-armament which we all rejected. We carried a banner with the slogan NO MORE WAR – NEVER AGAIN! We were so excited to have found a means of public debate on political issues in this small, conservative town that we convinced our class teacher to attend a Young Christian Democrats' meeting. He followed our advice and joined us. Later he became a Christian Democratic Party (CDU) member and carved out a great career for himself. He climbed the ladder to ultimately become Minister of Economic Affairs in the Land Rheinland-Pfalz. It is still incomprehensible to me how he could do such a U-turn – from the idealistic teacher and philosopher of our school days, to the Minister of Economic Affairs, responsible for executing the capitalist course of the CDU. Perhaps it was his belief in our new constitution and its commitment to social justice. Or perhaps his idealism was replaced by a kind of Wallensteinian 'realism'. "Ideas may dwell together in your mind. But in reality things clash."[4]

Love and friendship

We were inspired by the ideas of German Idealism. But we were also young. Because of the war we were slightly older than young women in secondary schools today – and like all nineteen-year-olds we also were interested in *Love*.

For many of us, love was not just a theoretical idea. There were many close friendships among us; some of us were perhaps in love. Yet to my knowledge, none of these developed into open lesbian relationships. In my case, two of my classmates became my best friends. This friendship has remained stable and enduring; it has lasted to this day. If possible, we try to meet once a year.

Although we were aware that lesbianism existed as an alternative to heterosexual relationships, it did not really count. In any case, it could not be shown openly. Some of us were interested in the boys at the Cusanus Gymnasium which was in the same building as ours. But the most romantic and dramatic relationships developed between women students and some of the French soldiers who were stationed in a garrison in Wittlich. Our boarding home director and our teachers were very tolerant, and we had no regulations. Like us,

---

4 The original German reads: "Eng beieinander wohnen die Gedanken. Doch hart im Raume stoßen sich die Sachen."

the director and the teachers knew of the love affairs. But the teachers trusted us. They issued no bans or prohibitions. How could they? We were all more or less adult women.

And myself? What was my attitude towards love? I was perhaps the most idealistic of all idealists. On the wall next to our group table I wrote the following inscription in pencil: "Ama et fac quod vis" (Love and do what you will). But where was the appropriate object for this ideal love? I was not at all interested in the boys from the Cusanus Gymnasium. And the French soldiers were out of the question, too. I found them stupid. No, I was not looking for a man. My yearning for love was a vague, foggy, idealistic feeling that evaporated instantly as soon as a member of the other sex came close.

Men

I really was not interested in men. My experiences with strange men had been rather unpleasant and were limited to my dancing partners at major festivities in Steffeln: fun fairs, Christmas and Easter parties where old and young people would come together. Young men came from villages far and wide. As a girl, you had to wait patiently until one of the men invited you to dance. I always felt this to be an indignity. Moreover, I was not really pretty and could not dance well. We did not have dance classes although my older brothers who had returned from the war, were all crazy about dancing but did not have the patience to teach me the foxtrot, waltz, rhinelander, etc. I did not like the male-female relationship expressed in these dances anyway. The man 'led' and the woman had to 'follow' his movements. The worst thing about it was that some men had to have drinks at the bar first before they had enough courage to ask a girl to dance. Sometimes, I would sit around like a wallflower toward the end of the evening until some rather drunken man came to recite his ritualised "May I?" in High German. Then he would hold me so tight, the smell of alcohol emanating from every pore of his body, that I was unable to move and put some distance between us. As a girl, you were forced to either 'yield' or run away.

So when dances were announced, I ran to the woods. Alone. I would walk for hours through the Auel and Steffeln forest, explore new and untrodden paths, or tramp straight through the thicket until I came to a clearing. I always expected to find something new.

Sometimes, I took my sketchbook to the woods. I drew whatever caught my eye. I learned about plants and trees, came to love their character, their aura. Without knowing at the time what that was. Beech trees became my favourite: their wonderfully smooth and high trunks, the imaginative patterns formed by their branches and twigs, the leaves of which would glow with light green colour in May and explode in a firework of gold and rust-red in autumn.

When I first became conscious, even if unclearly so, that issues about men and everything to do with them such as marriage, housework, children, etc., was not *my* thing, I also understood I would probably live my life alone.

"I'll just hug a tree then", I once said to myself. Sayings involving trees continued to inspire me later as well. Such as a quote from Kleist's *Penthesilea* tragedy, "The dead oak stands against the storm. The healthy one he topples with a crash. Because his grasp can reach into its crown."

Perhaps I was in love with my French teacher, at least I adored her. Her name was *Yvonne Gellier.*

Our French Teachers

Yvonne was an attractive, dark-haired and very passionate woman. She lived in a neighbouring village and always rode her bicycle to Wittlich. She taught French very passionately and at times said, "anyone who does not understand French does not understand German, either." In her opinion, French was the epitome of *rational thought* in theory and in practice. (She often compared French Rationalism with German Romanticism. Yet it was said she was in love with a German.) Students who could not comprehend this rationalism would be punished by her contempt. "I could shoot you!" she would bark at students when they were not able to understand French grammar or the meaning of a poem.

Under Yvonne Gellier we not only learned French grammar but were also introduced to the history of literature. She raved about poets such as Rimbaud and Verlaine, and philosophised with us over Ronsard's sentence 'Carpe diem'. I still know the poem Verlaine wrote in jail by heart:

> *Like city's rain, my heart*
> *Rains teardrops too. What now,*
> *This languorous ache, this smart*
> *That pierces, wounds my heart?*[5]

I loved Yvonne Gellier and learned French and French literature easily and well. However, she did not stay with us for long.

Her successor was a very different type of person, *Geneviève Schmittheisler*. She was small and gaunt, wore her hair in a duchess braid and came from a rich tobacco manufacturing family in Lothringa. Geneviève loved Germany and the Germans after the war. She came to Germany to follow a 'mission'. In short, her mission was to promote peace between peoples on the basis of the Gospel. She, too, was an excellent teacher, but more lenient than Yvonne Gellier. She particularly impressed us by her attempt to take the teachings of Jesus literally and follow it on a daily basis. This included following the commandment of poverty. She felt that Christians – like us – were much too rich. She had just one skirt and a blouse for the summer and one piece of clothing for the winter. She never wore stockings as a matter of principle. She owned only

---

5 Translated by Norman Shapiro (1998, p. 78).

one pair of shoes, and was a vegetarian, of course. Sometimes she said, "I can get drunk on vegetable juice!"

Once, when one of her family members married, she borrowed a dress and stockings from one of the students – which was a great concession on her part because she had allowed herself to become disinherited by her rich family. Her long-term goal was to become a missionary in India, for which she learned Sanskrit. Gandhi's teachings inspired her greatly.

She also belonged to a progressive French movement, well-known under the name of 'Renouveau Catholique'. The initiators of this movement included Georges Bernanos and Paul Claudel. Geneviève was not interested in the theory, but in the practice of the Gospel. She lectured the Wittlich municipal church's dean on the contradiction existing between Jesus's teaching and the church's actual practice. He never had much to reply, since she was *living* the Gospel.

We all loved and cherished her, and we became good friends, even if we were much more lax in practicing the Gospel than she was. She loved to take us on pilgrimages to holy places in the area. On one occasion she went barefoot to an old monastery. And to intensify her asceticism she put an iron or stone in her rucksack. Her aim was to march as far, and with the same weight on her back, as a foot soldier. "What they can do, I can do, too", she said.

In the end she left us because she had been accepted into a missionary order. But she did not stay there long. She did not have a problem following the vow of poverty or celibacy but rather the vow of obedience. She was to eat what everyone ate: meat and much more than she was used to. She was no longer allowed to eat oatmeal, even though it helped her counter the stomach problems she was prone to. At first she tried obediently to follow this new discipline – she still wanted to go to India. But then she could no longer bear it and left the order to return to France.

I do not know what happened to her after that. I do, however, remember a sentence she said to me at her departure, "Experience many miracles!"

Love

The miracle our teacher Geneviève spoke of happened to me when I was nineteen years old, one year before finishing school. *I met the love of my life.* In retrospect, this encounter was a *turning point* in my life. The course of my life took on a completely new and definite direction. This turning point gave me the necessary energy and strength to explore ever new horizons, to acquire ever new insights and perspectives, to dare to make ever new encounters.

This love was the 'red thread', a strong current that continued to carry me throughout the course of my life. It gave me the courage to do anything and the feeling that whatever I did would ultimately succeed. The idealism of my school years, my romanticism and vague love of love took on a very concrete, human form in this encounter.

In short, here is the story:

Zulfiquar

The German Railroad announced an advertising competition and invited the surrounding secondary schools to participate. I took part and submitted a large painted poster depicting the history of traffic – from the invention of the wheel to the development of the railroad. And, who would have thought, I won first prize, which consisted of a free roundtrip ticket through Germany to whatever sites I chose to visit. I had never taken a big trip before which is why I asked one of my school friends, Mechthild, if she wanted to go with me. She did. In the following summer vacation we took off.

Our goal was to visit the cities, churches, castles and other tourist attractions we had heard of in our classes. This included the *Deutsche Museum* in Munich, a museum of technology and science. Not that

I was particularly interested in science and technology, but someone had said that the *Deutsche Museum* was definitely worth visiting.

We arrived in Munich on 24 August, 1950. Standing before the gate of the *Deutsche Museum*, a tall, dark man suddenly approached us and asked, "Do you speak English?" Mechthild shook her head. I immediately answered, "Yes, I do." Although my knowledge of English was minimal and limited to what I had learned in my two years at the school in Gerolstein (and most of which I had also forgotten since then), I somehow had to say, "Yes, I do." This dark man standing before us appeared to me as a messenger from a different world. I had to follow him. To me this was a miracle – I had never seen such a man before.

He asked if we would accompany him through the museum and help him translate the exhibit labels. I boldly answered, of course we would. He must have noticed Mechthild's hesitation, and in an attempt to lessen our fear he said, "I am your brother."

His words struck the very core of my heart. They seemed to me the height of marvellousness: a completely strange person suddenly appears from a country I had never heard of, and like an angel from heaven says, " I am your brother." For years afterwards I continued to philosophise over this sentence. The most strange and foreign of persons says he is my brother. What a miracle!

Back then I did not know that Muslim men often said this to women they were unacquainted with as a means of communicating to them that their intentions were honourable.

His name was Zulfiqar, and he was a Muslim. He told us he was a radio operator on a Pakistani ship, now docked in Plymouth.[6] He was from East Pakistan – which is today's Bangladesh.

---

6 The British government had sold the ship to the newly established state of Pakistan. Pakistan was founded as a new state for Indian Muslims in 1947 after the British left India. It consisted of West and East Pakistan (Bangladesh). This represented the first division of a country allegedly based on purely religious criteria. It created immense misery and lasting hate between the two population groups, which continues to this day. A consequence of this has been 'ethnic cleansing' and major waves of refugees. Hindus, primarily from the Punjab region, fled the new state of Pakistan to India; Muslims fled to Pakistan . . . resulting in brutal massacres.

When India was still a British colony he had left his home and gone to Mumbai (formerly Bombay) on the western coast to become a sailor. He was now on holiday and visiting Germany to see General Rommel's grave and the *Deutsche Museum*. In the museum he was able to explain more to us than I could to him, for instance, how a Morse device functioned. Despite my lack of English we were able to communicate with each other. Mechthild was probably bored, but I was fascinated and could not keep my eyes off him. After visiting the *Deutsche Museum* he offered to buy us an ice cream. He was planning to visit the mountains the next day and asked us if we would like to go with him. But we had planned to visit the cathedral in Bamberg next, so this meant the end of our first encounter. I could not accept this and asked him to give us his address in England. When I returned home I wrote to him and even received an answer.

It was the first of many light-blue envelopes smelling of tar and the wide world. They brought me news from a man who, I thought, loved me. *I*, at least, was head over heels in love with *him*. Whether he truly loved me is something I still do not really know.

In his holidays the following year – his ship was again docked in Plymouth – he planned to visit me. I, too, wanted to spend some time with him and told my story to my class teacher, requesting one week of vacation to accompany my Pakistani friend during his visit to the Rhineland. He and the other teachers consented which was very unusual because our final examinations were planned to take place shortly after that week. Yet our teachers trusted me, which shows how liberal the atmosphere was at our school.

I was in love but completely naïve regarding men and love. I had no idea of what awaited me. Zulfiquar suggested we meet in Trier, and we agreed on the Dom Hotel as our meeting place. When I arrived, he was nowhere to be seen. Confused, I returned to the train station. On my way, I suddenly saw him approaching me among the crowd of people on the pavement. Another miracle, I thought.

I showed him the Roman ruins in Trier, the *Porta Nigra*, the *Imperial Baths*, *Constantine's Basilica*, and after a protracted walk on foot, the *Amphitheatre* at Trier's south end. Sitting on one of the tiers there, he explained that he wanted to marry me.

Despite all my romanticism and infatuation, this hauled me back to reality. Marriage? Between a Muslim and a Catholic? That was just not possible. Completely impossible. I held off his caresses. He was patient and said I did not have to decide immediately. I should take time to think about it. Obviously, he was serious about marrying me. As far as I was concerned, religion stood between us. It seemed to me an insurmountable hurdle. I said this to him very clearly, despite the butterflies in my stomach. Yet I also could not just get up and leave.

He returned with me to Wittlich and took a room at the station hotel, where I visited him every day after classes. For the first time in my life I felt that trembling beneath my skin. For the first time I had met a man who I was really attracted to and who embodied all the aspects of my yearning for foreign places in one person. He was tall, attractive and dark. He was a sailor, a foreigner and an idealist. And he was as much in love as myself, or so it seemed to me.

Luckily, he did not take advantage of my naivety. We met in the station's empty restaurant in the afternoon. He ordered tea for me. It was the first time I had tried real Darjeeling tea. And he told me of his work as a radio operator on his ship, the HMPS TIPU SULTAN.

Formerly a British warship, it had been bought by the Pakistani government and was docked at Plymouth Harbour where it was to be overhauled before being commissioned. As an electrician and radio operator, it was Zulfiquar's task to inspect the ship's entire radio communication system. This was also considered to be his further training. As soon as the ship was refitted, it was to sail to Karachi via Gibraltar, the Mediterranean, the Suez Canal and the Arabian Sea.

He departed after three days. From then on, and over many years, our relationship was limited to communications by mail. Before he left he gave me a genuine Parker fountain pen which I used to write hundreds of letters to him. I also received mail from him from the most exotic places on earth. He wrote regularly and gave precise accounts of what he was doing. In our correspondence we also discussed various philosophies of life as well as political issues. It became clear that we were often not of the same opinion. Like many Bengal men, ambition and enthusiasm had motivated Zulfiquar to enter the navy. He admired Germany, the German military, military theorists and diplomats such as von Clausewitz, Rommel, Bismarck and others. I was completely uninterested in all of this. I admired Gandhi and his non-violent struggle against British colonial power in India. Zulfiquar was of a totally different opinion on this. He was apparently a follower of the *Indian National Army* under *Subhas Chandra Bose*. They did not believe in non-violence, but in military solutions to attain independence from Britain. In his mind, it was not Gandhi who liberated India, but he thought that Hitler's war had weakened England, forcing it to give up India as its colony.

Back then I had little knowledge of the history and politics behind the developments on the Indian sub-continent, and my anti-military position had more or less been built on sentiments seeking to promote international understanding after the ravages of World War II. I did not like Zulfiquar's position. I also did not like his admiration for Germany. Admiration for all things German was frowned upon in our post-war climate. Later, when I worked as a lecturer at the Goethe Institute in Pune (formerly Poona), India, I did meet many Indians who learned German because they admired Germany and Hitler, but this admiration was part of an anti-colonial strategy within the Indian independence movement. Already by 1911, the first Indian school had been established in Pune which taught German instead of English. The intellectuals of Pune did this to disconnect themselves from English language imperialism.

Yet in the years 1950 to 1952 I was unaware of all of this. I also did not know that Zulfiquar's definite plans to acquire a German wife may have been part of his personal strategy to maintain connections to Germany.

Religion

The question of marriage continued to appear in Zulfiquar's letters to me. He could not accept religion as a real hindrance to marriage. He listed many famous men in India, Pakistan and Ceylon (Sri Lanka) who had married European Christian women. And these women had actively taken part in India's struggles for independence. He was not a religious man himself, but he would not have been able to renounce his religion to marry a woman. In his opinion, a Catholic woman and a Muslim man could indeed enjoy a happy married life together. Religion was not important. Today I would say he was right. Back then, I was not able to do so yet. Our most important point of dissent concerned children.

Although both Islam and Catholicism do allow their members to marry outside of their religion, both religions claim the children from these marriages for themselves. The Catholic church was particularly intolerant in this respect. It demanded the Muslim or non-Catholic partner become Catholic. Which was impossible for Zulfiquar. And I could not imagine my children becoming Muslim. I, too, was not particularly religious. But I could not imagine any other children but Catholic children.

I began to examine Catholicism and Islam. I studied the Catholic dogmas; I went from one priest to the other in order to find a hole in the orthodox teachings with regard to non-Christian marriage partners. I could not find a thing. I read the Koran and also sought loopholes in its laws. But both religions' dogmas appeared to have erected an impenetrable wall. As yet I was not a feminist. The word 'patriarchy' in its historical and political context was still foreign to me. I felt these walls – erected by each religion to protect and increase its members – to be an absolute prohibition against my love for a Muslim man. I realised I would have to relinquish my love – which I ultimately did. At least it seemed that I did. Had we been consistent, we would have ended our correspondence completely. Which I did try to do, and for some months I completely refrained from writing. But love is inconsistent. I received another letter from him, *"Why have you been silent for so long? Why don't you write to me any more, my love?"* This was followed by passionate declarations of love and the same repeated request to marry him. Which I answered in the negative. He was distraught and could not understand me and no longer understood what was going on. *"I am an unhappy man and will die unhappy,"* he once wrote to me. I did not understand myself, either. I loved this man whom I hardly knew, but I resisted all efforts to realise this love with the argument that our religions differed too much. He finally said he did not believe that religion was the only reason that was keeping me away from him. He was sure I had other reasons and speculated that another man was behind my resistance.

Although there was no other man, he was right in thinking I had other reasons for not marrying him. Actually, I did not want to marry at all. Much later I asked myself whether my refusal to marry Zulfiquar was truly motivated by religious reasons. Or whether there were other reasons?

Our platonic relationship obviously satisfied my need to be loved, even if this love did not find sexual expression. At the same time it gave me the freedom to continue with my own plans which back then would not have been possible after marriage. I wanted to be free to do whatever I wanted without having to be bound by a husband and family. My refusal to marry apparently based on religious grounds was probably part of an unconscious, feminist strategy which gave me the feeling of being loved without having to limit my freedom.

Since Zulfiquar did not accept my religious arguments I had to have other reasons for my refusal, such as the argument that in Oriental and Muslim cultures women did not enjoy equal rights.

He reacted angrily to my stereotypical prejudices and instructed me that, in fact, in South Asia – Pakistan, India and Ceylon (Sri Lanka) – there were more female professors, politicians and even heads of state than in Europe. He was right. Indeed, at that time there were many more women professors in India than in Germany. And there were also many more active women politicians in parliament than here. India, Pakistan, Ceylon (Sri Lanka) and later Bangladesh all had women heads of state long before a woman became chancellor in Germany.

Zulfiquar did not have a particularly high opinion of European women's morality. There were so many divorces taking place in every country, and in England there were also reports of trafficking in women and of prostitution as an accepted trade. As a sailor he had had relevant experiences in various European and non-European seaports. Today I ask myself why he was so completely convinced of my 'faithfulness'.

Lessons from Love

Today, when I look back on the many years of my 'love story', a strange feeling overcomes me. Why was I satisfied to live with dreams for so long? Why did I not understand patriarchal structures earlier and realise what they do to men and women? But the women's movement did not yet exist back then, and I had never even heard of the term 'patriarchy'.

On the other hand, I do know that much of what I learned, I learned from this love story. It 'carried' me for many years: from my school years through my studies to become a teacher, up to my first years of work, and even beyond the time I ended the relationship completely. My encounter in front of the *Deutsche Museum* in Munich in 1950 was a stroke of fate, not only for myself but also for my 'eternal sailor', as he called himself. It was the moment when the entire world opened up for me, when my feelings and thoughts, my learning, took a completely new direction. What began in 1950 became a 'red thread', first in the form of a stream and then as a strong current, continuing to swell throughout the course of my life and branch out into what has meanwhile developed into a huge web/network of relationships. It has carried me and given me the inspiration and energy needed to follow up on new ideas and projects.

I can only list a few of the most important lessons I learned from this love story. The first and most important one was an unimaginable *expansion of my horizon*. Whereas from the time of experiencing my first intense homesickness I had been very fixated on my home and my village, my romantic love now opened a whole new world for me: the East, the Orient. While most people in the post-war years looked more to the West, or more accurately, towards the United States or Canada, I was attracted to the East. I therefore unconsciously followed my great grandmother's advice, "Children, do not cross the Rossbach!" meaning, don't go past Steffeln towards the west.

Carried by love's emotional strength I took what seemed to be the first right step and learned proper *English*. The little English I had learned in the two years of modern secondary school in Gerolstein did not even allow me to write intelligible love letters. Zulfiquar encouraged me to learn more English. I began to do so amateurishly with a dictionary and vocabulary cards. Later I took an English course offered by the BBC.

English skills were very necessary if I wanted to study the history, culture, economy and society of the Indian sub-continent. Although some universities in Germany had departments on India, most of them were exclusively specialised in the study of ancient Indian philosophy and philology, particularly in the study of Sanskrit.

However, I was less interested in the ancient holy texts and philosophy of India. I was also not drawn to yoga or Indian spirituality and art – as the hippie generation was to be later. I just wanted to learn about life and society in South-East Asia – India,

Pakistan, Ceylon (Sri Lanka). There was not much to be found on that, even at the South-East Asia Institute in Heidelberg.

As mentioned before, my love story also led me to do intensive research on the fundamental ideas of the two irreconcilable, patriarchal and monotheistic religions of Catholicism and Islam which seemed to form a wall between myself and Zulfiquar. Long before *religion* became a political issue, as it is today, I read the Bible as well as the Koran with *the eyes of a woman in love*. I soon realised then that these two religious communities are not divided by their differences, but by *their very far-reaching similarities*. Along with Judaism, these two religions are deeply rooted in the Old Testament, a *book of 'revealed truths'* written by prophets and a priestly cast. The revelations of this book are centred on a jealous, monotheistic and patriarchal God who demands that his people be faithful and obedient to him, just as a husband demands faithfulness and obedience from his wife. Monotheism and monogamy, particularly women's monogamy, are closely interlinked. The animosity developing between these three patriarchal biblical religions is of a different quality than between 'Christians' and 'heathens'. The animosity is basically all about the jealousy and competition between the sons of a patriarch. It is about maintaining control over women (see Mies, "Globalisierung und religiöser Fundamentalismus", 2005a).

The most important lesson I learned from my love story was, however, that you can only understand something when you love. "On ne voit bien qu'avec le coeur" ("One sees clearly only with the heart"), as the fox says in Saint-Exupéry's *Little Prince*. My friend Claudia von Werlhof put it this way, "Who does not feel, does not understand, either." This early insight into how things are truly connected to each other, even if they are considered to be very different, divided and strange, retained its relevance throughout my life. In the story of my 'great love', the two strands of homesickness and yearning for foreign places came together. The 'other', the 'stranger' is not the 'enemy' or 'hell', as Sartre writes, but is the 'beloved' and 'heaven'. This far-off love not only provided me with the most important experience which later helped me to become a feminist. It also provided me with the keyword of my social critique: the term patriarchy. Because of this love story, the term had a very definite international dimension for me from the very beginning. Yet after my final exams it still took many years before I finally let go of my very idealistic concept of love. I had to face reality. That meant I had to finish school and become a school teacher if I wanted to become economically independent.[7]

Academic Studies and First Years as a Teacher

In 1949, after the four Allied occupation zones were dissolved, West Germany was granted its sovereignty. This meant school and cultural policies of Germany were now under German ministerial jurisdiction. The French occupation zone was transformed into the 'land' (state) of Rheinland-Pfalz with its capital, Mainz. This is where the Ministry of Culture responsible for our schools was based.

Our 'Pedagogical Institute' was turned into a 'Secondary School for Girls' offering the final Abitur examination.[8]

---

7 After receiving my doctorate (in 1972) I went to Bangladesh and had the opportunity of meeting Zulfiquar one last time. He looked older, had grey hair, and he left me with the impression of being hard and authoritarian. He had married in the meantime and had children. When I met his wife – she knew of our story – she said, "You have been saved." I thanked fate for 'being saved' once more! He said he regretted that we did not marry. I answered, "Things would not have gone well between the two of us." I probably would have divorced him. He was horrified. Divorce? Upon the wife's request? That was the worst scandal a Muslim man could experience back then.

8 In Germany, the final exam after completing a secondary school (gymnasium) was, and is, called Abitur. Only those who have successfully passed the Abitur are allowed to go to a university for higher studies.

After passing the Abitur, German students are usually nineteen years old, older than British or American high-school students. The Abitur is equivalent to the French Baccalauréat.

The first completed Abitur at our school was a big event and great success. The kind of fear of exams or failure that turn school into torture for young students today was completely unfamiliar to us.

I gave the Valedictory speech at the end of the Abitur ceremonies. I unfortunately no longer have the text, but I do know that in my speech I particularly emphasised the *trust* our teachers placed in us. The typical old German style, where the teacher was a disciplinarian, was unknown to us at that school. In particular, we never had teachers who were interested only in achievement and passing examinations.

Representatives of the Ministry of Culture and other official persons came to the Abitur celebration. Our parents were also invited, and it was the first time my mother and father came to Wittlich. Of course, they were very proud of their daughter.

For a short time after this high point in my young life I lived with the feeling that things would continue like this – that I would stride, dance and fly from one summit to the other. The elation, however, did not last.

My Studies at the Academy of Education in Koblenz

Studying at the Academy in Koblenz[9] was quite a disappointment. To begin with, there was no way for me to study at an art academy, because being able to attend the Pedagogical Institute (and later the gymnasium), was based on the condition that I would become a public school teacher and, after completing my studies, work as a teacher for five years in Rheinland-Pfalz. I had nothing in general against doing this, since I needed a job that would feed me, and I also convinced myself I could always try attending an art academy later on.

But what disturbed me from the very beginning was the narrow-minded and doctrinaire standard of teaching practised by the professors at the Academy. They were still of the 'old school',

---

9 Rheinland-Pfalz being primarily Catholic, men and women were trained in separate academies at that time: the men in Trier, the women in Koblenz.

meaning they had obviously completely missed the developments of the German progressive education movement from the turn of the century and the first half of the twentieth century. They were ignorant of – or did not talk about – play pedagogy or vocational pedagogy, and saw no reason to promote our creative abilities. They also had no passion for political discussions and international understanding. In a punctilious manner, they quickly taught us whatever young school teachers needed to know to work in a village school. Tests and exams served to measure our performance. Of the professors, there was not one I was enthusiastic about. As a result, I have forgotten all of their names.

My first years as a teacher

Compared to the high-spirited intellectual and emotional atmosphere of our years at the gymnasium, the years in Koblenz were 'grey years' to me.

I completed all the necessary exams well and became a teacher. I had a good job, a secure livelihood and was independent: I should have felt happy and satisfied. I was not. I wanted more.

It therefore came as a certain deliverance when immediately after completing my teaching exams I was offered a job at a small, two-classroom public school in Hohenfels in the county of Daun which is my home county. That suited me well, as it meant I could go home on the weekends. And I was already familiar with the kind of teaching necessary in a one-classroom public school from my own childhood years.

I liked being a teacher, and I think I was, and still am, a good teacher. I could inspire children. My maxim was, "I want to make life interesting for children." In doing so, I could draw on the experiences with my brothers and sisters. I knew that children only learn when their interest is aroused.

Back then there was no standard curriculum, there were no static regulations or performance standards as there are today. A young teacher had ample scope to find creative means of instruction – and with very little material available in those days: a chalkboard, chalk and the entire school of nature outside. As a result, instruction often took place outside which the children and I liked very much. We took walks through the meadows and woods. The children learned about plants and trees, they drew them and learned to sing songs according to the particular season. I enjoyed developing their creativity.

What I did not like was the school board's bureaucracy and authoritarianism and the world view of the Catholic church which exerted quite a deal of influence on the Catholic regions of Germany. The influence became very palpable from the moment I started my work as a teacher. Without being asked, young women teachers were immediately made members of the Catholic Women Teachers' Association. At the first meeting of the Association, the chairwoman proclaimed that women teachers were to live a celibate life, as the teaching profession was a mission similar to that of a priest. Women teachers were to be role models for the village. I found this shocking, even though I was not interested in marrying myself. I soon left the Association.

Art

As said before, my 'mission' was not marriage and family, nor was it a celibate life. My primary mission, or so I thought, was to become an artist.

More than any other profession, being a teacher provided me with the time and opportunity to draw, paint and sculpt. Which I did. Yet, again and again I was confronted with the limits of my technical abilities. Although I often had wonderful ideas, when I tried to carry them out, the result was less than satisfactory. I was frustrated. I realised I was lacking real training as a painter, let alone as a sculptor. I particularly loved working with clay: I modelled heads and torsos, not pots and vases. Whatever I produced in these first artistic attempts I gave to my friends, brothers and sisters. I have almost nothing from this time. One leftover, a tapestry, was made of cloth scraps from our box of material odds and ends. It depicts the bottom of the ocean, the grave of sailors.

But I realised that none of this was enough to turn me into a true artist. I had talent, but I was really just an amateur playing around with different materials. I wanted to change that. I wanted to attend a proper art school and have training in the various fields and eventually become an art teacher. Because I did not have the money for such training, the only chance left was for me to transfer to a city with an art academy.

I applied for transfer to Mainz which was granted. However, I was not given a post there but was transferred to a village far away from Mainz and the art academy. I was miserable. What was I to do in a place totally unfamiliar to me, where my aim of attending an art academy did not seem feasible? If this was impossible, I at least wanted to return to the district of Trier where I felt more at home. Again I applied for transfer, and again it was granted.

I was assigned to a public school in Hermeskeil in the Hunsrück mountains. This see-saw of job changes took place within a short period in the spring of 1955.

In Hermeskeil I realised I had to forget about making art my profession, not only because the circumstances did not allow me to do so. I had finally understood that the reason was to be found within myself. If I had truly had enough inner drive and endurance, I would have continued with my efforts. But I was probably not only lacking the passionate will to concentrate on art, I also did not have enough talent to become a successful artist.

So I abandoned the idea of becoming a real artist. And I stopped drawing and painting because they were no longer pleasurable hobbies for me. I felt I had probably been deceiving myself all those years.

At the same time, being a teacher in school was not enough for me. Living and working in the small town of Hermeskeil made me particularly realise how narrow and limited my life was. My job as a civil servant[10] provided me with economic security and it was a respected profession for women. So what more did I want? There was nothing around to inspire me. Everyone was concerned with material reconstruction after the devastations of World War II. Everybody was literally preoccupied with building and refurbishing their houses. Germany's 'Wirtschaftswunder', or economic miracle, was beginning to unfold. But all of this did not attract me one bit. I wanted something else. I wanted to escape this narrow, grey world.

I began to learn English properly. I was no longer satisfied with the English of my love letters, since I had acquired the language just as amateurishly as my art skills. I first began to take BBC English courses regularly and finally took the BBC course exam, which granted me a Cambridge University Lower Certificate of English.

My English studies were based on a very practical goal: I wanted to go to a developing country. I understood that my teaching diploma and my German and French language skills would not help me much there.

A branch of the Institute for Education Sciences of the University of Münster was located in Trier (at that time Trier did not yet have a university), where it was possible to study languages on weekends and acquire a 'Realschule', or junior high school, teaching diploma. I studied English and German. In 1962, I passed my teaching exam for these languages.

Before completing my studies, I was transferred to a school in Morbach (again in the Hunsrück mountains). The reason for this was that after Germany became a sovereign state, English became the primary foreign language. However, there were hardly any English teachers in Rheinland-Pfalz. For this reason, I was

---

10 In Germany, teachers and professors are civil servants even today. This means life-long job security.

immediately in demand as an English teacher and transferred from the public school to the junior high school in Morbach.

But I wanted *to go out into the world*, and I wanted to help change it. My desire to leave my small world behind and the dawning of new horizons were not only a result of my love story, but also, to a much greater extent, a result of my participation in the camps of the *Service Civil International*. From these new experiences and ideas, new and greater international horizons opened up for me.

Service Civil International (SCI)

The SCI was founded by Pierre Ceresol, a Swiss, together with others after World War I.

The main idea of this international movement was to abolish military service and to reconcile former 'enemy states', as for instance Germany and France, by voluntary service for peace. The volunteers of these SCI work camps came from all over the world to carry out different social projects like reconstructing workers' houses, digging trenches for water pipes, helping to build schools in remote areas and helping rebuild destroyed communities after wars. The main principle of the SCI was 'deeds not words'. That meant the founders were of the opinion that *practical work* performed together with members from all nations would promote understanding and peace more than endless discussions.

The SCI also fought for replacing *military service by civil service*. It was thus a place where *conscientious objectors* from all countries could meet. The SCI helped in making conscientious objection accepted in Switzerland and other countries, even in Germany. This struggle demanded a lot of perseverance and patience.

These international work camps were organised in an astounding number of nations, for instance in India, Great Britain, France, Spain, Switzerland, Algeria, Lebanon, Yugoslavia, Belgium and the United States. The SCI was not restricted by any religious, national, cultural or class borders. Volunteers included both men and women who had to do the same work. The SCI therefore went further than the French Revolution with its principles of 'Liberté, Egalité and Fraternité'. In these work camps I found for the first time that a hierarchical division of labour between women and men did not exist.

During my first years as a teacher these SCI camps were a great inspiration. Every year during my holidays I would go to one of the SCI[11] workshops. Carrying out common work on one of the projects was a great joy. As in my childhood, I experienced that work and joy are not separate dimensions of life. But this time it was an international community. One other result of these camps was the abolition of common prejudices.

We lived in temporary shelters: tents, ruins, half-built houses. We carried out our reconstruction work and helped the local people in a number of common tasks. After work we had a lot of fun. We learned and sang songs from different countries of the world, and people would play different instruments. We also talked with each other and discussed all kinds of issues; we received information on the problems of countries that existed only in name to us.

And of course, in these camps friendships and love relationships developed which lasted long after the work-camp. One of my old friends is a Swiss woman with whom I am still in contact. I also had relationships with some men: a communist from Calabria, a man from Egypt who wanted to escape military service, a Belgian. But I made sure that they were kept at a distance.

In Lebanon, where we built a village school in 1957, I met Petra from Holland. We slept in army tents – women and men separately. At night, Petra and I would tell each other our love stories. I told her about my 'great love'. Petra listened patiently. When I finished, she said, "Maria, a less-than-perfect reality is better than a romantic dream!" Her words struck me at the core of my heart. From then on,

---

11 The SCI went through a number of changes in the course of time. But it still exists and has an office in Bonn, Germany: SCI, Blücherstrasse 14, 53115 Bonn.

this sentence became the guideline of my life. I realised that up to now I had only been *dreaming* of love, that I did not even know, or really know, the man I thought I loved. I did not know his country, I knew nothing of Pakistan, nothing of South-East Asia where he came from. I knew nothing of his language and his actual culture. I only had some very romantic and idealistic ideas of love and international 'brotherhood' in my head. Petra's statement that a less-than-perfect reality is better than a romantic dream finally turned me right-side-up and placed my feet firmly back on the solid ground of reality. I underwent something like a conversion: I changed from an idealist to a realist. Petra's statement alone had accomplished what religion, with its absurd dogmas, had been incapable of doing.

4

Departure for India

Goethe Institute Pune

As soon as I received my junior high school teaching diploma I applied for a job as a lecturer at the Goethe Institute (GI) – with South Asia or the Near East as my preferences. To my great surprise, my application was accepted and I was offered a post at the Institute in Pune (then Poona), India. That was in 1962. I was overjoyed and requested a leave of absence from the German school authorities.

I was to leave in September of 1963 which meant I had to prepare my departure very quickly. I attended the Goethe Institute's preparatory classes in Germany and not only learned the methods of teaching 'German as a foreign language', but also the goals pursued by the German Federal Republic with regard to their cultural policies abroad, particularly with regard to developing countries. My initial idealism evaporated quickly when I heard that Germany's cultural policy was, in the end, to profit the economy. I had to pack up and leave my apartment in Morbach and make very practical decisions on the kind of things I would need in the tropics. The central office of the GI warned me that it was not easy for women to live in a country 'such as India'. There was only one other woman working at the five GI branches in India, and she was in Pune as well. We were the first women worldwide to work for the

GI, but this fact did not alarm me at all. At that time, some of the Institute's colleagues also shipped their car to their overseas assignment. I did not want to do that, but I did quickly set out to get my driver's licence and, fortunately, I was able to pass the exam right off. I am still proud of that to this day.

Things began to happen very quickly and everything seemed to go well. The current of my life rushed on – towards unknown shores. This is what I had always wanted. The ship that took me from Genoa to Mumbai (then Bombay) in September was called the *Victoria* and was one of two *Lloyd Triestino* ships to sail this route.

The trip took three weeks: from the Mediterranean, through the Suez Canal, the Red Sea, the Gulf of Aden and the Arabian Sea to Mumbai. For me it was truly a trip out into the open. I do not think I have felt that kind of elation ever again.

At night I lay directly on the rough ship planking – the further we sailed the warmer it got – and verses and songs kept going through my head, verses such as Nietzsche's:

That way is my will; I trust
In my mind and in my grip.
Without plan into the vast
Open sea I head my ship.

All is shining, new and newer,
Upon space and time sleeps noon;
Only your eye – monstrously,
Stares at me, infinity![1]

---

1 Translated by Walter Kaufmann (1974, p. 371).

When the *Victoria* landed at Ballard Kay in Mumbai, I knew I had arrived. I had finally arrived in the country I had spent so much time thinking about. I was in the area of the world where my heart felt at home. India had become my country.

When I left the ship I was met by my new German colleagues, Fräulein Frings Geiseler and Herr Hülsen, the director of the GI in Pune. They greeted me in the traditional Indian manner with a garland, and Herr Hülsen said to me, "Welcome home!"

From the very beginning, "Welcome home" were not just empty words to me. I experienced none of the things that many travellers to India call the 'Indian Shock': the unbearableness of seeing the poor sleeping on the streets, or being repelled by the noise and smell. Often I heard from people, either in India as tourists or on business, that India's spicy foods did not particularly agree with them. Some people suffered so severely from Indian Shock that they were forced to return to Europe prematurely.

I experienced none of this. I was not disturbed by the dirt, nor by the smell of urine and excrement, nor by the noise everywhere. And I enjoyed the food from the very beginning, a fact that naturally plays an essential role in being able to feel 'at home' in a country. Later on, I understood that one's stomach – or 'gut' – reaction is very much related to whether one generally experiences a situation as familiar or enjoyable, or rather as a threat.

For many people the Indian Shock is also often triggered by a sudden encounter with so many foreign people and with the 'masses' on the streets of India. Many population experts develop their theories of overpopulation from this first emotional reaction, which they then attempt to substantiate by scientific analysis and statistics. However, in my opinion, the reason for experiencing a gut-level sense of immediate threat when faced by masses of strange people is to be found here. One just needs to witness Mumbai's suburban trains crowded with people – the windows and doorways are jam-packed with whole clusters of individuals, and people even sit on the top of the trains.

All of this I saw as well. But my primary feeling was curiosity. With great curiosity I observed people, and I found them beautiful, every one of them. Men and women. Not only because of their beautiful clothing, their saris, but also because of their faces, their beautiful hair and skin. I compared them to Caucasians with their rough, often chubby or square faces and asked myself how it became possible for our ugly white race to colonise the world. And as far as the 'masses' were concerned – I felt comfortable among them.

One of the consequences from my first encounter with Indians, however, was that the romantic sentiments which had elated me for so many years since meeting Zulfiquar vanished immediately. Here were millions of good-looking, dark men. Many of them were to become my students in Pune, but I no longer developed any feelings in the direction of romantic infatuation.

Not only was this due to having taken Petra de Vries's guiding principle, that a lousy reality is better than a nice dream, to heart. It was also due to a conscious act of will on my part. I did not want to become distracted by a – possibly hopeless – love story yet again. I wanted to concentrate on my immediate tasks and on the many interesting and new things I would be able to learn in India.

To begin with, these were my students themselves. The GI in Pune was at that time the first in the world to maintain a training programme for non-native German lecturers. Students came from all over India to study in Pune. They attended first- and second-grade courses in German at the GI, and after successfully completing their final exams, the German government granted them a scholarship to attend a one-and-a-half-year training course in Munich. Once they passed their exams, they could get jobs as German lecturers at one of the five branches of the GI in India. They were in Mumbai, Kolkata (Calcutta), Chennai (Madras), Bangalore, Pune. In this way the German government sought to remedy a lack of qualified Germans who were willing to go overseas for five years to promote their native language and culture there.

This measure shows the great importance the German government placed upon pursuing its cultural policies in Asia, South America and Africa. All this has radically changed since then.

The GI in Pune was an exception in so far as it also had boarding homes where students could live for four months. The homes, naturally separated by sex, were situated on the *Mullah Muta* river, on *Boat Club Road*, a few hundred metres away from the Institute and its classes.

The Institute itself was housed in a large modern bungalow built by a Parsi who went bankrupt. The GI was originally planned to be a part of the *Deccan College* which already included the *American Institute of Indian Studies*. At first, the GI was also called the *Indian Institute of German Studies* and was indeed part of the renowned *Deccan College*. As an institution it could have continued to fit well within Pune's German-friendly tradition – a tradition that developed as a consequence of anti-colonial sentiments during India's independence movement. At that time, Pune's education elite wanted to break the English language monopoly in their schools and in 1911, the *Deccan Education Society* founded the *New English School* which offered German as the first foreign language. Many residents of Pune deliberately went to Germany, and not to England, to study.

However, the GI's director in Pune did not want it to become incorporated into an Indian research institute. When I came to Pune in 1963, the GI was already an independent, completely German institution with its own campus.

Besides teaching German we were also supposed to instruct our students in the geography, history and culture of Germany. I discovered, however, that some of our students knew more about Germany than I did. My students were adult men and women, some of whom already had work experience. Some had studied philosophy and were familiar with German and Indian philosophy. Others were scientists or engineers who wanted to go to Germany. They came from various parts of India, and through them I learned about this vast country. I learned that there are seventeen major languages – each of them with its own alphabet and literature. I learned about the country's various marriage customs and rituals, and began to understand India's caste system and its diverse local and regional traditions. I also learned something about its political struggles which, especially in the late 1960s, led to farmers' and students' revolts in Bengal and Kolkata.

Yet at that time I was still very 'apolitical'. I believed in 'development' and considered my work at the GI as a contribution to India's development and to international understanding. When one of my students wrote an excellent essay on Hegel and Marx in German, I became aware for the first time that the thoughts of these men were still very much alive in far off countries such as India and other, to me, remote places of the world. Although I knew these men by name, I knew almost nothing of their thoughts. Throughout my entire school and student career after the war, West Germany avoided making serious efforts towards addressing the history of Marxism, socialism and communism. Discussion was limited to German Idealism and post-war literature. But it was in the 1960s, in particular during Germany's reconstruction and 'economic miracle', that the country was re-integrated into the Western capitalist system.

From the very beginning I was driven by the question why these Indian students wanted to learn German. As far as the men were concerned it was fairly obvious: most of them were scientists and wanted to go to Germany to continue their studies or work. But what about the women? After all, a remarkably high percentage of the students were women. How could it be natural in such a patriarchal country, for young women to live – even if in separate boarding houses – and work together with men for four months in a strange city? After all, a division of the sexes was maintained everywhere. In the trains there were even special 'Ladies' Compartments'. What kind of women were these? What motivated them to study German? Some of them were already married or were about to marry, and it was clear they would not be able to do much with the language. In discussions with various students I came to hear the most incredible stories. One young woman, let us call her Pushpa, came from a *Jain* family in Rajasthan. Although she had just been married, she was able to convince her husband and father-in-law that their family would profit from her going to Pune for some months to study German. How was this possible?

When she told me this story I also learned that Rajasthan was one of the most conservative, patriarchal regions of India dominated by Rajputs, a warrior caste and class. *Jains* (followers of the Jain sect) treated their women even more strictly than the Rajputs and other Hindu sects and castes. For instance, it was prescribed that all women and daughters-in-law rigorously observe *Purdah*.[2] Her father-in-law represented the absolute authority in her large 'joint family'. Pushpa's mother supported her in her thirst for education. Pushpa invited me to Rajasthan to meet her family. When I arrived, I began to understand what *patriarchy as a system* really meant.

---

2 For instance, a daughter-in-law was not allowed to talk face-to-face with her father-in-law or any of her husband's older brothers. A *Purdah*, or cloth curtain was to hang i.e. in the door between two rooms separating father-in-law (as head of the family) and daughter-in-law. The same had to be observed for brothers-in-law. If no such curtain existed, a young woman was at least obliged to cover her head – particularly her face and hair – with a *pallau*, the end of her *sari*.

Purdah was not just a piece of cloth, but encompassed all the symbolic and technical provisions to keep women, especially young women, not only separate from men – called the segregation of sexes – but also within an absolutely hierarchically structured system of dependence and authority. In their youth these women were dependent upon their fathers – or eldest brother. After marriage, they became dependent upon their husbands, as widows they became dependent upon their sons.

The authority of a family's eldest male member was particularly based on his being the head of the 'joint family', the wealth of which was not allowed to become divided up, not even after death. The patriarch's family wealth was considered communal property and belonged to its sons. Daughters were not entitled to any part of this wealth.

I would like to mention here that the *purdah* system was not imported to India by the Muslim conquerors, but was already based on gender relations shaped by Hinduism before the Muslims arrived (see Mies, *Indian Women and Patriarchy*, 1980).

I learned from my women students that patriarchal norms are also the determinant factors for Muslim as well as Christian women. I remember one of our students – a young Muslim woman from Mumbai – who had successfully deferred *marriage talk* by taking up one course of study after the other. She had already acquired a BA as well as an MA, and had even studied in France. Her family was progressive and enlightened. She finally came to the Goethe Institute in Pune to learn German. Actually, she did not know what she wanted to do with German, but she knew her family would not press her to marry as long as she studied.

Among the educated middle class, pursuing education and an academic course of study was an accepted social norm, even for women. As long as a woman studied, she did not have to be bothered by *marriage talk*. Yet at some point she did have to marry. The Indian social system, even its modernised version, did not and does not allow, in the main, for independent, single women. As a consequence, this young Muslim woman, too, had to marry. It was an arranged marriage – as many of them were and still are mostly today – and was carried out according to the traditional Muslim rite.

At this point I once again experienced one of those *happy coincidences* which played such a decisive role during all of my life. I met Dr Iravati Karve from Deccan College. Dr Karve was a world renowned anthropologist and ethnologist. Like her husband, D.D. Karve, she had studied in Berlin in the 1930s and published a highly regarded book on kinship organisation in India (see Karve, 1953).

When I told Dr Karve of my interest to better understand the social origins behind our students' motivation to study, she suggested, "Why don't you carry out an empirical study. I'll help you develop the questionnaire."

Even though I had never studied sociology or ethnology, I was full of curiosity and began to carry out my little research on what motivated our students to study German. It was titled "Why German?" and was the first of my sociological studies. I enjoyed it very much. It also was a first effort in the direction of sociology/ethnology, a field I was later to 'properly' study upon my return from India. My essay was ninety-two pages long and was published in the *Deccan College Bulletin* – my first sociological publication (Mies, 1967/68).

Iravati Karve was an exceptional woman. She belonged to the generation of women who had participated in India's independence struggle. These women were not explicitly feminist. They had yielded to some of the patriarchal norms of their society: they were married, had children, and were obedient daughters-in-law. And yet, they exhibited personal strength, courage and independence in a manner I had never experienced in German women. Iravati Karve dedicated her famous book to her husband with the words, "I place my head on your feet and ask you for your blessing."[3] She was a tall, strong woman who impressed her entire surroundings with her self-assurance and poise. She was not concerned with what people in Pune or anywhere else thought of her.

At one point, sitting on her desk in her office, she told me angrily that her son who had married a German archaeologist, was not willing to take a new post at a university in Kolhapur, a provincial city in the south, because his wife would not go with him. "Well, he should take a new wife, then!", she cried so loudly that everyone in the offices of Deccan College heard her. I understood that she demanded obedience from her son because she felt it very important for India that qualified young people not remain in comfortable positions in the cities but go and work in the country. A son of the famous Karve family was not allowed to shirk this important national responsibility.

She was active in the city's politics because she realised that the ideals of India's independence movement would soon be betrayed. Some called her the only 'man' in Pune.

---

3 The placing of the head on the foot is, to Indians, what shaking hands is to Westerners, or bowing is to the Japanese.

I often asked myself where Iravati Karve's and other Indian women's strength came from. I could not understand the contradiction between the patriarchal Indian norms on the one hand, and the actual behaviour of these women in society and in the family, on the other hand.

A part of Iravati Karve's political consciousness and strength was derived from her background as a Brahmin and daughter-in-law to the renowned Maharashi Karve. Maharashi Karve was one of the great Indian social reformers who, like Raja Ram Mohun Roy and Vidysagar in Bengal, linked the struggle for national independence with the struggle for women's liberation. They fought against child marriages, against killing girls, and against the burning of widows on their husbands' funeral pyres (*sati*). They fought for the right of widows to remarry and for the education of girls who, until the nineteenth century, were excluded from going to school.

Another great reformer of this era was Mahatma Phule. Phule linked the fight against Brahminism – the pervasive rule of the Brahmins – with the struggle for women's independence.

These movements led to a series of legal reforms, even under British rule: in 1795 and 1802, killing young girls was forbidden by law in Bengal. In 1829, *sati* became prohibited. In 1856, the *Hindu Widow Remarriage Act* allowed widows to become remarried.

Maharashi Karve himself married a widow in order to promote these reformist ideas. Their son, D.D. Karve became Iravati's husband. Maharashi Karve founded a school for widows in Pune and *India's first women's university* in Mumbai. Together with *Ewha Women's University* in Seoul, Korea, they were the first and only universities for women in the world at that time.

Iravati Karve was very conscious of this history. Although she was not a feminist, she sought to follow this history according to the possibilities open to her. For instance, she fought for a universal, secular family law that would apply to all religious communities equally. However, after independence, the Indian government under

Jawaharlal Nehru made concessions to Hindus and Muslims, allowing them to retain their own family law, in particular their own marriage and inheritance laws. This later led to horrible conflicts between Hindus and Muslims (the current fundamentalist massacres, such as in Gujarat in 2002, are ultimately still all about women). Also, the current Islamist struggle to enforce *Sharia Law* based on their religious tradition, in opposition to the secular state laws, is primarily about maintaining control over women.

Yet at that time, I had little knowledge of this history. I was simply impressed by strong Indian women such as Iravati Karve or even by some of our women students who, though not openly opposing the patriarchal norms of their Hindu or Muslim societies, did enforce their will, for instance by taking up a further course of study.

The most important result from my small empirical study was that most men learned German in order to promote their careers. In contrast, quite a few women came to Pune in order to postpone further *marriage talk* by taking up language studies.

The questions that arose and the contradictions that became apparent to me during my first stay in India concerning the societal norms on the one hand, and the actual behaviour on the part of Indian women on the other, also led me to make this the theme of my dissertation when I returned to Germany.

My First Women's Group

At that time, Dr Charlotte Vaudeville, a French Indologist, also worked at Deccan College. She carried out research on the literature and mysticism of the medieval Hindu poet *Kabir*. In summer, she worked at the Sorbonne in Paris and during winter she was in India. I met her at various events organised by the GI.

Charlotte Vaudeville was a follower of Charles de Foucauld's spiritual teachings, and had established a small Charles-de-Foucauld group made up of two Indian women teachers from Mumbai and a woman student from Pune.

Charles de Foucauld had already fascinated me when I was still in Germany, in particular his desire to put the 'little Jesus' – meaning Jesus the worker, the man of the poor and humble – at the centre of his spirituality. The Worker-Priests and the Little Brothers and Little Sisters of Jesus were influenced by him, and there were also lay groups who followed his spiritual teachings.

Charlotte's group was a lay group of professional women with chapters all over the world. Perhaps this is the reason why I joined the group. Although I was not very religious and felt repulsed by the official Church, I was looking for a spiritual community in which I could address the deeper questions I had been confronted with since the time of my love story. It was another *happy coincidence* that led me to such a secular women's group in Pune.

This did not involve any great changes to my practical life. The only spiritual obligation I had was to identify with the poor, to meditate and read the Gospels regularly.

In accordance with my identification with ordinary people I did not move to one of the large bungalows in Koregaon Park where the former English rulers had their summer residences and where my colleagues lived, but to a refurbished garage. The director of the GI in Munich was not at all pleased with this very humble, unrepresentative abode for one of the Institute's employees. But our women's group met at my place regularly and I felt very comfortable in this small residence. Students also gladly came. For the women in Mumbai it was like a summer resort, as Pune is situated on the higher Deccan plateau.

However, what I did have difficulty with was the fact that one was forced to have domestic servants if – whether woman or man – one wanted to live a 'normal' professional life in India. It was impossible to combine one's profession with housework. My German colleagues each had a chauffeur, a cook, a cleaning woman, a *Dhobi* (clothes washer), a gardener, and, if they had children, they also had a nanny.

I simply had *one* woman, Laxmi, who did everything for me. She went to the market, she cooked, cleaned my home, and washed my clothes. At first, I did not have a car and rode a bicycle to the GI. Later on, I bought an ancient, two-seater Italian Fiat that always kept breaking down. But I liked this life. It did not stop me from making contact with those I wanted to meet, those *on the other side*, meaning the side of the simple folk.

Most of the people who visited India then – and even more so later and today – were, and are, seeking new spiritual orientation and illumination, whether through Buddhism, through one of the many Gurus or in an *Ashram*.[4] I myself did not feel this desire, but I was curious.

When an acquaintance told me she was going to Puducherry (Pondicherry) to visit *the Mother* and asked me if I wanted to go with her, I accepted. Puducherry, a former French colony in the south of Madras – today's Chennai – was a city to which *Sri Aurobindo* fled during India's fight for independence. He was branded as a terrorist and pursued by the British colonial government. Sri Aurobindo founded an Ashram in Puducherry with the goal of connecting Eastern and Western thinking. A woman from Paris followed him as her guru. It was said that she came from a Turkish-Egyptian family. After Aurobindo's death she became the centre of the Ashram, quickly becoming renowned as *the Mother*, first throughout India, and then throughout the world.

Those wanting to join the Ashram were required to place their wealth 'at her feet'. As a result, the Ashram became wealthy very quickly. It maintained modern schools where children and young students could study whatever they wanted: music, art and even natural sciences. Sports also played a very large role. One often saw

---

4 An Ashram is an estate similar to a monastery in which people who are looking for a particular way of life or salvation come together. Most of the Ashrams have been established by spiritual, sometimes also political, Gurus (i.e. Gandhi). In contrast to monasteries, Ashrams are often open communities.

them wearing shorts and riding their bicycles through Puducherry, or lying on the beaches in bathing suits. This was an unusual sight for Indians at that time. Of course, those who came to Puducherry were the children of the wealthy. What struck me was that the city was one of the dirtiest I had seen in India. In contrast, the Ashram compound with its high, protective walls, its bougainvillea plants, tropical trees and all of its comforts appeared to be a small paradise. Sri Aurobindo and the Mother had acquired the compound from the French colonial rulers. Yet upon leaving its gates you first had to jump over open and stinking sewer drains. Later I heard that Puducherry had the highest rate of leprosy in India. When confronting the members of the Ashram with this contradiction, they said they expected their example to ultimately 'spread' over all of India.

Later the Ashram developed into *Auroville*. People are still waiting for its example to spread out over India.

In the leap year of 1964, the Mother planned to celebrate her birthday on 29 February. Thousands came to Puducherry to celebrate this memorable event. On that day, all of those who came for this event gathered in front of the Mother's residence to meditate. For the first time in my life I experienced a mass meditation. Like all the others I sat on the ground in a cross-legged position and waited to become 'empty' and experience some kind of illumination. Nothing happened. Only my legs hurt. At last, the Mother stepped out onto the balcony and said a few words I did not understand. After that, one was allowed to get up and go. I was not convinced.

After this we visited one more Ashram which had become famous through its founder *Sri Ramana Maharshi*. This Ashram was much more modest and I liked it better. But my first Ashram tour and a visit to southern India's great temples completely satisfied my initial curiosity.

I realised it was not my thing. I was not looking for salvation and my scepticism and sense of reality always intervened when I tried to meditate. The same also occurred when I tried to meditate on the Gospel or on Jesus and his parables. I could never close my eyes to the real existing Church. My critique of the Church as an institution grew when I listened to the stories my women friends – the two teachers from Mumbai – told me about the serious deficits existing in the Catholic schools there. They said the Church continued to differentiate between rich and poor children, between children from higher and lower castes and the untouchables, the *Harijans*[5] as Gandhi called them. How was this to be reconciled with Jesus's teachings?

The years working at the GI in Pune was a very happy time for me. I had a profession that deeply satisfied me, I got to know many interesting people, I had friends, both male and female, with whom I was able to communicate on a deeper level and with whom I also had a lot of fun. I also belonged to a worldwide community. I came to really know and love India. This country became my second home. I had never felt so free, and I was able to take the initiative on some projects myself.

For instance, in 1966 and upon my suggestion, further training courses for Indian teachers of German were set up in the summer months of May and June for the first time. It was often incredibly hot then, between 40–50° Celsius. But I rode my bicycle to the Institute and enjoyed it. Back then, there was no air-conditioning, only ceiling fans. I remember these courses with great joy because we did so many interesting things together and all of us enjoyed this time. In the evenings we often went together to the only Chinese restaurant nearby or organised theatre shows.

I remember one dinner in particular, it was in May 1967. All the others had gone and I was still sitting with a German lecturer from Hyderabad. He was one of our former students, Saral Sarkar. We got involved in a discussion over religion. Mr Sarkar was an atheist

---

5 'Harijans' means 'Children of God'.

and came from Kolkata. I asked him where an atheist derived his inspiration for wanting to make the world a better place.

Of course, we were not able to bring the discussion to a satisfactory conclusion in the course of this first evening. We did, however, begin to correspond on various societal questions. But I made sure the exchange did not get too personal. I did not want to enter into another platonic relationship with a man, as I had enough of the first one. And I did not want to marry and give up my freedom. Yet in the mid-1960s, I was still not a feminist. And I had no idea of the political-ideological struggles that were already going on in India and everywhere in the world at this time.

Some contemporary history

By 1964, the Communist Party of India (CPI) had split into a soviet-oriented radical wing – called the *Communist Party of India (Marxist)*, *CPI(M)*. The CPI(M) ruled the government in the federal state of Bengal (and still rules there today). The CPI ruled and still rules in Kerala.

But the ideological conflict did not end with this split. Students and peasants, particularly in Bengal, felt that the CPI(M) was too bureaucratic and slow. 1966 marked the year of the Chinese cultural revolution. This motivated student uprisings in Bengal and led to a split from the CPI(M), with the establishment of the CPI(ML)[6] in 1967. In this year, the peasant uprising in *Naxalbari* in Bengal also took place. Followers of this 'Chinese line', who propagated the 'violent struggle' against the feudal class, were called *Naxalites*. They were particularly active in the remote mountainous areas of Bengal, Bihar and Andhra Pradesh.

At the GI in Pune one heard nothing of these uprisings. I myself was still very apolitical and, although I had in many ways witnessed

---

6 Communist Party of India (Marxist-Leninist).

and experienced the class, caste, and patriarchal system as well as its consequences, I was still not in a position to understand what I saw.

Later I understood Marx's statement, "How can class struggle be understood once it is seen?" The fact that *seeing* and *understanding* are not identical is something I did not realise until I became a feminist and began to join in the struggle for women's liberation.

This also began in Pune. One day our librarian, Ms Parekh approached me. She was very excited and held a book under my nose. It was Betty Friedan's *The Feminine Mystique* (1963) which signaled the beginning of the women's movement for many in the USA. Ms Parekh was a German who had married an Indian. I knew she was not happy in her marriage, but she saw no way out. This book showed her the way. I read the book too, and much of what I had observed in India and Germany became very clear to me. I also realised that women's liberation would become my theme in the future.

5

Back Home,
Renewed Studies and Teaching

1968 – The Student Movement

Sociology and Marxism

In December 1967, I received a letter from my sister informing me that my mother was very ill, and that they were not sure if she was going to live. Immediately, I wanted to go home and be with her. I applied to the GI headquarters for a leave of absence and for a premature termination of my five-year contract which was to end in May 1968 anyway. The GI agreed and I left Pune very abruptly. I went home to my mother and noticed that she got well fairly quickly after my return. Perhaps I just imagined it; nevertheless, after a short time she was able to leave the hospital.

I now had to think about how I wanted to live in Germany. As a junior high school teacher I had only been granted a leave of absence from the German school system for five years to work for the Goethe Institute abroad. This leave of absence was to end in April 1968. This meant I would have had to take up my profession as a teacher of English and German again – possibly under the direction of a small-minded headmaster – which was an intolerable prospect. After having the world open its doors to me, I was now to return to live in a provincial nest? Impossible! To quote a phrase my mother always used in such a situation, "It was as if death had given me a nudge."

In the past few years I had stormed out into the world according to the motto: FORWARD EVER – BACKWARD NEVER. A motto, by the way, that seemed to stand for the entire era of the 1960s and 1970s. Was I to go 'backward'? I could not, and did not want to. What, then, could I do?

I wanted to continue working on the issues I had started on in India. I wanted to know more about India's society, particularly about India's women. As a result, I began to look for German universities offering courses of study that had something to do with the sociology of India. However, as already mentioned, the few universities with courses of studies in Indology, such as Bonn and Cologne, were limited to Indian philology and philosophy, and in particular to Sanskrit. I was not interested in that. I was interested in India's modern society. I turned to the South-Asian Institute in Heidelberg, but no one could help me there either. Moreover, no contemporary literature on women in India was to be found all over Germany. The only books available were by British colonial ethnologists, such as Robert Briffault's *The Mothers: The Matriarchal Theory of Social Origins* (1927).

I finally decided to study sociology at the nearest university which was Cologne. Cologne was only 100 kilometres away from my village. This meant I could visit my mother regularly which would do her good. Once before, in 1963, when three of us left to go overseas (one brother to Chile, one sister to the USA, and I to India), she had also become sick.

I acquired a university catalogue of courses and visited the director of the sociology faculty at the University of Cologne, Professor René Koenig. He greeted me warmly, and listened to me with interest, as I gave him a detailed account of all I had done in

India and what I wanted to study. When I said I was interested in knowing why Indian women were able to enforce their will with respect to studying and taking on a profession even though they lived in a patriarchal society, he became enthusiastic. He was fascinated by the country's beautiful women and their saris, and was particularly impressed by Indira Gandhi who was prime minister of India at that time. He had little knowledge of India himself, but he was open and curious and encouraged me right away to not only study sociology under him but start writing a doctoral thesis. "Why don't you begin with your doctorate right away?" he asked. I answered immediately, "Well, if possible, why not?"

I had not given any thoughts to acquiring a doctoral degree, I just wanted to continue pursuing the subjects that interested me. I was not ambitious and was not thinking of climbing the career ladder.

This encounter was again one of those many *happy coincidences* I experienced in my life. Professor Koenig was a liberal and generous man of the old school. He not only had the authority to award doctorates in sociology, a field of study incorporated into the economic sciences at the University of Cologne at that time, but he also had the authority to award doctorates in the humanities. He was actually one of the last universal scholars of Germany. His major field of study was the sociology of families which also corresponded to what I wanted to study. In addition, he taught the sociology of law and medicine, and did research on the ethnology of American-Indian tribes. My studies with him were interesting from the very beginning.

Germany: A foreign country

My return from India, from the 'wide world' to Germany, to this small, even small-minded country, was quite a shock for me. Although I was lucky and had found a new and very interesting field of study, I still felt like a stranger in this country which was supposed to be my home. In the first six months of my new life as a student I walked through the streets of Cologne and felt lost. I kept asking myself, "What am I doing in this country? What do I have in common with the people here?" I could not get rid of a feeling of alienation.

In the five years I spent in India, Germans had become wealthy, they had ascended and were busily constructing their economic miracle. There were more cars and new shops than before I had left. More than ever before, I felt the chasm that divided India from this German 'Wirtschaftswunder'. When I tried to speak to people about India and explain why I felt comfortable in that 'poor country' I was met with disinterest and incomprehension.

The student movement and my discovery of Marxism

When I returned to Germany in 1968 and began my sociology studies, the student movement had reached its high point. I had landed in the middle of this movement and began to learn things I had never heard of. Students held courses on *Das Kapital* by Karl Marx everywhere. They organised sit-ins in the offices of professors they considered too apolitical or traditional. The slogan UNTER DEN TALAREN, DER MUFF VON TAUSEND JAHREN (Under their robes, a thousand-year-old fustiness) was applicable to the University of Cologne as well. At that time, the controversy on positivism was raging between Cologne and the 'Frankfurt School'. It was an absolutely fascinating theoretical debate on the methods of social research. But in Cologne this debate was not only limited to civilised discourse.[1] After the University was occupied by leftist students, it was eventually vacated by the police, during the course of which eggs and tomatoes were thrown – as in many other universities at the time. Nonetheless, Cologne students were not as radical as

---

1 As reported by Kurt Holl, the University was occupied on various occasions. On 30 May, 1968, on the occasion of the third reading of the Emergency Acts, leftist students blocked the major entrance to the venerable Albertus-Magnus-University and hung a large banner with the following inscription: ROSA LUXEMBURG UNIVERSITY. Rightist students wrote above this, 'Radio Luxemburg'. The student protests of these years were characterised by humour and creativity.

students in Frankfurt, Berlin and Munich, although the Socialist German Student Association (SDS) did call the shots, and sociology students set the agenda for the student protests.

Although I was much older than most of them – I was thirty-eight – I joined the student movement. I participated in one of its self-organised study groups, and I read core Marxist literature and all the old texts republished by students in unauthorised copies: Karl Marx's *Manifesto of the Communist Party* (also known as *The Communist Manifesto*, 1848), the writings of the Frankfurt School, especially essays on the positivist dispute, Max Horkheimer, Theodor W. Adorno, Jürgen Habermas, also William Reich and Erich Fromm. I went to the library and delved into Georg W. F. Hegel's *Phenomenology of Spirit* (1807) and his *Lectures on the Philosophy of History* (1837).

I was particularly interested in Marxism. As was the case for many young people in post-war West Germany, this part of our history was more or less unknown to me. The 1960s student movement made sure that this whole topic was no longer branded as a taboo subject. With great interest I read Marx and Engels's *German Ideology* (1845a); and Marx's *Theses on Feuerbach* (1845b), where he criticises German idealism, inspired me. Particularly his 'Eleventh Thesis' became my future leitmotif, "Philosophers have only interpreted the world, in various ways; the point, however, is to change it" (Karl Marx, 1845b, pp. 14–15).

The 'Eleventh Feuerbach Thesis' and *The German Ideology* as a whole, marked the beginning of what seemed to be a new era for me. I discarded my preceding idealistic concepts and for the first time discovered a clear theoretical foundation upon which to base my previous critique of the Church, giving up a metaphysical-idealist view in exchange for an historical-materialist one. I began to understand that all religions had developed historically, and also understood to a certain extent why all the major religions I had become familiar with – Christianity, Islam and Hinduism – were essentially patriarchal and why they oppressed women. Although I had experienced oppression and suffered from it, I previously had no *concept* to explain what I had experienced. Marxism gave me these concepts: *patriarchy and capitalism*.

It was all new and exciting to me. I not only studied at the university with great enthusiasm, but also analysed whatever I saw on the streets and everything else the student movement had criticised. I participated in international protests against the Vietnam War and against the implementation of the emergency laws. I took part in the Easter Peace Marches and helped to make public the so-called Third World countries' fight against American imperialism. When *Benno Ohnesorg*, a student, was shot and killed in Berlin by a policeman during a demonstration against the Iranian Shah's visit on 2 June, 1967, the entire student movement became radicalised and increasingly focused on state repression and on bourgeois majority politics, implemented by the coalition government of Christian Democrats (CDU) and Social Democrats (SPD). *Rudi Dutschke* became the leader of this movement. He called for a revolt against the Springer press because its *Bild* newspaper had created a 'witch-hunt atmosphere' against intellectuals and students with long hair and jeans, branding them as enemies of the 'democratic state of law'.[2]

In February 1968, the *International Vietnam Congress* was held in Berlin. Five thousand people participated. The concluding demonstration was disturbed by a counter-demonstration organised by the Springer press. The publishing company's intimidation campaign not only resulted in the demonisation of people with long hair but also led to Rudi Dutschke being shot on 11 April, 1968 by a young man (who later was identified as an agent of the USSR).

---

2 Several women were among the most radical wing of the student movement. The most famous was Ulrike Meinhof. A film has recently been produced on the members of this radical wing called "The Baader Meinhof Complex" (2008), based on a book written by Stefan Aust (1985/1997).

Dutschke never really recuperated from the shooting and died a few years later.

In the aftermath, anti-Springer demonstrations were organised all over Germany, and the extra-parliamentary opposition APO (*Ausserparlamentarische Opposition*) was established. Based on their experience, these radical youths had lost their faith in parliamentary democracy. They called for schools, universities and workers to participate in the extra-parliamentary revolt and in a boycott of Springer publications.

The student movement not only taught me about Marxism, but most importantly allowed me to gather theoretical insights from practical actions and struggles, and not only just from reading books. Since then, the realisation that practice and theory belong together has remained my leitmotif. Marx's statement "... the point is to change it" has kept me active up to the present.

Political Night Prayer

The spirit of the student movement permeated all of society: you could not miss it, nor could you ignore it. In all families, and throughout all social classes, intense debates were taking place on 'the long-haired hippies' and their disrespectful behaviour toward authority, particularly toward their professors, and with regard to their new forms of protest: their *sit-ins and direct actions* such as their occupations of public offices and universities, as well as their fights with the police. It was no longer possible to put down the movement as a marginal phenomenon carried out by a social minority. Bourgeois circles who detested the students' radicalism, were themselves forced to deal with the issues raised by the movement. For the first time in my life I learned what a *social movement* was.

Following the assassination of Benno Ohnesorg in 1967, critical Christians began to question whether it was time for them to join students in publicly protesting against the Vietnam War. Church leaders, like the rest of the 'establishment' – a term that became standard vocabulary from this time on – had so far refrained from issuing any critique of the USA.

In Cologne, thirty Protestants, Catholics and various non-believers initially came together with the goal of carrying their protest into the church. The initiative was led by *Dorothee Sölle*, whose book *Christ the Representative* (1967)[3] had just shortly before been criticised and rejected by the official Church. The group organised a demonstration and a Good Friday mass in 1968 on Cologne's Neumarkt Square. This was followed by the establishment of the *Political Night Prayer* movement. Its goal was to unite faith and politics – in public. Dorothee Sölle wrote later that, in their meetings, the ecumenical group became increasingly aware of the fact "... that theological contemplation without any political consequences is tantamount to hypocrisy. Therefore, every theological statement must also be a political one" (Sölle, 1999, p. 71).

A friend of mine took me to one of the group's Night Prayer meetings at the Antoniter Church in Cologne and I decided to participate. I was a student, and despite my critique of religion, I was still a member of the Church. I liked the Political Night Prayer's approach and method. For the first time I witnessed political issues being addressed, information being provided and debates held on these issues in a church setting. Church members were no longer doomed to keep silent while being preached to 'from above'.

Moreover, the group not only provided information and discussed socio-political problems. Each group developing a 'Night Prayer' also had to think about concrete actions and steps to be taken to change the situation. Pure analysis and critique were not enough. And ample room was given for 'prayer', or meditation as it was called, for which passages from the Gospels or the Old Testament prophets could be taken, but also excerpts from a poem by Bertolt Brecht, a

---

3 The book was first published in Germany in 1965 under the title *Theology after the Death of God* (*Theologie nach dem Tode Gottes*).

song by Helder Camara, or a quote from Marxist authors. The four-part process, encompassing *information – discussion – meditation – action*, was a truly revolutionary method. Dorothee Sölle emphasised the necessity to outline the Night Prayers' themes as concretely and precisely as possible. "The more an issue is kept within definable limits, the more possible it becomes to provide information; the more concrete an issue, the more fruitful the discussion and action" (Sölle, 1999, p. 72).

The issues were not specified, but one or more persons could make a suggestion on a problem to be taken up. They then formed a group to prepare and carry out a Night Prayer as well as do follow-up work on it. It was not enough to just make *suggestions*. Time was spent during the following Night Prayers to inform people on how the action went. The group was also responsible for typing, copying and laying out the script for each Night Prayer – as in a screenplay – so that people could have material to take home.

These small brochures were distributed widely beyond the city boundaries, and the Cologne Night Prayer was copied in many other cities in Germany and abroad. The Political Night Prayer developed into a radically new political movement within the established churches, the traces of which have not yet completely vanished. The group was able to gather its information from experts, but it remained a lay group of people who used the church setting to organise public debate on major social and political problems of our societies.

I worked on three of these Night Prayer groups. The first one was titled *Development Aid – A Vicious Circle*. I asked some of my fellow students in my sociology group if they wanted to join and some of them agreed. When reading this Night Prayer now I am impressed by the actuality of the issue and also by our analysis. An anthology of the first Night Prayers was published by Kreuzverlag in 1969 (Sölle and Steffensky, Eds) including the following lines:

because you are poor you have to die
poverty keeps you from saving
without savings you can't build capital
without capital you can't invest
without investment you can't increase production
without an increase in production: poverty
because you are poor you have to die.
(*Politisches Nachtgebet in Köln*, 1969, p. 86)

The discovery of patriarchy as a system

The second Night Prayer I worked on was called *Emancipation of Women*. It was based on my initiative, because during my fieldwork in India for my dissertation, and due to my studies of ancient Indian texts on gender relationships, I had discovered *patriarchy as a system*. At the same time, I realised that in our modern Germany we were still living in a similar *patriarchal* system. As a result, I stated, "In studying the Indian system of patriarchy I also discovered Germany's patriarchy." I wanted to portray, criticise and call for a change of these patriarchal structures in a Political Night Prayer. Dorothee Sölle, Ursula Erler and Erika Klug joined in preparing and carrying out this prayer. We took a quotation from Ernst Bloch and modified it as the slogan for our flyer: DIE FRAU LIEGT [IMMER NOCH] UNTEN (Women are [still] on the bottom) which was printed on the cover of the brochure (*Politisches Nachtgebet*, 1971).

It was the first time the issue of women's discrimination and oppression was publicly discussed in a church in Germany. When the Night Prayer was carried out on 5 January, 1971, the small Antoniter Church was packed full. Not only Christians, but also many women from the still fledgling Cologne women's movement came. The major point of our critique was directed towards the traditional division of labour within the family: while the male is the 'provider' who earns money, women's work at home does not count. We compiled a long list of common prejudices:

> The man is the head, the woman is the heart. The man is a specialist in the sciences, arts and creative design of the world. The woman is a specialist in love. Her role in life: to please (*Politisches Nachtgebet*, 1971, p. 7).

This Prayer had a great impact: our demand for establishing open women's consciousness-raising groups at the School of Adult Education (Volkshochschule Köln) was successfully met, and these groups continued for many years. This particular Night Prayer did much to promote the women's movement in Cologne.

The third Night Prayer I worked on was titled *Bangladesh: Beginning or End?* As of 1971, a political liberation movement in East Pakistan had been struggling to secede from West Pakistan. The population in East Pakistan felt that they were oppressed, exploited and colonised by its Western counterpart. The new, autonomous (Bengal) state that was to become established was called Bangladesh (country of the Bengal people).[4]

This Political Night Prayer took place on 11 January, 1972. Those who organised it were Claudia von Werlhof, Jochen Kaufmann, Barbara Skriver, Maria Mies and Jaspal Singh. The choice of this topic shows that the Political Night Prayers were not only limited to pressing local and national problems, but in fact extended to international issues. At that time, we endeavoured to create a link between what was happening in India and Bangladesh with what we were dealing with in Cologne. It was our – and my particular – wish to further an international perspective.

---

4 Pakistan was established in 1947 when India became decolonised and divided into 'Hindu' and 'Muslim' sections. The major portion of Muslims lived in western India, Punjab and Sind. A considerable portion, however, also lived in Eastern Bengal, thousands of kilometres away from West Pakistan and its capital of Karachi.

The student movement and the Political Night Prayer not only politicised me, but I was also finally freed from that strange feeling of alienation that had been holding me hostage since I had returned from India.

The 'Women's Question'[5]

From the time I worked at the Goethe Institute in India I had been confronted with the glaring effects of patriarchy as a system. And before that, during the time of my unending love story with my Muslim sailor, I had experienced the dogmatic harshness of this system as maintained by the major religions of Christianity and Islam. I also knew they held all more or less similar views with respect to women's rights, Hinduism included. Male subjugation of women was the basic principle underlying all of these religions and the cultures based on them. The Hindu Law codes provide a particularly clear example of this. When I studied them in preparation for my doctoral thesis I found this sentence in the *Laws of Manu*, India's earliest Hindu legal treatise: "Her father protects [her] in childhood, her husband protects [her] in youth, and her sons protect [her] in old age; a woman is never fit for independence" (Bühler, 1886, *Laws of Manu*, Chapter IX).

In our brochure on the Political Night Prayer *Emancipation of Women*, an entire chapter was dedicated to women's exploitation by the Christian churches. Our reasoning was based on the Christian texts. We wrote (pp. 10–11):

In formulating their concept of women and family, the Christian churches have created religious justification for male domination of women. They have created the ideal of 'the handmaid of the Lord' from woman's role as a dependant and servant. Lord and God, however, was a man ...

---

5 In the nineteenth century, the discourse on women's emancipation in Germany used the concept of the 'women's question'.

'The head of a woman is her husband' is not only a statement to be found in St. Paul's letters and in multiple variations written by the church fathers. Still today, sacrifice and service, subservience and renunciation are the most important virtues – not of mankind, but of women.

Josef Kardinal Höffner, in *Marriage and Family in the Light of Faith* (*Ehe und Familie im Licht des Glaubens*, 1969) wrote the following on the role of the mother and homemaker: "Selfless and with untiring effort she carries out her office, without claim to pay and holiday; workdays and Sundays, often more than twelve hours a day" (p. 11).

Our question was, "Why is not the same spirit of sacrifice demanded of men? Are they not also Christians without claim to pay and holiday, workdays and Sundays?"

Dorothee Sölle added (p. 11):

And in a manner typical for the kind of semi-enlightenment existing in Protestantism it was granted that ' ... although all of the professions are open [to woman] in principle, it should not be forgotten that because of her natural disposition towards motherhood, the family is her primary sphere of influence. Therefore, she should only carry out a profession outside of the home if it also complies with the family.

All of the prejudices existing in bourgeois society regarding 'the role of women' were reiterated by the men of the church: the male is more 'free' of 'personal emotional attachments' than the female because of his 'stronger leadership qualities' and his 'objectivity'.

In conclusion to our critique of the Christian patriarchal system I wrote (p. 12):

How can theologians make a patriarch out of God and a master and king out of Jesus – instead of giving him the title he gave himself: Son of Man? The Christian churches have continuously trivialised, concealed and betrayed Jesus's intentions. They have acted as henchmen to the ruling classes and have presented the existing patriarchal system of power relations as an eternal, divine right. The same is being done today when the systems of exploitation are obfuscated by exhortations on the family as 'an oasis in the anonymous landscape of modern life' (J. Höffner). They talk of partnership but do not lift a finger towards laying the axe at the root of the problem, namely at the economic and social relationship of dependency between man and woman.

We were not feminist theologians – this did not yet exist in Germany in 1970 – but we incorporated Jesus into the circle of great revolutionaries (p. 12):

Believers in the Bible believed in a humane society. It was self-evident to them that a humane society can only be established when it is taken possession of by all equally and without discrimination. Not only Abraham and Jesus, but also Joachim de Fiore, Thomas More, Marx, Engels and Castro worked on acquiring a 'consciousness of the matter' of which the world has only possessed the dream. All of these struggled to make the world a better place. As in Marx's analysis, we are not the first ones to think about the past; it is important to take action on those thoughts ... *the point is, to change it.*

We quoted women of the 'past, present and future' who testified to our desire for liberation, such as Antigone, Jeanne d'Arc, Clara Zetkin, and Rosa Luxemburg, who "until her murder on 15 January, 1919 worked, suffered, laughed and enjoyed a life that was dedicated to the emancipation of the working people ..." (p. 13).

However, our long passages were not used to criticise 'men' as such, but rather to criticise the sex, class and power relations that were obstructing the realisation of our 'dream' of emancipation. This included also criticising the *deformations* we had begun to identify within ourselves caused by this patriarchal-capitalist system. Dorothee Sölle wrote (pp. 13–14):

> It is our object to prolong the perseverance of those who believe and to pronounce solidarity with those who are rebelling, breaking out and going on strike ... It is not our object to replace domination with domination. As women, we have understood how to take revenge against the male law with which men ruled over us. We did it secretly, in the evening after his work day ... We got so far as to wear him down with the pettiness, lack of sympathy, and animosity that accrued during the course of our empty day of housework ... and to prod him on his way up the economic ladder. Rarely did we encourage him to resist and to demand action in the common interest at work and in public ...

In the discussion on what action needed to be taken, we not only demanded that consciousness-raising groups be established for women, but that a new division of labour between men and women was necessary. Men and women should divide housework between them, both should work and contribute to providing for the family. Not only women, but also men would profit from this new division of labour (p. 16):

> A man would no longer be subject to the non-stop compulsion of always working for more and better things. He would be able to go on strike against exploitation and injustice without being in continuous fear of not being able to provide for his family.

He would be free to make use of his civil rights; threatening to fire him from his job would no longer be a means of blackmailing him.

Some of the demands formulated in this Political Night Prayer were met immediately: discussion groups for women at the Volkshochschule came into being and existed for many years. But even today our demand for a different division of labour in society and the family has not been completely met. Politicians still call for 'family and work balance'. Most of the issues addressed in this Night Prayer were also being discussed in the international women's movement at that time. For the Cologne women's movement, this Night Prayer represented an important impetus, because in 1971, there were still no other women's groups addressing the issue of a new division of labour between men and women.

Working on the issue of women's emancipation for the Political Night Prayer was a decisive turning point for me personally. Through my own earlier experiences and my doctoral studies I had already understood that the patriarchal system was one that oppressed women, that it formed the basis for all major religions, including Christianity. Yet this insight was not enough for me to leave the church. Not until our public critique of this system by means of the Night Prayer on 5 January, 1971 was I able to take this step. It took two more years until I left the church, and set a seal on it by writing a poem I later always recited when someone asked me, "Maria, what do you think of religion?" Here it is:

We Women are God-less

We women are god-less
we have gotten rid of God

The God of Abraham, Isaac and Jacob,
The patriarch of patriarchs

Who subjected the world to their rule
With their herds and wars
And destroyed the fields of the women gardeners

It is this God they invoked
When they divided life
Into man and woman
Above and below
Heaven and hell
Head and belly
Spirit and matter
Headwork and handwork
Theory and praxis
Lord and servant

His name
Jehovah
Will not pass our lips
And the other
Father
Is like saw dust on our tongues
And on those of our children

And what is Allah to us?
The one and only
who needs no one?
His jealousy imprisons us here
in the harem
And there we are to serve
The men as houris[6]

And Jesus?
The brother?

---

6 In Islam, a beautiful maiden who awaits the devout Muslim in paradise.

Look what they've done to him
From his blood they have made a mass
And in his name
They took our sisters
The witches
and murdered them

Neither do we know Shiva
Who erects his phallus
On the deflowered earth
Which he turned into a desert
Now the poor call in despair
To Bhumi Devi
And paint the stones on the field red
But Magna Mater has become infertile
The Brahmins of East and West
Have been repulsed by her menstrual blood for too long
Now she has become frigid

Krishna, too
Is not the God of women
Disdainer of the human heart
He sent Arjuna into war against his brother
'As the law commands'
Let him remain the God of lawyers
With his nishkama karma[7]
He leaves us cold

Yes, my sisters
We have gotten rid of God
There is no place for us in their heavens
And none on the earth
Of fathers and sons

---

7 "Act. But do not expect any gratification for your acting" (Hindu philosophy).

Of lords and servants
Of priests and professors
Of warriors and capitalists
(Maria Mies, Cologne, 1973)

Later, I added:

And the age-old young one?
The one that was always there
The life in us
And around us
Why do we call it Goddess?
(Maria Mies, Cologne, 1984)

Doctoral Degree

As was often the case in my life, everything happened *at the same time*. I studied sociology, became acquainted with Marxism, participated in the student movement, took part in the Political Night Prayers, was active in the women's movement and worked on my doctoral dissertation.

I had already outlined the theme of my dissertation the first time I met with Professor Koenig: to analyse the contradictions encountered by educated and/or working middle-class Indian women. I had come across these contradictions and conflicts when working with my women students in Pune.

Professor Koenig accepted this theme immediately. He, too, was working on the conflict between *tradition and modernism* in developing countries.

The title of my doctoral thesis was, "Indian Women between patriarchy and equal opportunity: role conflicts for women students and working women." In order to acquire a thorough, empirical basis

I had to return to India to carry out fieldwork. Professor Koenig provided me with a letter of reference which helped to open doors for me at Indian universities.

I did not receive any money. I financed this fieldwork, as well as my entire sociology studies, by myself. I also did not apply for a scholarship. During my work as a Lecturer at the Goethe Institute I had been able to save some money and the costs of living were very low in India; thus I could pay for my studies from what I had saved. This did pose somewhat of a risk because I had left my job as a teacher and had relinquished my status as a civil servant when I started my second academic studies. However, I was confident I would be able to find a job immediately after completing my dissertation, and if not, I could always go back to teaching at the Realschule. Hence, I did not burn my bridges rashly. As the daughter of a peasant, I knew that it was absolutely necessary for a woman who did not want to become dependent on a man to have a firm economic base upon which to live.

In India, I sought to make contact with middle-class women in Mumbai and Delhi. This posed no problems, as I had many friends from my days in Pune who now lived in various cities.

In Mumbai, Suma Chitnis, a professor at the *Tata Institute of Social Sciences (TISS)*, helped me to make contact with her women students. She was very interested in my thesis, as she herself was a perfect example of how women of her caste and class were trying to reconcile the various social roles assigned to them. They combined the roles of wife, daughter-in-law, and mother with the roles of student, working person and often also as a politically active woman. This kind of role diversity for women was unthinkable at that time in Germany. I witnessed the same when interviewing her students and other women in Delhi. All of them knew they would have to marry, because unmarried women in India did not have any means of existence and no social status. Despite these difficulties, most of the women not only wanted to study but also carry out a profession.

What surprised me most about the diversity of roles was the fact that there were far more women working as professors and in senior jobs in this patriarchal country than in Germany. Even more surprising was the fact that men had no problem working 'under' a female boss. This was something I could not imagine in Germany, let alone in the whole of Europe.

I have often been asked to explain this fact, especially because India seems to be the patriarchal country *par excellence*. I have answered that Indian women are 'strong women'; in addition, women in higher positions also mostly belong to the privileged classes and castes. Today I know that Indian men accept 'strong women' – such as Indira Gandhi – because the basic structure of Indian society has remained matriarchal. Its mother-centred heritage has never been completely destroyed.[8]

I received my doctoral degree in September 1972. Professor Koenig, my doctoral adviser, was enthusiastic about my dissertation. It was the first sociological study on women in India to have been written in German. It was published by Anton Hain Publishers in 1973. After this company was sold, my book passed from one publisher to another until it landed at the Europäische Verlags-anstalt (EVA) in 1986. It was re-titled *Indian Women between Oppression and Emancipation (Indische Frauen zwischen Unter-drückung und Befreiung)*. Saral Sakar, by then my husband, also translated the book into English, and it was published in 1980 under the title *Indian Women and Patriarchy* by Concept Publishers in New Delhi.

---

8 That Indian culture was originally a matriarchal one is quite obvious even today. Not only are goddesses like Lakshmi, Durga, Kali, Sarasvati and others venerated in big city temples, but also in village temples. They are also often the main family deities. The Marxist philosopher Debiprasad Chattopadhyaya has shown that the veneration of Mata Devi (Earth Mother) was necessary in old times to make the soil fertile (Chattopadhyaya, 1959).

Even in modern patriarchal India men have not totally forgotten that patriarchs need *mothers* if they want to have sons. This may explain why Indian men accepted women in higher positions much earlier than was the case in the West.

Teaching: Fachhochschule Köln
(University of Applied Sciences, Cologne)

In September 1972, I received my doctoral degree, and in December of that year I got a job at the newly established Fachhochschule Köln in the Faculty of Social Pedagogy. I did not waste time looking for a position at another university. Cologne was not far from my village and the Fachhochschule Köln had the further advantage that, as a legacy from the student movement, it was dedicated to connecting theory with practice. This appealed to me very much. In my interview for the job I suggested that the faculty's commitment to practice be realised in the form of a *project-based course of study* as was already established in various universities and colleges of applied sciences across Germany (such as Oldenburg, Bremen and Osnabrück). At that time I had read Paulo Freire's book *Pedagogy of the Oppressed* (1970) and was enthusiastic about his method of 'conscientisation'. It seemed to me that Freire's method would be just the right thing for this new approach to social pedagogy, in particular to adult education. It resolved the problem of purely transmitting knowledge as practised in the universities, and connected the knowledge that was to be transmitted with political consciousness-raising and political practise. I had personally met Paulo Freire at a congress in Paris in 1972.

The nominating committee agreed and I was given the job with two fields of specialisation: sociology of the family and sociology of social minorities. In addition, I was given the task of establishing a project-based course of studies for the Faculty of Social Pedagogy. After a short time, a colleague, *Mechthild Höflich*, joined me in this task.

I had already become acquainted with Mechthild through the Political Night Prayer where she had worked in a project with homeless youths, called 'Die Etage' (The Storey). She was able to continue this project within the framework of our newly established project studies.

I asked my students what projects they were interested in. Many of them had not come from secondary schools or gymnasiums but had already held a job. It was important to us as colleagues to include their experiences in our teaching. Moreover, many of our students as well as our colleagues were still inspired by the spirit of the student movement, and any authoritarian behaviour on the part of the professors would not have been tolerated. It was impossible to put on airs as the 'knowers' whose only task it was to transfer their knowledge to the minds of 'unknowing' students in order to test that knowledge in exams. Discussions, group work, cooperation instead of competition, practice, independent initiative, and a view from below – meaning from the parties involved – played an important role.

Project-based course of study

Our innovative approach found its clearest expression in the faculty's project courses. The students (project groups were mixed at first; as yet there were no women-only projects) were asked to form a group which would then choose a specific project to work on: either in the area of youth work, adult education and training, the homeless; later on also on specific women's projects and other social-pedagogical fields. Contrary to the traditional internships carried out in existing institutions, our students had to create something new: besides giving help to those who needed it, their activity had to have an *emancipatory quality*. Moreover, the emancipatory goal of these projects not only applied to the target groups as such, but also to the students themselves. In my understanding, their group work, shared practice and reflection on their work, as well as the necessity to cooperate on bringing out a project report, was to be a *practice of freedom*, as Paulo Freire called it. This project-based course of study was an effective method in

BACK HOME, RENEWED STUDIES AND TEACHING

overcoming the pressure on individualism and competition that traditionally ruled in universities, and it was effective in allowing the students to *directly* learn about the problems of society. It was about developing the capacity for teamwork and social creativity, and, most importantly, it was about acquiring experiential knowledge *before* acquiring theoretical insight, as well as understanding that theoretical studies are imperative for praxis. In effect, I reversed the traditional sequence of first teaching and learning theory and then putting it to practise. *For me, praxis precedes theory.*

It was important to me that our students acquired direct *experience* from real social life situations and encounter the problems that particular groups of people have – youth, children, the elderly, the homeless, migrants and women – so that they could work with them in developing concrete solutions to their problems. It was a very creative and mutual learning process for both the students and those 'suffering' from the situation. Only with this first-hand experience as their base would they be able to develop a genuine interest in theoretical knowledge.

From these project groups developed life-long friendships which, in the amicable atmosphere, extended to us teachers. As at all universities back then, the students and professors addressed each other informally, and not in formal terms as was traditional.[9] Malicious tongues even spoke of 'the red student/professor collective in Cologne-South' where our university was housed.

All of this does not mean that we did not encounter any problems in our project studies. Not all of our project groups accomplished their self-set goals. And within the groups the usual group-dynamics also took place. Some individuals could not continue working with their peers. Yet all of these difficulties were discussed in our weekly project meetings. My motto was, in principle, that there was no

---

9 The student movement in its anti-authoritarian drive dropped 'Sie' (You) to address people in higher positions. They simply used the familiar 'Du' to show that we are all equal.

such thing as a failed project. Even if a group did not achieve its goal, they were able to gather important experiences from real-life situations and learn something from them.

One of the 'failed' programs in this sense was a bilingual language project I initiated for migrant Spanish women who primarily worked at the Ford automobile plant. I had designed the project according to Paulo Freire's method where the Spanish workers were to learn German from our students, and the workers were to teach the students Spanish. Both groups were students and teachers at the same time, and in the process of learning the language they were to become politically *alphabetised*, meaning the experience was to raise their political consciousness. In our alphabetising campaign we wanted to implement the method successfully used by Paulo Freire in rural Brazil.

After a shared discussion of an important problem, we developed a so-called code: a certain picture or a role play that illustrated the problem we had just discussed. After that, key words were developed, written down, learned, and finally put together in a sentence. As a consequence, learning the language turned into a process of becoming politically conscious, whereby the usual hierarchical relationship between teachers and students was broken down.

The language course took place in a boarding house maintained by the Cologne chapter of Caritas, Germany's largest Catholic welfare organisation. It worked out quite well. We had actually gotten as far as being able to put together a small primer from the codes, key words and sentences we had developed. Everyone involved in this bilingual language course had fun, even if the Spanish women learned more than we Germans.

However, the language course had to end abruptly. The director of the boarding house informed us that the Bishop of Cologne would not allow the project to continue in Church-owned facilities "because Paulo Freire was a communist."

Perhaps we would have been able to carry on our project in a different place, or we could have fought with the episcopal authorities to continue our course. But we could not, and did not, want to do so over the heads of the Spanish women. They did not want to 'quarrel' with the Church leaders. And after their day's work, they also did not want to drive somewhere else to learn German. Both reasons made sense. We were forced to give up our project. However, we all had learned a lot. I not only was able to put Paulo Freire's method into practice, but I also learned how quickly this method worked and how negatively the Church reacted to any attempt to help people become more aware and politically conscious!

Accusing someone of being a communist was a knock-out argument. Yet I continued to offer regular seminars on the methodology of social action and on Paulo Freire's *Pedagogy of The Oppressed* (1970).

In the context of our practice-oriented pedagogy we also carried out various actions. One of these was our *garbage action*. After one of my seminars that dealt with the issue of 'structural violence', a concept created by Johan Galtung (1975) with regard to the 'Third World' and the environment, my students asked me, "What can we do to stop structural violence?" In turn I asked them, "What concrete problem is bothering you here?" Someone reported that the canteen had replaced its porcelain dishes with plastic ware. The Student Service responsible for the canteen wanted to save costs and personnel. We said, "This has to change. The plastic stuff only creates garbage and has to disappear from the canteen!"

Our anti-garbage action began with the students gathering all of the plastic dishes and cutlery used in the canteen and throughout the entire university and dumping it all onto a huge pile in the university's foyer. The next morning, when students and professors streamed into the university, they tripped over our mountain of plastic. The students distributed a flyer explaining the action. We also theoretically documented where all the plastic stuff came from, where the natural resources for making it were taken – namely from the oil fields in the South, and finally, whether it was possible to limit the huge production of garbage in our wealthy countries.

Lothar Gothe, one of my friends from the Socialist Self-Help Group Cologne (SSK),[10] told me he knew of a man who did not produce an ounce of garbage. I invited him to come to our seminar where he explained how he organised his garbage-free life.

I also invited a Hungarian friend, a chemist, to give a lecture on the chemistry of plastics. He told us how much petroleum is needed to make plastic and what types were recyclable or not.

The students also invited a representative of the Student Services to explain why it made economic sense to replace durable porcelain with plastic ware that had to be continuously replenished. He presented us with a classical cost-benefit analysis and claimed the conversion to plastic was an 'economic necessity'. The students countered, "What a naïve assessment, because if you include *all* the costs in your calculation, even the 'invisible' ones such as oil production, transportation, unemployment and garbage disposal, the plastic stuff becomes absolutely unaffordable."

Our expert had just one thing to say to that, "Such considerations had nothing to do with normal business-management calculations." It was beyond his responsibility. Now we had a very concrete example of what 'structural violence' was.

In the end, our anti-garbage action was successful. The plastic stuff disappeared from our canteen and the Cologne press also reported on it. On Cologne's Municipal Environment Day we were invited to publicly present our garbage action on Neumarkt Square.

---

10 The Socialist Self-Help Group Cologne (Sozialistische Selbsthilfe Köln, SSK) was established by two students, Lothar Gothe and Rainer Kippe, to prevent homeless youths from becoming criminals. At the same time it sought to encourage students to form and develop an anti-authoritarian and self-determined community. At first the City of Cologne supported the project. When the authorities tried to close the facility – due to rumours of drug abuse – our faculty provided asylum to the youths at the university. It was quite an adventurous story which, due to lack of space and time, I cannot elaborate on here.

Not long ago a colleague told me, "The garbage action was really a total success. Our canteen still has porcelain dishes and proper knives, forks and spoons, and no plastic ware."

Sociology of social minorities, sociology of the family

I also applied a practice-oriented approach to my other sociological seminars. I always attempted to include my students' experiences in my teaching to create a link between the practical knowledge they had, and theoretical knowledge.

My two fields of specialisation – sociology of the family and the sociology of social minorities – were particularly conducive to this approach. Social minorities – called 'marginalised groups' at that time – included a broad range of people with problems that our nascent social pedagogues were supposed to help solve, at least in part. I left it up to the students to determine for themselves which group they wanted to concentrate on in theory and in practice.

In the sociology of families I proceeded in a similar manner. Everyone had experiences with families. Yet there was very little knowledge about the *history of families*. Family sociologists who reflected critically on the history of the family were hardly known. Most of them were conservative or liberals and presented the *bourgeois nuclear family* as the eternally unchanging model for all families in all cultures. In order to rectify this deficit, I introduced Friedrich Engels's *The Origins of the Family, Private Property and the State* (1884/1942) as mandatory reading, despite some feminist critique of Engels at that time.

No social institution to date has been so heavily debated ideologically as the institution of family. *The sociology of families* has therefore also been influenced by the respective ruling parties and their *family policies*. This example in particular made me realise that the social sciences are not, and cannot be, value-free. You cannot speak of 'families' without also speaking of men and women and of the *relationship between the sexes*. As a consequence I placed great value on illustrating the *historical changes* that these relationships have undergone, as well as the huge cultural differences in the relationships between the sexes throughout the world – an exciting, and still very topical issue that fascinated me as well as my students.

Since taking part in the Political Night Prayer in January 1971, I was not only actively involved in the women's movement, but I also called myself a *feminist*. Like many of the women involved in the movement I tried to include the dimension of *women as a minority* as well as the *relationship between the sexes* in the focus of my teaching and research. At that time, none of the academic disciplines, neither the humanities nor the social sciences, and especially not the natural sciences, were even aware of any 'gender' categories. In discussions on theory, women did not exist.

In my two fields of specialisation this systematic disregard of the female sex was particularly scandalous. Back then, hardly any of the social studies using statistics were differentiated according to sex. That is why, in teaching, I put particular emphasis on the fact that our human society is comprised of both sexes, of which the one – the female – is treated as a *social minority*, although statistically it represents the majority in the world.

6

The Women's Movement

WOMEN TOGETHER ARE STRONG / SISTERHOOD IS POWERFUL!

When I applied for my job at the Fachhochschule Köln (University of Applied Sciences, Cologne) I said I was active in the women's movement. Hence, from the beginning I made it clear that I was a feminist.

New social movements do not take place in the office or the library. They happen *when the time is ripe*. When a child is born after long months of pregnancy it is suddenly just *there*! So it is with social movements.

This is how the new women's movement happened. It just suddenly seemed to appear. Almost simultaneously, women stood up all over the world. They stood up and protested against exploitation, oppression, and against direct and structural violence which affect all women. This movement did not have its origins in any single place, such as in the USA, as many claim. Women were also rebelling in India, Bangladesh, Egypt, Thailand, Hong Kong, Korea, Japan and in many other countries. The international women's movement seemed to *be suddenly present on all continents*.

What still fascinates me the most today about the appearance of the new international women's movement in the 1960s and 1970s is the *simultaneity* with which women's liberation struggles developed throughout the world. I do not mean this with regard to time and space alone. What I perceived was that women all over the world discovered they had one thing in common despite their differences in culture, religion, class and race: *no matter where they came from, being a woman meant being a second or third class human being.*

Experiencing the movement's simultaneousness and realising its community of interests led to a great feeling of strength and bonding with other women. SISTERHOOD IS POWERFUL was the slogan of the era. No woman was alone any more and everyone seemed to be connected. Every woman involved in the movement also developed the feeling that we were *strong*.

Our strength and our momentum led to the will to change the structures hostile to women, to change the world, and this was reflected in another slogan, WOMEN TOGETHER ARE STRONG! Projects, activities, various forms of protests and demonstrations sprang up everywhere, and songs were composed that quickly spread all over the world (even without the help of computers).

Women established women's centres, bookstores, women's newspapers and associations and in doing so they not only attacked the ruling male society but also sought to develop true alternatives to patriarchy.

The problems concerning women becoming apparent in this context necessarily resulted in a renewed search for valid answers to age-old questions of humanity, for instance, when did this patriarchal and misogynistic system begin to exist? Why has it continued for so long? Why does women's work, in particular housework, have no value? Does this system exist throughout the world? Or is it an invention of capitalism? Such theoretical questions were not the result of academic studies – although women academics were involved in finding answers to them.

The movement's general climate resulted in a great desire to *think*, in an "Erotik des Denkens" (an erotic of thinking) as Veronika Bennholdt-Thomsen called it. Theory was fun. It meant taking old questions, posing them anew and providing new answers without having to heed the proclaimers of 'eternal truths'. As already mentioned, I insisted on combining practice and theory. This produced so much creativity and energy that everything seemed possible. It gave us the momentum to address even the most difficult problems of women's oppression and attempt to solve them.[1]

One such ancient problem was *violence against women*. This problem not only existed, and still exists, in 'backward', 'traditional' societies, but was found in the midst of our modern, 'civilised' industrialised nations. In 1976, some of my women students and I began a movement to fight violence against women in our immediate surroundings – in families in Cologne.

The struggle to establish the first autonomous women's shelter in Germany

Inspired by the first *International UN Women's Conference* held in Mexico in 1975, I began to offer courses on this topic at the Fachhochschule Köln. Many women students at that time began to develop an interest in the women's movement. We realised we hardly had any knowledge of Europe's *previous* women's movement, let alone of women's movements in other parts of the world.

After a seminar on the nineteenth and early twentieth century women's movements, some students were amazed to discover that many of the current problems and demands had already been formulated by feminists in the mid-nineteenth century. Why had women's liberation not made any progress since then? Why did the women's movement peter out during the Weimar Republic? Why did we forget our history? Why did no one tell us about it?

---

1 As a symbol of the movement's simultaneity and power, the Indian feminists chose the image of the great, ancient, multiple-armed *Mother Goddess* which is present in many forms and has been given various names in all areas of the country. *Durga* or *Kali*, the most powerful manifestation of this Great Mother, has eight arms and hands in which she holds different objects: tools, instruments, a flower, and also a sword (she is by no means a pacifist). Two of her hands are raised in blessing. Durga/Kali rides a tiger.

"This must never happen again," my students said, a group of fifteen. They got together and discussed what they could do. One thing became very clear: they did not just want to form a *consciousness raising group*, nor did they just want to be an informal discussion group. They wanted to take the issues they had reflected on in their discussion rounds and apply practical-political measures to solve them. The most important issue was *violence* against women in the family. Around this time *Erin Pizzi* founded the first shelter for battered women in England, in the London district of Chiswick. My women students decided to establish the first shelter for battered women in Cologne.

In order to launch this project, the students sent a delegation to the social welfare office and presented their request to *Herr Körner*, the head of the social welfare department. However, Herr Körner was of the opinion that there was no need to open a women's shelter in Cologne because no woman had ever sought help from the facilities maintained either by the city or any charitable institutions. He advised the students to first present a study on the extent of violence against women in private homes in order to statistically determine the need for a shelter or a crisis centre. It was clear that his aim was to shelve the problem by requiring a study.

When the students returned and reported on their meeting we decided to organise a street action on the issue of 'violent husbands' rather than carry out a statistical study. We had no money to finance such a prolonged study in the first place; secondly, we knew that the results of such studies often do not reflect reality and, thirdly, that such a study would not lead to social or political change.

In the beginning of the spring semester in 1976 we held our street action on a Saturday in the Schildergasse, Cologne's most busy shopping street. The women students painted posters, collected newspaper articles and pasted them onto cardboard. We talked to people on the street and asked them if they were aware that women in Cologne were being beaten by their husbands and whether they considered this to be a serious problem. We also asked them whether they thought Cologne needed a house for battered women. We informed them that, according to the head of the social welfare department, the problem of battered women did not exist in Cologne. People immediately told us of the many examples they knew of where women were beaten by their husbands. We then asked them to sign a petition openly identifying violence against women as a problem and demanding the establishment of a *shelter for battered women*. With the help of a cassette recorder I documented the reports we heard of violent husbands. On this day alone, we collected 2,000 signatures in support of a battered women's house in Cologne.

A friend of mine, a woman journalist who worked for Cologne's daily newspaper the *Kölner Stadtanzeiger*, took part in the action and reported on our results the next day. In the article, the telephone number of a students' commune where some of the students lived was published so that women seeking protection from their violent husbands could call there. The report also advertised the date of a meeting to discuss where and how a shelter for battered women should be established.

Approximately seventy women came as well as a few men. We told them clearly that a house for battered women would primarily be a shelter for *women* and that men would not have access to it. At this meeting the participants decided to establish an association named *Women helping Women* (Frauen helfen Frauen e.V., FhF), which would create an autonomous shelter for battered women in Cologne.

At this meeting we introduced our concept for the shelter. We launched a lively public relations campaign on the issue of *violence against women*, in the course of which students responsible for the action were invited to regularly report on their project for a women's shelter. These invitations were also welcome opportunities to collect money contributions for our endeavour.

At this time the *Kölner Express* published an article on *Christa Thomas*, at that time a seventy-year-old resident of a municipal senior citizen's home. She demanded that the municipal authorities offer one of its buildings in the senior citizens' complex as a battered women's shelter, a request the municipal authorities rejected.

Lie Selter, however, one of our project's initiators, immediately set out to meet her. Together with her friend, *Anke Rieger*, Christa Thomas quickly joined our 'Women helping Women' initiative and actively became involved in all our events. As a result we learned about another chapter of women's history in Cologne, as Christa Thomas had been actively opposing war and militarism ever since World War II. In the 1950s, she – a Catholic – had vehemently opposed the Christian Democratic Party's support of re-arming the Federal Republic of Germany, for which she was even arrested. Christa Thomas clearly saw a link between public militarism and private male violence against women.

Until her death she continued to fight for peace and disarmament, against nuclear technology and the patriarchal system. We were glad to have three generations of women represented in our association: 'daughters', 'mothers' and 'grandmothers'. We organised a celebration to honour the revival of the *Matrons*. Christa Thomas had collected much material on the ancient matron cult which had existed in the area around Bonn, Cologne and throughout the Rhineland.

The founding members of our FhF (Frauen helfen Frauen), women's shelter association included Birgit Hanner, Lie Selter, Frauke Mahr, Ulla Struwe, Annette Löning, Conny Pätzold, Astrid Frazer-Schilling, Ursula Viefers, Anke Rieger, Maria Mies and Christa Thomas.

Equally important as our public campaign was the fact that directly after our association's telephone number was published, many women called seeking shelter in a women's house that did not even yet exist. Since we could not send them back to their violent husbands, we temporarily housed them – and often also their children – in our own homes. This continued during the entire summer of 1976, and the situation became increasingly difficult. Although the FhF association had been established, not only did we not have any money, but we also did not have a building or paid employees.

Yet the problem of violent men, of violence against women in private homes, had now been brought out of the closet and made *public*. The city's authorities, that is the Social Welfare Department, could no longer claim that the problem did not exist in Cologne. During all of this time we, the association, had continued negotiating with the city authority for a building that would house our battered women's shelter. We also successively reported on the number of women who had already sought our help. Pressured by these facts and by the broad public interest in this issue, the municipal authorities had to give in.

They finally decided to carry out a study in their own municipal and private charitable institutions to find out how many women were seeking refuge from their violent husbands. At the end of the summer in 1976, the findings were made public: the city had to admit that, on the average, 100 women each month called the police or appeared at other social facilities seeking shelter from male violence. They also discovered that these women could not be helped, because violence in the family was considered to be a private matter. Therefore, unless women made formal charges against the offending men, which happened rarely, the police were forced to send them back to their husbands.

Once this study came out, the municipality was under *political* pressure to act, especially since there were women in our FhF association who were also active members of the churches, the Social Democratic Party and the press. The association had meanwhile become well-known beyond Cologne. Women's groups in other cities also began to establish associations with the name 'Women helping Women'.

One of our most important events was a benefit concert for the FhF performed by a famous local music group. This concert provided an ideal opportunity to make our organisation and our concept known to a broader public. The benefit concert also provided us with the financial basis we needed to carry out our fight for a women's shelter.

Our negotiations with the city were difficult because we insisted that a shelter be established according to our concept. We did not want to erect a new social facility in which women seeking help would become 'objects' under the administration and control of social welfare. According to our concept, the city would not have the right to limit the number of women or places, nor should it request documentation on those seeking help. We insisted that the women's shelter be an *autonomous* facility in which adult women in an emergency situation would be able to organise their lives independently, cooperatively and in solidarity. The association and the social pedagogues working at the facility were to merely play the role of initiators, mediators and supporters.

In accordance with the principles of grassroots democracy which we adhered to, the women of our association rotated in negotiating with the social welfare authorities. We wanted all of the women to become familiar with the bureaucratic way in which the authorities dealt with people seeking help. We wanted to provide them with the experience of what women can do against the arbitrary use of power. This, too, annoyed the city's authorities. The civil servants who negotiated with us felt it a continuous nuisance to deal with different student representatives instead of one experienced and 'capable' board of directors, as they described it. Moreover, they demanded that the FhF association join one of the established social welfare institutions. Despite our reservations – we wanted to maintain our principle of autonomy – we finally joined the most secular institution, the German Joint Association of Charities (Paritätische Wohlfahrtsverband, DPWV).

The city's manoeuvres and the frictions these entailed had the effect that by the autumn of 1976 a house for battered women in Cologne was still nowhere in sight. Although the city had promised to establish one, no one knew when they would carry out their promise. Meanwhile, more women continued to call us seeking shelter from their violent husbands.

Since the situation had truly become unbearable, we decided that the FhF would rent its own house. Women seeking help would have to pay a flat rental fee for which they would legally have to receive reimbursement from the Social Welfare Department. In this way, the municipal authorities ultimately had to pay for the battered women's shelter.

One of the initial successes of our action was that women seeking help from the FhF were legally acknowledged as *special emergency cases*. This status forced the Social Welfare Department to grant "aid in special life situations" according to paragraph seventy-two of the Federal Social Welfare Law (Bundessozialhilfegesetz, BSHG) which also entailed paying social welfare and rent for shelter.

The house we rented was a building marked for demolition in a Cologne suburb. With the help of many friends, sympathisers, association members, and the women seeking shelter we furbished the house with furniture, laundry, household goods, etc. The house was ready by November 1976 and from the very beginning it was overcrowded with women and their children.

Presented with a *fait accompli*, the city authorities were now under pressure to provide the FhF association with a suitable building. Moreover, in December 1976, the city council also decided to finance a full-time position for a social worker to supervise the shelter.

Meanwhile, the students who had initiated our project had completed their studies and were now looking for appropriate jobs. Four of them decided therefore to work at the shelter and share the one full-time job available.

Yet weeks and months went by before the pay for these jobs was forthcoming. During this time, the association set up a 24-hour service of volunteers staffed by the association's women members. We felt it necessary to have women present at all times who had *not* been beaten, since there was always the danger of having a violent husband appear at the doorstep wanting to take his wife back by force. To protect the women at the shelter we not only kept its address secret, but we also maintained a complicated system of bringing a battered woman to it. Those seeking help from us had to come to a specific place where a woman from the association would meet her and bring her to the shelter. Often valuables, documents and children had to be snuck out of the house as well, in clandestine operations, in which case several women from the association had to be present.

During those times when I was 'on duty' I witnessed how the women in the shelter kept wanting to talk about their experiences, asking themselves over and over again why their men were so violent. They needed us so they could unburden their often incredible stories of violence. It became clear to me after a while that talking about their experiences was a kind of healing process. I therefore suggested that we record their stories. We tried to determine *at what stage* 'a career of violence' had begun in their families, how the women dealt with it, why they often let the cruelty go on for so long, and finally, at what point they began to change the situation.

A group of students decided to record and review the women's life stories as a study project. It was conceived as an *action-research project* in which we not only wanted to gain deeper insights into the 'careers of violence' existing in German families, but also to help the women understand and change their situation themselves.

The project's results were published, along with the life stories, in the book *News from the Ghetto of Love* (Frauenhaus Köln, *Nachrichten aus dem Ghetto Liebe*, 1980). Writing down their stories helped the women in the first place to document their case in the event they wanted a divorce or demanded financial support. The female students involved in this project could make visible the link between what we call 'love' and male violence.

I included all of these stories in my essay "Towards a Methodology for Feminist Research" (1983a, pp. 117–139).[2] The most important insight gained from this practical and theoretical research project was that *if women really want to understand a terrible situation, they have to change it.* If we had conducted 'standard' statistical research on women seeking help from our shelter, they would never have admitted they were suffering from violence. Only by beginning to *change* their miserable situation were they in a position to speak out about their experiences openly.

While a shelter for battered women had been opened in Berlin with the support of the Ministry for Family Affairs, our women's shelter in Cologne was the first in the Federal Republic of Germany to be established without government aid. Many other 'Women helping Women' associations were established in Germany according to the same principle of autonomy.[3]

A new research approach: action research

The struggle for a battered women's shelter in Cologne opened my eyes to the true condition of our society, especially with regard to how much violence is concealed behind the supposedly peaceful middle-class family façade, violence that is particularly directed against women – a complete taboo until our actions – and against children as well. I also understood that what had commonly been called, and is still accepted as, *objective science* did not comprehend

---

2 The essay was first published in German in 1978 under the title "Methodische Postulate zur Frauenforschung"; it was first published in English as "Towards a Methodology for Feminist Research" in 1983 in *Theories of Women's Studies* edited by Gloria Bowles and Renate Duelli Klein.
3 In December 2007, many representatives from 'autonomous battered women's shelters in Germany' came together in Cologne to celebrate the movement's thirtieth anniversary.

this reality at all, and in fact could not, and did not want to, make it visible because the victims of domestic violence were women. These women did not speak to the social scientists – who were mostly men – of the violence they had suffered, often because they were ashamed, and because doctors or the police generally did not give credence to their stories.

As a social scientist myself I felt I had to take my *anger and concern (Betroffenheit)* from hearing the women tell their stories day and night, and then to *act together with others* to change it. I soon realised that the traditional methods of empirical and quantitative social research would not allow me to do this, as this methodology was taboo for 'objective science' which does not allow for any form of partiality and solidarity with those afflicted, as well as any form of subjectivity on the part of the scientist theorist. This was impossible for me to adhere to. I developed my own methodological approach for an involved form of women's research. In this approach, based upon a critique of the prevalent *"uninvolved observer research"* (Gerrit Huizer, 1973) with its false claim to objectivity, I developed seven fundamental methodological postulates for feminist research in the new field of women's studies. These postulates evolved from the experiences gained in our struggle for a women's shelter in Cologne.

This approach was not created in an ivory tower but was the result of our practical and theoretical battles in the universities and in society. It soon had further consequences. When, at the yearly convention of German sociologists in 1976 in Bielefeld, we realised that *die Frauenfrage* (the 'women's question') was not being addressed in any of the sections or working groups, Claudia von Werlhof and Veronika Bennholdt-Thomsen set up a table, and hung a poster in the foyer of the university calling for the establishment of a *Women's Studies Section within the framework of the 'German Sociology Society'*. Seventy women came together and formulated a petition. It was rejected, of course. We did not give up, however. We decided to form an association with the name *Sociological*

Theory and Praxis for Women. We agreed to come together again in the winter of the following year; until then we divided up 'homework' amongst ourselves, such as: "What does theory mean in the light of the women's movement?" "What research methods are appropriate in the context of the women's movement?"

I chose to work on the second question. Since I was involved in fighting for an autonomous women's shelter in Cologne with my students day after day, I had no time to produce a 'scientific' paper. While Carola Möller and I were driving to Frankfurt in February 1977, I quickly wrote down the points that, based on my practical experience with the battered women's shelter, seemed to me the most important. I called them the 'methodological postulates of women's studies'[4] and introduced them at our meeting in Frankfurt. I did not write them up until later, where they were presented to a larger public in the autumn of 1977 at the 'Heksencollegen' (Witches' College) at the university in Nijmegen, Holland. It was then first published in Dutch in the Heksencollege's documentation.

My seven postulates on a *methodology of women's studies* were not developed to only help battered women and assist women in universities to fight for a better status in the prevailing fields of

---

4 Summary of the Methodological Postulates for research in women's studies:
   i   The postulate of value-free research, of neutrality and indifference towards the research participants is replaced by conscious partiality.
   ii The vertical relationship between researchers and researched is replaced by the view from below.
   iii The contemplative, uninvolved attitude of the researcher vis-à-vis the researched is replaced by active participation in actions, movements and struggles for women's liberation. Feminist research must serve this goal.
   iv Participation in social actions and struggles means that the change of the status quo becomes the starting point for a scientific quest. "If you want to know a thing you must change it."
   v   The research process must become a process of 'conscientisation', both for the researchers and the researched, and all other participants in the research process.
   vi This process of conscientisation should be accompanied by recording women's individual and social history, so that women can appropriate their history.
   vii Women cannot reclaim and appropriate their history unless they begin to share and collectivise their experiences, insights and theories. Feminist research must help to overcome the competitiveness and sterile individualism of academia.

research. Rather, the postulates were designed to completely revolutionise dominant social science.

The *Methodological Postulates* soon became the classic text for feminist research around the world. This may have brought them more critique than praise in the beginning, but it led to a lively and still continuing controversy over an approach to research fundamentally different from the prevailing patriarchal one. It started with a critique of social science methodology.

Except for feminist circles, my approach was less popular in the scientific 'mainstream' in Germany. The opposite was true in other countries. The *Methodological Postulates* were translated quickly into Dutch and English and were re-printed repeatedly in journals and books, even in those addressing the issue of how to generally conduct research among discriminated, colonised, and oppressed people to ensure that they not be instrumentalised by scientists, politics and the economy.

No serious book on feminist research could ignore my seven *Methodological Postulates*. They last appeared in the *Handbook of Feminist Research* published by Sage Publications in London in 2006. In this version, I critically reassessed my methodological approach in the light of the experiences I gained in the context of the anti-globalisation movement (Mies, 2006, pp. 664–665).

Other Associations, Research and Theory

When we established the association 'Sociological Theory and Praxis for Women' we also decided to bring out a journal called *beiträge zur feministischen theorie und praxis* (contributions to feminist theory and practice). I remember debating heatedly whether we should use the term *'feminist'* in our title. Back then it was still taboo to call yourself a 'feminist'. I argued that 'feminist' is a historical term, a fighting concept with which we would clearly signal our position. This argument ultimately won.

The first issue of the *beiträge*, published in 1978, included ground-breaking essays on housework, such as: "Housework is Not a Science" ("Hausarbeit ist doch keine Wissenschaft"), by *Silvia Kontos* and *Karin Walser*; "Women, Colonies, Neo-Colonies" ("Frauen, Kolonien, Neokolonien") by *Ilse Lenz*; "Women's Work and Female Productivity" ("Frauenarbeit und weibliche Produktivität") by *Sigrid Metz-Göckel*; "Women's Work: A Blind Spot in the Critique of Political Economy" ("Frauenarbeit: Der blinde Fleck in der Kritik der Politischen Ökonomie") by *Claudia von Werlhof*; and my "Methodological Postulates on Women's Studies – Illustrated with the Example of Violence against Women" ("Methodische Postulate zur Frauenforschung – dargestellt am Beispiel der Gewalt gegen Frauen").

The things I had learned in the context of our struggles for a battered women's shelter in Cologne were key experiences for me: politically, scientifically, theoretically and methodologically.

The form of action-research we had practised, and I later continued to practise in all my research and teaching, as well as in my political struggles, was used *not* to make the individuals we were researching the *objects* of research, but to engage them as co-researchers. Over the course of my life this approach has proven to be very fruitful.

7

Women and Work

The Subsistence Approach

Subsistence and capital accumulation: housewives,
peasants, colonies

I also applied the new form of *action research* to a project on
women's subsistence production in rural southern India which I had
carried out from 1978 to 1979. In preparation for my dissertation,
I had previously conducted a research project on Indian middle-
class women. Now I wanted to study the subsistence production of
rural women.

Our campaign for a battered women's shelter in Cologne had
successfully made domestic violence against women a public social
issue. However, in the context of my teaching position at the
Fachhochschule Köln (University of Applied Sciences, Cologne)
which did not finance research at that time, it was difficult to clarify
the kind of extended theoretical issues which developed out of the
women's movement. One of these issues was that *in capitalism,*
housework is not considered to be 'work' and is therefore unpaid. Many
feminists in Germany and from around the world were dealing with
this issue at that time (see *beiträge zur feministischen theorie und*
praxis, 1/1978).

This issue was important to myself and my friends, Veronika Bennholdt-Thomsen, who I had known since studying ethnology, and Claudia von Werlhof, who has been a close friend since my postgraduate seminars with Professor König.

Like many of those involved in the women's movement of the 1970s, we approached this issue from the perspective we had acquired from Marxist theory. We were not willing to accept endless descriptions, and besides Marxism we knew of no other theoretical approach which had dealt with the term 'work' specifically in the context of housework. In addressing this issue, all three of us profited from having lived, worked and researched in so-called developing countries for a considerable period of time: Veronika among Mexican peasants, Claudia in Central America, and I in India. What we observed was that many people worked for little or no pay and that this work was not considered to be *wage labour*. The goal of their work was not to produce *goods* for an external, capitalist market but rather to secure their *survival*, their subsistence.

Most Marxist, Western theoreticians did not know how do deal with this kind of work. Established terms such as the proletariat, working class, sub-proletariat, productive work, etc. could not be applied to these workers. All of them, whether they were peasants, rural labourers or slum dwellers, were assigned to the *informal sector*, as the UN described it. Apparently, their work lay *beyond* the capitalist means of production.

Around this time left-wing intellectuals in Latin America were having debates on the various *means of production*. For the first time the term *subsistence production* appeared. However, the entire subsistence sector was described as pre-capitalist and backward. It was argued that this sector would have to be subject to the kind of bourgeois revolution and proletarian transformation that accompanied industrialisation. Only then could a proletarian revolution take place which would overcome capitalism.

Veronika had written her dissertation on Mexican peasants and was familiar with these debates. Yet, from very early on, she and André Gunder Frank argued that the subsistence sector was neither backward nor outside the capitalist system. On the contrary: it was the very essence of capitalism. She rejected the stages-theory and fought the idea that peasants and their rural areas were backward, while workers and their cities were considered progressive – an opinion that is still rampant today.

After Veronika and Claudia acquired positions as research associates at the University of Bielefeld with a focus on the Sociology of Development, we continued this discussion amongst ourselves. At first our approach was called the 'Bielefeld approach'. However, we have continued to call it the *subsistence approach* to this date. Many of our male colleagues initially agreed with our subsistence approach, but they could not accept the fact that we included housework in this sector.

In order to clarify the many unsettled, practical and theoretical issues accompanying this discussion, various international conferences were held between 1978 and 1979 in Bielefeld on the theme 'Subsistence, Development and Accumulation'. I took part in one of these conferences in 1979.

Before the 1979 conference, in our discussions on *housework and capitalism*, the three of us had already formulated our preliminary theory that the subsistence production of women, peasants and other people including children and non-peasant men, should not be considered *pre-capitalist* but rather part of the *informal* sector which certainly contributes to capital accumulation.

Our hypothesis was this: unpaid housework, the work done by colonised peoples and the free production from natural resources, also belong to subsistence production and are being exploited for capital accumulation.

Rosa Luxemburg shows us the way

The issue of housework and capitalism was the most discussed topic among feminists in those days. Some of them called this work pre-capitalist, the others considered it to be a feudal relic. Many questioned whether domestic work was only 'reproductive' or whether it was in fact 'productive'. *Maria Rosa Dalla Costa* argued that it is indeed productive because it produces the commodity of 'labour power' (Dalla Costa, 1972).

We liked this approach, but felt it did not go far enough. While working in the rural areas and city slums of Latin America and India, we had encountered working conditions which were structurally similar to those of housewives: they were unpaid, or at least so poorly paid that the workers could not secure 'reproduction', which was why they often had to be employed at various jobs at once. Their wages were so low that they could barely survive on them. Yet where was the connection between subsistence and domestic work?

Rosa Luxemburg helped us further here. Among the three of us, Veronika was the one who had the most in-depth knowledge of Marx's theories. She had not only participated in the so-called courses on capital[1] at the University of Cologne but she had also taught her own courses. In contrast, my knowledge of Marx was eclectic. I took down Marx's blue volumes whenever I sought to clarify a certain term, for instance the term 'work' or 'productive work'. Yet in my opinion, Marx's definitions did not satisfactorily explain the meaning of domestic work in capitalism. It was Veronika who read Rosa Luxemburg's *Accumulation of Capital* (1913) in 1972. She told us about how Rosa Luxemburg had proven in 1913 that in order to 'extend the accumulation of capital' it is not enough to exploit the classical proletariat, but that more and more 'non-

---

1 After 1968, students everywhere held their own 'courses on Capital' because they could find *nothing* in the universities that would inform them of Marx's 'Critique of the Political Economy'.

capitalist milieus' must also be exploited. She argued that these were peasants, small-scale craftsworkers, day labourers and also workers in the colonies. The exploitation of the non-capitalist sectors – later described by the UN as 'the informal sector' – therefore perforce leads to the destruction of these workers' livelihood (Bennholdt-Thomsen, 1981, pp. 16–21).

"That is what women's work is in capitalism," Veronika said, "housework only ostensibly belongs to the so-called non-capitalist sector. It is exploited and appropriated in the same manner by capitalists as the production of peasants, of the colonies, and of nature."

Rosa Luxemburg was not a feminist. But she showed us the way in which we could explain what we called *subsistence production* from then on.

This insight represented a decisive theoretical and practical break-through not only for myself but for all of us. In 1983, we published our view of these issues in the co-authored book *Frauen, die letzte Kolonie* (1983b; the English version, *Women: The Last Colony*, was published in 1988).

However, there were many theoretical questions left which we wanted to answer. And in order to test our hypothesis, we carried out further empirical studies. To this end Veronika went to Mexico, Claudia went to Venezuela, and I went back to India.

8

Return to India

Women and Subsistence in India

In 1977, I received a small sum from the International Labour
Organisation (ILO) to carry out a research project in India. The project
was part of the ILO's *World Employment Program* (WEP). I wanted
to study the situation of women in rural subsistence production.

The Lace Makers of Narsapur

My first empirical research project with Indian women was when I
prepared my doctoral thesis on the role conflicts of educated and
working middle-class women (see Chapter Four). After our discussion
on subsistence production, I now wanted to know whether our thesis
about the connection between subsistence production and capital
accumulation would also be valid for rural women in India.

I carried out the study[1] in two districts in the state of Andhra
Pradesh. The first in the town of Narsapur in the district of West
Godavary, the second in the Telengana district near Hyderabad. Since
I did not know Telegu, the local language, two assistants helped me
as translators: Lalitha and Krishna. The first part was about women

---

1 Maria Mies (1982a) *The Lace Makers of Narsapur: Indian Housewives Produce for the
World Market*.

who worked in a household industry where they made crochet lace for the world market. Narsapur was a small town in the delta region of the river Godavary on the eastern coast of south India. This household industry was organised according to the classical putting-out system which existed in Europe in the beginning of the nineteenth century. This meant that poor women would sit in their huts and make crochet lace goods which were then collected and exported by a 'manufacturer' to the world market – to the USA, Europe, Canada or Australia. Crochet lace was very popular among middle-class women around 1900. Lace items such as tablecloths, pillowcases, or borders on blouses were a sign of the ladies' higher status. Irish nuns introduced lace making in Narsapur and the surrounding villages during a time of famine because they wanted to help poor women. Ideologically, this industry was based on the definition of women as housewives by nature who were sitting idly in their houses with a lot of leisure time. They were not 'workers' but had husbands as breadwinners. Even today many women, when asked about their work, say, "I do not work, I am a housewife and mother." The Irish nuns thought that these Indian women 'sitting in the house' could use their time more productively. By producing lace for the Western market, they could conveniently combine their duties for the family and work for an external market, and thus earn a bit of extra money.

The wages the lace makers got were abominably low, much lower than the minimal wages of a day labourer who worked in the fields of a landlord. From childhood to the age of eighty, the women would crochet lace in their huts from morning to night, and combined this work with their household tasks. While studying the work conditions and the work organisation of the lace workers, I began to understand why the lace exporter – there was only one in the whole of Narsapur – could make a huge profit which was very obvious by the size of his mansion.

I found that the reasons for the profitability of his business were mainly the following:

- The lace makers had the lowest wage in the whole economy. The exporter had hardly any labour costs to pay.
- There was no need to build a factory where the women could work together. They were scattered all over the place and sat isolated in their huts. One woman would collect the lace pieces and bring them to the exporter.
- Due to this atomisation, the women could not form a trade union. They belonged to the so-called unorganised. Even the trade unions were not interested in them, because they were 'just' housewives.
- The women did not make a whole product, like a tablecloth for instance, but only a small component which they called a 'flower' and which another isolated woman had to then join together so that a whole product would be made. By this division of labour the exporter made sure that the lace workers could not sell a whole piece themselves in the local market.
- This industry was totally invisible. It was 'submerged' as I called it. When entering Narsapur or one of the villages one could not see any woman doing this work because they were all working in their own huts. For the lace exporter this was one of the most efficient forms of labour control.
- The exporter carried hardly any of the costs for the raw material. He gave the women the thread they needed, but deducted the price for the thread from their wages.
- If there was no demand for lace in the rich countries, the women had no work and the exporter did not have to pay any money for their sustenance (which happened during the great depression in 1929–1933).
- Women buying the hand-made lace in the rich Western countries had no idea of the lace makers' work conditions. Nor did they understand that their luxury items were the result of extremely bad labour conditions. This exploitation was none of their concern.
- Another aspect of this industry making it so attractive to the exporter was that the lace workers had to combine 'reproductive

work' – meaning housework – with 'productive work' for an external, even global, market.

I began to understand that such a household industry was the most profitable form of labour for capitalism. In fact, it was the optimal labour for any capitalist.

This is why I called this type of work 'housewifisation of work'.

It is still the most profitable type of labour for capital accumulation even today in our globalised economy with its principles of liberalisation, privatisation and universal competition. Today, even men have to do this 'housewifised work' (see our book *Women: The Last Colony*, 1988). The only difference is that the workers usually do not sit in a hut, but in a modern flat in front of a computer and do all kinds of work for an unknown corporation or an outsourced entrepreneur for unknown consumers in the 'free' world market.

No one today speaks of 'housewifised work'. The term used is 'flexible work'. That sounds more decent. Yet the organisation and the purpose of these labour relations are the same as those of the women lace makers of Narsapur in the late 70s. The term 'housewifisation of work' became an important term for our discussion on subsistence and accumulation. It has remained a controversial one.

In the conference in Bielefeld, mentioned above I introduced this term. It was met with fierce protests. From the beginning it was clear to my two friends and I that the 'housewifisation of work' represented – and still represents – the optimal type of work for the modern economy, and that it determines the future of work. The 1983 German version of our first joint publication, *Women: The Last Colony* (1988), had the subtitle *On the housewifisation of labour*. The book includes a ground-breaking essay by Claudia von Werlhof "The Proletarian is Dead. Long Live the Housewife!" ("Der Proletarier ist tot. Lang lebe die Hausfrau!") in which she not only analyses why housework will become capital's most desired and optimal form of labour relations, but also predicts how men too will be forced to carry out 'housewifised work'. The goal is not *proletarisation* of all workers, as Marxists expected, but their *housewifisation*.

Poor Peasant and Agricultural Workers in Telengana

I carried out the second part of my research in the villages surrounding the provincial city of Bhongir in Telengana. After analysing the connection between home industries and capital accumulation, I was now interested in the question of whether the same link also existed for female rural labourers.

Lalitha, Krishna and myself lived like the women peasants and rural labourers; we cooked as they cooked, hauled water from the well and accompanied them during their house and field work, that is, while they planted rice seedlings after the monsoon rains; and we sang and danced with them in the evenings after their work. Although I could not join in their activities much since I did not understand their language, based on my experience as the child of a peasant myself, it was easy for me to understand things and I quickly became integrated. Lalitha was a wonderful singer. She knew the women's songs and also sang the revolutionary songs she had learned as a member of a radical student organisation.

I was astonished by how these women still had the time and energy to sing and dance after their long hard days of work – which they did for themselves, not just to please us. Singing while working was their recreation.

They also made their own inquiries into our lives. Women would come to us in the evening and into our yard which men were prohibited from entering. They asked us questions:

"Are you married?"

"Yes," we said.

"Do you have children?"

"No."

"Why not?"

We shrugged our shoulders.

"What do you do when you have your menstrual bleeding? What do you use?" We explained that we used sanitary towels.

They were insatiably curious. When a Dutch woman came to visit us – she was very big – they wanted to see her naked. They wanted to know what a white woman's skin looks like under her clothes. They found out that underneath their clothes white women do not look different from themselves. They also wanted to get to know our husbands and invited them to come to their villages. And the men actually came from Hyderabad. The village women were finally satisfied that we were just ordinary women like themselves.

Rukamma

In conducting this project I applied the principles of action research as I had developed them in the context of our struggle to establish a shelter for battered women in Cologne. Lalitha, Krishna and I began our fieldwork in villages in which a private development organisation – CROSS – had already begun to organise landless peasants in 'sangams', or village committees. But women did not go to sangam evening meetings. After their work as day labourers on fields owned by landlords, they had to take care of the housework and their children. In addition, women hardly had the chance to speak at the men's meetings. As a consequence, a CROSS representative suggested that separate women's sangams be formed. They were a success from the very beginning. When we arrived in the region surrounding the provincial city of Bhongir, there were already seven villages with women's sangams.

I decided to carry out our fieldwork in cooperation with the women from the sangams. In accordance with my methodological approach I did not want to conduct single interviews but to discuss with all women the problems that were most urgent for them. Besides specific questions regarding subsistence (such as pay, cost of living, work hours, etc.), the major issues of our discussions were violence and oppression on the part of the landlords as well as their own husbands' violence and alcohol consumption.

These women were all 'untouchables', meaning they were casteless and outcasts. In order to raise their status, Gandhi called them *Harijans*, meaning 'children of God'. The higher castes despised them and did not allow them to use the same village well, for example. Women of higher caste asked me why I went to 'those' women and not to them. They said they knew much more about what was going on in the village. Yet this would not have been consistent with my 'approach from below'.

I also placed particular value on carrying out what I called 'reciprocal research'. This meant, while studying the village women's life and work, they should also be able to study us, if they wanted to. Which they did as soon as we arrived in their villages.

Our research in the field was not done with the traditional distant 'observer research' approach. The goal of our studies was to *change the status quo*, to change the oppressive situation in which these women lived. We as researchers also did not exclusively seek to 'take' the results of our research and publish them in a foreign country, but 'give them back' to the women at the end of our work.

This point in particular shows how productive our methodological approach was, which is why I would like to describe in detail the events that followed our fieldwork.

We invited the women we had worked with to take part in a week-end camp organised at a college in Bonghir so we could report our results to them. Seventy women came from the various villages. For the first time they had a whole weekend to themselves, undisturbed by men and children. We spoke of our observations and insights and showed them slides. The women were enthusiastic, but also told us where they disagreed with our findings. By means of role plays, they clearly expressed what they felt to be their most important issues. As a consequence, we learned a lot about the deeper connections between caste hierarchies, landlord violence, male violence, alcoholism and the vicious circle of exploitation and poverty.

Most importantly, the Harijan women had a great deal of fun on this weekend, especially because they could make public fun of their 'masters'. They laughed, sang and danced and decided to come together in weekend camps on a regular basis, at least once a month. Which they did, at first with the support of CROSS. Later, when the CROSS people recognised how much the men considered these camps a problem, they wanted to stop them. However, the women countered, "We will continue these camps, even if we have to stop drinking tea or even save a portion of our day's wages to take the bus."

A year after our fieldwork I learned that thirteen such weekend camps had already taken place.

These weekend camps were not only successful in that the participants demanded, and received, higher wages for women's work in the fields (in fact the same wages as their husbands), but also by making sure that so-called specific 'women's problems' such as marital disputes are treated as *general* problems. The women additionally formed regional committees in which village representatives came together to discuss and develop solutions to such problems.

I once experienced the kind of revolutionary force these women's meetings represented in a camp that took place in the village of Viravalli. Because there was no room, the gathering took place out in the open on the village square. Only a makeshift canopy had been set up to protect them from the sun. An innovation was that the women also organised a microphone. The children and men in the village could hear and see what the women were debating, and many women came to attend, including women from the upper castes and classes. They wanted to speak first and instruct poor women about the importance of sending their children to school. They understood themselves as the 'leaders' of the village women. The Harijan women allowed them to speak first. After a while, one of the Harijan women went to the microphone and berated the rich women for being exploiters and oppressors. They had no right to talk here. Where did they think the Harijan women would be able to get the money to pay for their children's school uniforms?

After this, a downright class war between the poor and rich women began. The Harijan women refused to be silenced and made the most astonishing suggestions for improving their situation. These not only pertained to the landlords' exploitation and violence but also to the violence of their own husbands who were all the while standing in the background and listening with astonishment and dismay at what their women were saying. In role-plays they cut right to the core of the matter and at the same time made fun of their 'masters'.

During this camp, the women experienced for the first time that *together they were strong*, that they could act with self-confidence and attack their oppressors *publicly*. This had never happened before.

Rukamma was one of the most courageous and powerfully eloquent women there. After the Viravalli camp she was elected as speaker of the regional committee which met every two weeks. However, every time she came back from one of these meetings, her husband would beat her. He could not forget that she had publicly exposed him as a drunkard during the camp. Rukamma discussed this with the other women at the next meeting. They debated and decided that his beatings had to stop immediately. Rukamma should not allow herself to be beaten by him any more. He should prostrate himself before her and apologise. If he refused, none of the women would ever give him water, bread or food. Which meant he would have to go back to his mother. The greatest dishonour for a patriarchal man!

These women did not treat Rukamma's story as an isolated problem. Violence against women existed everywhere. In this context the women made a truly revolutionary resolution:

When a woman and man cannot live in peace together they should separate. In this case the man must leave the house because *the house belongs to the woman!* The woman must remain in the village with her children, where she has her work and her house. The man can move to the city and look for work there!

I will never forget the sentence: *The house belongs to the woman!* Only over the course of time did I realise how revolutionary this sentence was. It stood in complete contrast to the strategy we had used in Germany to fight male violence: we had taken the women out of their homes to protect them from their men. As a consequence, they were forced to abandon their material basis and infrastructure and start from scratch again. The Harijan women held on to their material basis. Moreover, they attacked the patriarchal ownership/property structure straight on. They did not wait for laws to change but applied immediate methods of social boycott.

However, they were also in a much better condition to do so than Western middle-class and working-class women, who live in isolated private homes with their men and have no community to support them. Moreover, the sentence: *The house belongs to the woman* is not to be understood symbolically. In rural India, people live in mudbrick houses primarily built by women. They first mix the mud like dough and then form it into bricks which are placed on top of each other to make walls. The men help, but are not in charge.

I was so excited by the force, clarity and wisdom exhibited by the Harijan women that I recounted Rukamma's story over and over again to my students after returning to Germany. The story also impressed my students so much that some of them decided to implement this strategy in carrying out their projects to protect women.

Yet it still took about five years until Germany passed a *law* allowing a woman to file charges against her violent husband and force *him* to leave their shared home. In contrast, the rural women in India achieved this much more quickly and directly (Mies, 1982a, pp. 18–46).

Of course, in my study I also posed 'scientific' questions pertaining to their level of income, their working hours, their property, etc. I also asked whether they owned a share of their husband's land and whether they were able to sell something. Dumb questions. Most of the men were landless. Yet the mudbrick houses belonged to the women because they had built them. The fields they worked on from morning to night belonged to rich *landlords*, which meant the men were at most tenants or day labourers.

These were the heydays of the 'Green Revolution' and the landlords made huge profits from the sale of rice. Women working as day labourers for them only earned a minimal wage: back then it was three rupees a day.

Again, it was very obvious: here too, as in the lace industry in Narsarpur, poor women made up the subsistence base not only for their families but also for the capitalist local landlords and international companies. Without these women's subsistence production, their profits would not have been possible. Subsistence production was, and still is, the necessary prerequisite for all production.

Today we are not only witnessing this condition in the so-called Third World but also in our industrial countries: as women and men teleworking from their computers at home, as out-sourced subcontractors producing components for parts which are put together in some distant place across the globe, all of them carrying out housewifised work. The structure of their employment hardly differs from that of the laceworkers in Narsapur in the late 1970s. The advantages to capital are obvious: no, or very low, fixed costs for factories and machines; isolated and individualised male and female workers worldwide who combine production with housework; workers who are not organised in a union and who do not strike, in fact *cannot* strike because once their orders stop coming in, they are left to themselves. Companies do not take responsibility for them. Innovations in computer technology lead to more housewifised work – today one speaks of *flexible* work. Although the majority of people in the world are now employed in such 'flexible' housewifised work, I know of no other analysis that addresses this new form of employment in globalised capitalism. To date, one still considers a *normal labour condition* as that of a male as *production worker*. As head of the family he is considered the *provider*, whereas the female, as exclusively the housewife, carries out *reproduction work* and often *production work* as well.

The findings I formulated and published at that time were greeted with enthusiastic approval from different parts of the women's movement, but they were also greeted with intense critique from others. The critique often also came from those few men who went so far as to even read feminist publications. As a rule, male members of academia just ignored our feminist writings, since they considered them to be 'unscientific' *per se*. This view has changed somewhat since then. My friends Claudia and Veronika, however, personally suffered from male-dominated academia's blanket rejection. Despite their prestigious doctoral and postdoctoral degrees, they could not find positions in German universities. Claudia finally went to Austria, where since 1988, she holds the chair for Political Science and Women's Studies at the University of Innsbruck. Veronika has remained unemployed, despite bringing out many publications in Germany and abroad. This is a scandal many colleagues abroad just cannot understand.

What men in dominant academic positions disliked was not only our public avowal of feminism, our critique of the Marxist definition of work and our theory on the housewifisation of work. What they particularly rejected was the conclusions we drew from our analysis of housework, of rural peasants and of the workers in the 'informal sector', meaning all those we described as *subsistence producers*. Our main theory was *that subsistence production – the production of life – is not only the permanent precondition for all forms of production, including capitalist production, but it represents the only, viable perspective for the future.*

This point still irritates all those who believe *that life comes out of the supermarket* and that the problem caused by industrial society and its technologies – ecological destruction, pollution, climate change, unemployment, exploitation of other countries and peoples, social injustice, violence against women, children, minorities and new wars – can be solved by means of industrial society and its new technologies. Moreover, ever since the fall of socialism in eastern Europe, solutions are now only being sought within the context of capitalism, and currently particularly in its globalised, neoliberal form. More on that later (see Chapter Nine).

I personally did not suffer much from the academic, and predominantly male, elite. I profited from the advantage of my 'early birth': I was about fifteen years older than Claudia and Veronica, and by 1972 I had already gained a position at the Fachhochschule Köln (University of Applied Sciences, Cologne) before anyone knew what feminism was and what theoretical position I would later hold. In addition, I had stressed the *international* character of the women's movement from the very beginning – my first feminist seminars dealt with the old and new international women's movements. I wrote my first essays (for instance on feminist methodology, on the peasant revolts in India) and books not only in German but also many of them in English, and they were published by English-language publishers. However, my research results on women's subsistence production in rural India appeared in English; to date those results have not been published in German.[2] This led to the fact that I became well known in the English-speaking world

---

2 See Maria Mies (1984) *Indian Women in Subsistence and Agricultural Labour*, World Employment Programme (WEP), Working Paper No. 34, International Labour Office, Geneva.

My major work *Patriarchy and Accumulation on a World Scale* (1986a) Zed Books, London and Spinifex Press, North Melbourne – appeared first in English before the German translation.

from early on and received invitations to the USA, Canada, Holland, and of course to India, where I have regularly spent my semester holidays since completing my doctorate.

After completing my research in India, and in the course of many discussions with other feminists in Germany and abroad, I formulated my insights into the structure of the economy in industrialised society in the form of the following diagram:

The Iceberg Model of the Capitalist-Patriarchal Economy

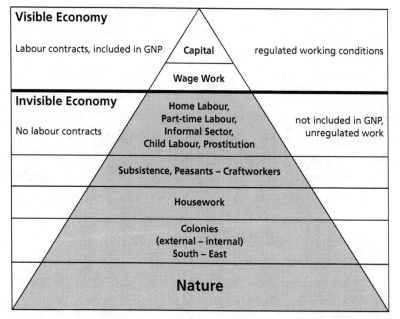

The dominant concept of the economy is limited to the *visible* economy placed *above* the water line, that is, capital and wage labour or the so-called *formal* sector.

The *invisible economy* is comprised of various levels of work which are almost completely hidden and ignored by mainstream economists. Or they are defined as 'free goods', such as the production of nature.

These levels are ordered from the bottom up according to their respective proximity to the economy above the 'water line'; that is to the money or capital economy of the formal sector.

We consider that all levels of the invisible economy belong to the *subsistence economy* (Bennholdt-Thomsen and Mies, 1997, p. 38). Later on, I will explain why subsistence is not only the key term in our critique of the capitalist-patriarchal society and economy, but also, why it represents our perspective for a better economy and society.

A piece of contemporary history of India 1978–1979

Since living in Pune, I had maintained my contact with India, but with a new emphasis. While working at the Goethe Institute from 1963 to 1968, I had believed that all the problems of India and the 'Third World' could be solved by development aid. This belief changed after the 1968 student movement, my participation in Cologne's Political Night Prayer, and my activities in the early years of the women's movement. When I returned to India in 1972 after receiving my doctorate, I wanted to find out whether a similar student or women's movement existed there.

I went to Hyderabad in the State of Andhra Pradesh where one of my earlier students, *Saral Sarkar*, was now a lecturer at the Goethe Institute. I was able to stay at his flat and I wanted him to tell me something of India's student movement.

Saral was not only particularly well informed about the Hyderabad student movement but was also something of a guru for these young people who were enthusiastic about the idea of revolution but who had little knowledge of Marxist theory. Young men and women met at his small flat to discuss the principles underlying Marx's critique of the political economy, to prepare speeches or student actions, and to sing those revolutionary songs, in the regional Telugu language which represented the most important means of political mobilisation for people all over India.

There were songs that people sang in different languages in the other federal states, but their effect was always the same: workers and peasants could understand and sing them and dance to their music. Most of the songs contained an accurate analysis of the political situation as well as a call to join in and change things. Most importantly, the songs inspired people more than speeches or written pamphlets. In a country where the majority of the poor, particularly the rural poor, were illiterate, there was no other way to educate people politically.

It was during Indira Gandhi's office as prime minister. Before being elected, she had promised to eradicate poverty. At first, the poor believed 'Indiramma' (Mother Indira) and voted for her. But after she was elected they saw her break that promise. In fact, the opposite happened: the rich got richer and the poor, poorer. Around 1976, it became obvious that the peasants and rural labourers were now more severely and violently exploited by the big feudal landlords than they had been before. I remember hearing one of these landlords say, "If you want to control the Harijans (the 'untouchables') then you have to rape their women, beat their men and burn down their huts."

And indeed, reports of such atrocities appeared in the papers every day.

The police sided with the landlords; they watched and did nothing. Politicians from the ruling Congress Party protected the landlord-class, and the only opposition parties – the CPI and the CPI(M) – were represented in just two of the Indian federal states: the CPI was in power in Kerala and the CPI(M) in West Bengal.[3] In all other states there was no real political opposition to the Congress Party under Indira Gandhi. It is therefore not surprising that, during this time, young and politically interested students were searching for more radical solutions, and, in doing so, they turned towards China and Mao Ze Dong's successful peasant revolution. A major peasant revolution had already taken place in India between 1946 and 1951 in Telengana in Andhra Pradesh, and a more recent wave of revolts

---

3 The party names are explained in Chapter Four.

The Mies family, 1940. Maria is on the right wearing a white dress.

Maria and her cousin Maria Agnes harvesting potatoes in Steffeln, 2008.

Shatrugna, Saral, Maria and Vina in Hyderabad about 1976. At that time Shatrugna and Vina were in jail as political prisoners during the Indian Emergency. This photograph was taken during their home-leave.

Maria and her sisters-in-law in Kolkata.

FINRRAGE Conference in Comilla, Bangladesh in 1989.
Farida Akhter (speaking), Paula Bradish and Renate Klein, sitting next to Maria.

FINRRAGE meeting at the World Women's Congress for a Healthy Planet in
Rio de Janeiro, 1991. This Congress produced the Women's Action Agenda 21
and was seen as a major preparation for the Earth Summit in 1992.

Protest against NATO at the US Airbase in Spangdahlem, 1999.

DWD Conference against the WTO in Seattle in November 1999.
The banner is by Theresa Wolfwood.

Maria Mies and Vandana Shiva in Oldenburg, 1995.

Diverse Women for Diversity Conference against War in New Dehli, 2001.

Stop the GATS Demonstration, Cologne 2003. After the Women Resist the GATS Conference we organised a spontaneous demonstration where we convinced a woman police officer that GATS would affect her too. She then escorted us on our way.

Maria Mies and Nawal el Saadawi.

The female trinity: Veronika Bennholdt-Thomsen, Maria Mies, Claudia von Werlhof.

Maude Barlow, Vandana Shiva and Maria Mies in front of a banner made for the conference by Theresa Wolfwood at the Women Resist the GATS Conference in Cologne, 2003.

was ignited by a peasant rebellion in *Naxalbari*, in North Bengal, an insurgency which gave its name to the Naxalite Movement.

The Naxalites

The peasant revolt in Naxalbari first began in 1967–1968. It did not last long, but it not only inspired oppressed peasants throughout India, it immediately also inspired the students in the cities: at first in Kolkata in West Bengal, and then in other Indian cities. When I came to Hyderabad in 1972, a majority of the students I became acquainted with were Naxalites or their sympathisers. The CPI-ML pursued an unmistakably radical and revolutionary course modelled on China. What this meant was that the revolutionary cadres went underground and became active in areas where feudal exploitation and violence against peasants was most extreme. In the mountains and jungle regions of Bihar and Andhra Pradesh (in Sri Kakulam in particular), they formed guerilla groups and killed the worst landlords, or extorted ransom money from them. In this way they tried bit by bit to create 'liberated areas'.

However, the CPI(ML) not only carried its armed struggle into the rural areas but was also active among workers and students in the cities. Armed conflict was definitely part of the ideology of the CPI(ML). According to the Naxalites, the CPI and CPI(M), being committed to the parliamentary system, were too revisionist and social democratic to be useful for the kind of social revolution they thought was imperative.

The men and women students who sympathised with the Naxalites believed that a new phase of revolution had begun throughout the world: in China, Vietnam, Cambodia, Palestine, Latin America and Africa. They thought that imperialism would come to an end in the near future. They considered themselves to be a part of this international, anti-imperialist world movement and, as a consequence, were also interested in the student movements in the USA and Europe.

I had closer contact to the *Progressive Democratic Students' Union* (PDSU), one of three groups headed each by a revolutionary leader. There are still many such Naxalite groups in India today.[4]

The new Indian women's movement

I did not really understand the ideological differences between these groups, but I was impressed by their revolutionary enthusiasm and their commitment. I was most impressed by the *female students* who had become members of the different groups. By 1973, they had already formed their own women's group within the PDSU called the *Progressive Organisation of Women* (POW). It was the first women's organisation to be established by the nascent women's movement in India, and it quickly became popular everywhere. I took part in their first meetings in Hyderabad, the capital of Andhra Pradesh. Because they did not have a space to meet, they gathered in a park and sat beneath a tree where they had a heated discussion on how they could solve the most immediate problems of patriarchal Indian society.

One of the problems they discussed was that parents demanded that their daughters who studied had to be home by 5 pm. Coming home later meant trouble. Another, more major social problem was the system of arranged marriages, particularly the *dowry* having to be paid by the bride's family to the groom's family. For families with a number of daughters this often meant having to go into great debt. It also led to the tragic burning-to-death of young brides[5] when the

---

4 They are now very violent and seen as terrorists, but see Arundhati Roy's 2010 essay "Walking with the Comrades."

5 While preparing my dissertation (1969–1970), I noticed an unusually high rate of so-called 'kitchen accidents' in the statistics on women's mortality in India. These cases concerned young women who – apparently – spilled kerosine for cooking over their saris which subsequently caught fire. Many women burned to death in this manner. Some social scientists spoke of suicides. The true cause of these tragic accidents only came to light when the nascent Indian women's movement started a nation-wide campaign protesting these kitchen 'accidents'. The campaign provided evidence that *murder* was the cause of most of these deaths and that the victims were particularly young brides who had just recently married. The crime was often motivated by the fact that the families of

amount of the dowry was too small. At all events, it was clear to these young women students that dowries had to be abolished.

They courageously started an Anti-Dowry Campaign which was the first of its kind in India. Members of the Progressive Organisation of Women travelled to all the colleges throughout the state of Andhra Pradesh. They lectured to young female student audiences, recruited new members and called them to fight the dowry system. The movement immediately became very successful among young women. Their young male counterparts were less enthusiastic. In my discussions with them, some made excuses that their parents *insisted* on a dowry. These young revolutionaries still often entered into marriages arranged by their parents, meaning their parents selected their brides. Caste, class and status had to 'fit'. These young men did not have the courage to rebel against their parents' will and against patriarchal tradition.

I did not understand the dichotomy between their revolutionary consciousness on the one hand, and their completely traditional and patriarchal behaviour, with respect to marriage and family and their relationship with the female sex, on the other. Later, I learned that this dichotomy also exists among the educated middle-class and I understood why not only parents, but sometimes young people themselves, prefer an *arranged marriage* instead of a *love marriage*.

Today, young men as well as women from liberal middle-class families enjoy a great many freedoms. They can go to the disco or watch a film together at the cinema. But when it comes to marriage, young people still often prefer their parents to choose their partner and arrange a marriage. They have more trust in their parents' greater experience and understanding of human nature. More importantly,

young daughters-in-law had paid too little in dowry and the daughters-in-law had to put pressure on their family to extract more dowry money from them. If they refused, 'kitchen accidents' in which they tragically burned to death were not uncommon. Their young husbands were then free to marry again and demand a new dowry. I joined the demonstrations against these murders in Delhi and wrote on the background of this phenomenon in *Indische Frauen zwischen Unterdrückung und Befreiung* (1969/1973).

they still consider it important that caste, class and wealth match each other. A young pair may now be allowed to go out and be seen in public together, but love and being in love is often not a pre-condition for getting married. *"Love comes after marriage"* is a popular saying. Even educated, enlightened young people would rather place the risk of a failed marriage into the hands of their parents.

On the background of this social reality, the Progressive Organisation of Women students' Anti-Dowry Campaign in Hyderabad was an incredibly courageous and revolutionary early action by women.

The Progressive Organisation of Women in Hyderabad may have been the first regular organisation to be established by the new Indian women's movement, but very soon many similar groups and organisations came into being in other cities: in Pune, Mumbai, New Delhi and Chennai. Contrary to the prevalent prejudice, it must be noted that they did not merely copy the women's movement in the West but that they immediately took up and launched campaigns against the most urgent problem Indian women suffered from, and still suffer from: *patriarchy*. Such campaigns addressed not only the dowry-induced murders (see above), but also Indian society's neglect of girls, the deliberate abortion of female foetuses (after the intro-duction of pre-natal testing), violence against women and girls, and the mass rape of women during and after the 1975 state of emergency. Nationwide, women went out into the streets to protest against the rise in prices of basic commodities such as sugar, oil, rice and flour. Everywhere, women from the new women's movement established autonomous groups and feminist journals such as *Manushi*, as well as feminist publishing houses like *Kali for Women*.[6] What they were far better at than we in the West was their ability to maintain their contact with the women of the old women's movement who had incorporated their struggle for women's rights into their fight

---

6 Kali for Women still exists today. It has produced two other associated feminist publishers: Zubaan Books and Women Unlimited.

against colonial rule. In this way, young feminists became far more widely accepted in Indian society than in Germany.

The Indian women's movement always inspired me. When I saw the problems these young women had to deal with and how courageously and creatively they accomplished so much over the course of the years, our problems in Germany seemed small and insignificant in comparison. Looking at what they were doing always helped me put my own situation into perspective and stopped me from losing courage. I learned a great deal from my Indian sisters. And they considered me to be one of them.

The impact of the New Women's Movement was in no case limited only to educated middle-class women. I found this impact even stronger among women peasants and rural labourers in the villages of Telengana where I carried out research on subsistence production. The majority of these women were illiterate, but they approached women's issues in a far more uncomplicated manner than urban women. Moreover, rural as well as urban Indian women were very aware that their fight to change the dominant patriarchal relationship between the sexes would have consequences: indeed violent ones. They not only had to reckon with violent reactions from their men, but also from their in-laws, the ruling classes and castes, and in particular from the police. Patriarchal male dominance is so deeply interwoven with the social fabric of India that a rebellion against it puts the entire structure of society into question. This was particularly the case when women joined revolutionary groups such as the Naxalites.

The waves of protest across the country caused Indira Gandhi to call a state of emergency for all of India in 1975. The emergency laws gave the government the power to ban all revolutionary parties, groups, movements and their writings, to put their followers into jail, repeal liberal laws and decree new ones – new laws which allowed people to be arrested without being informed of the cause and without being brought before a judge.

Civil rights were drastically cut and the climate in the country became totalitarian. Most people dreaded the decrees of MISA (*Maintenance of Internal Security Act*), the law against *sedition*, and the *Preventive Detention* law. What triggered these drastic measures were the mass protests of workers, peasants and students in 1973 and 1974, a major strike organised by railworkers in 1974, and the national movement led by the socialist Gandhian *Jayaprakash Narayan* (JP) who, under the slogan of 'Total Revolution' and 'People's Power', sought to bring together all the movements of the disaffected to create a major national movement.

Jayaprakash Narayan wanted to establish a democracy based truly on the people's wishes, one that was decentralised, oriented on village structure, anti-capitalist and against the centralisation of national government power. When the Allahabad High Court indicted Indira Gandhi of electoral fraud, she responded by proclaiming a state of national emergency. Besides instituting the new emergency laws, some of them originating from colonial times, she also decreed a twenty-point programme to eradicate rural poverty and accelerate development. This programme promised to bring higher wages to rural workers but also instituted drastic *measures to control population growth*. Western scientists had for a long time diagnosed India's 'unbroken' population growth as the main cause for poverty in the country and throughout the 'Third World'. The World Bank also put pressure on India to lower its fertility rate. It is said the World Bank recommended that India's government proclaim a state of emergency.

Backed by the emergency laws from 1975, the Indian government resorted to brutal measures.[7] It demanded that its civil servants not only limit the number of their own children, but also be responsible

---

7 In no other country I know of is patriarchy so closely interwoven with caste, class, politics and family. Even with the sudden economic rise of 'shining India', this pattern has not changed (see Maria Mies, new edition 1986, *Indische Frauen zwischen Unterdrückung und Befreiung*).

for reducing the birth rate to a particular degree in their jurisdictions which always involved force and corruption. The most drastic of these measures was the implementation of *forced sterilisations* of men in rural areas and among the urban poor. Men were taken and simply loaded on to trucks, driven to sterilisation centres and quickly sterilised regardless of their family status and the number of their children. This sterilisation campaign in particular caused Indira Gandhi's dramatic fall from power in the following elections of 1977, bringing the emergency to an end.

All of my friends in Hyderabad were affected by the emergency measures. A few had been arrested under MISA because they had published pamphlets sympathising with China. Many members of the Progressive Organisation of Women landed in prison as well; their leader was even arrested for sedition. Some spent as much as one and a half years in jail – longer than their male comrades – and were not released until the emergency laws were repealed. This shows that attacking the system of patriarchy was met with harsher punishment than mere revolt against class and imperialism.

After I completed my doctoral degree, I continued to visit India on a regular basis. I wanted to keep in close contact with 'my second home' on the one hand, and on the other, I also wanted to see Saral Sarkar, with whom I had entered into a closer relationship.

I went to Hyderabad as usual in 1975 and 1976, during my semester holidays, to visit him. I noticed I was not able to move around as easily as I had become accustomed to doing. Most of my friends were leftists, a few of them were in prison. I realised that my contact with them might make them more suspicious in the eyes of the police. I, too, was in danger of being deported as *persona non grata* (undesired person), since Saral was also known to be a leftist. Because of these circumstances, we decided it would be better to marry and legalise our relationship. We were married in September 1976. The ceremony was carried out according to the Indian Civil Marriage Law. It was completely devoid of pomp. Just a few friends came and brought us garlands which Saral and I took and placed around each other's neck.

Actually, I did not want to marry. As a feminist I considered marriage to be a trap. Saral thought the same. As a result, we had no problem in maintaining a partnership without a legal marriage licence, especially because our partnership was limited to being a long-distance relationship. I had no wish to move to India on a permanent basis as his wife. Nor did I want to give up my paid position in Germany to live as a dependent wife in India, even though I would probably have gotten a job.

Most importantly, I did not want to move to a country where I could not freely work politically. Had I done so, my friends would sooner or later have reproached me for coming from an imperialist country. I was afraid of having to face their bottled-up hate of Western racism and its imperialism. I did not want to experience that on a daily basis. It is why I decided to stay in Germany after marrying and restrict myself to visiting Saral once or twice a year. Saral also did not want to leave India and migrate to Germany.

Today, I sometimes ask myself whether we did the right thing to maintain this 'long-distance marriage', particularly in the beginning of our relationship. It was not until 1982 that Saral decided to move to Germany. He left his country, his well-paid teaching position at the Goethe Institute in Hyderabad and came to Germany to face unemployment, all for my sake.

Saral

Saral was raised in Kolkata and comes from a middle-class family which placed great value on education, particularly for the sons.

His father was a civil servant who spent a great deal of time away from his family in the course of his duty. He must have been a very strict man. When he returned from his trips, he always inspected whether his children had made good progress at school. Back then, daughters hardly learned English in Bengal as they would marry anyway. Saral later sometimes quoted his father's statement, "I'll send one of my sons to Cambridge and the other to Oxford." Saral was the most gifted of the six children. From early on he was proficient in English and was very talented in languages generally. He read a great deal and was interested in geography, history and politics. After receiving his Bachelor of Arts, he worked at a bank. His work consisted of adding together endless columns of numbers (of course without the help of a computer) which bored him. He was also frustrated by the vacuous, dull atmosphere of the bank.

He began to look for a more interesting intellectual activity. The idea came to him to learn another European language, and by coincidence he came across an advertisement for a six-month German course at the Kolkata branch of the Goethe Institute.

Saral enrolled in the course and for three years he learned German in the evenings after work. He subsequently received a stipend from the German federal government to take part in a training programme to become a German teacher. The stipend included a three-month course at the Goethe Institute in Pune. In 1963, he was one of my first students. His stipend also included further studies for German teachers at the GI's central office in Munich. In the summer of 1966, he passed his examinations there and immediately received a teaching job for German at the GI in Hyderabad.[8]

Once, a niece of mine asked me whether our different cultural backgrounds posed a problem. No, they did not. Our cultural differences do not play a role in our marriage. From very early on, Saral has been an atheist and cosmopolitan. He is not a religious Hindu. I, too, am no longer religious. We also share the same political opinions, although sometimes he has trouble with my feminism. However, what does lead to some irritation in our day-to-

---

8 Back then, the Goethe Institute was looking for Indian teachers of German, first of all because almost no applicants from Germany wanted to work abroad, and secondly, because Indian teachers of German were cheaper.

day life in Germany is not our difference in culture, but in class. Saral is the child of an educated and respected Indian middle-class family from a city famous for its culture and intellectual atmosphere, Kolkata. I am the child of peasants from a tiny village in the Eifel.

Before I continue with my life story, I provide some more details on my theoretical perspectives and insights derived from the research studies I carried out. This pertains in particular to the *subsistence perspective* I mentioned above.

9

Subsistence –
A Perspective for the Future

What is subsistence?

In the course of our research and of the global politico-economic developments it became clear to my friends and I that the subsistence approach not only constituted the starting point for our critique of the ruling system, but that subsistence also represented a new perspective for the future of the world.

Subsistence is generally understood to mean poverty, under-development and hardship. In contrast to this, Veronika Bennholdt-Thomsen, Claudia von Werlhof and I redefined this term in the context of the nascent women's movement as a way of working and producing that contradicts the general production of goods charac-terised by capitalism. I defined this term in the late 1970s as follows:

Subsistence production or the production of life includes all work that is expended in the maintenance of immediate life and which has no other purpose. Subsistence production therefore stands in contrast to commodity and surplus value production. For subsistence production the aim is 'life', for commodity production it is 'money', which 'produces' ever more money, or the accumulation of capital.

For this mode of production, life is, so to speak, only a coincidental 'side effect'. It is typical of the capitalist industrial system that it declares everything that it wants to exploit free of charge to be part of nature, a natural resource. To this belongs the housework of women as well as the work of peasants in the Third World, but also the productivity of all nature (in Mies and Bennholdt-Thomsen, 2000, pp. 20–21).

If humankind had solely relied on the production of goods it would not have survived, and it will still not survive and have a future if it does so today.

Women and subsistence production

The major share of subsistence production is carried out by women across the globe: they bear and raise children, carry out unpaid housework and care for the old and sick. In short, they carry out so-called wageless 'reproduction work'. Economists describe everything that can be appropriated without cost to capital as 'free goods', such as nature, sun and air. These 'free goods' not only include housework but also small farming, or peasant, subsistence, the colonies' production and, of course, not least, nature itself. For capitalist economists, only work that is *productive* and *visible*, is measured in money terms and included in the Gross National Product (GNP).

As feminists we discovered a link between women's invisible work and capital accumulation when we began to look at the role housework plays in capitalism. Those who want to appropriate domestic work without establishing wage relations must do so by means of structural and direct violence. Structural and direct violence characterise all exploitative subsistence relationships: between humans and nature, peasants and industry, capital cities and colonies. This is why we consider the man-woman relationship to be colonial at its very core. The liberal part of the women's movement has made a fatal error in that it has staked equality as its goal. In an exploitative, colonial system, equality can only mean rising to the same status as those who profit from this system. Obviously, equality does not mean equality with poor subsistence peasants. Subsistence as a *perspective* means the abolishment of all these colonial relationships. *The subsistence perspective has a history that many are still familiar with today.*

The subsistence perspective is not our invention; it was in existence in all industrialised countries until World War II. The remnants still survive to this day. The practice of subsistence includes a diverse range of activities directed toward satisfying human needs. Small-scale farming is included but also urban and rural gardening, preserving vegetables and fruits, craftwork (such as carpentry, sewing, smithies, petty trade), farmers' markets, trade in goods, all forms of repair work, often through neighbourly help.

The practice of subsistence requires a functioning local community: Commons – or at the very least neighbourhoods in which the principle of mutual help exists – reciprocity, responsibility for the community and the willingness to carry out community work without wages. Historically, these principles not only existed in rural but also in urban areas. Research studies carried out in the USA document that such subsistence activity existed in the industrial cities well into the 1960s.

Subsistence production by no means disappeared 'by itself' quasi-automatically. In the USA, it was deliberately extinguished by the government by means of new family and wage policies during the New Deal, initiated by President Roosevelt in the 1930s. These policies centred on the individual, the bourgeois/middle-class nuclear family and the 'non-working' housewife. In Europe, new agricultural policies and a shift towards industrial, chemical and export dependent farming, led to the liquidation of self-sufficiency and small family farms. It was considered 'progressive' for an 'industrialised' country such as Germany to reduce its number of farmers. To date, the

European Union (EU) has continued to pursue these agricultural policies even though it has become widely known that they devastate the environment, are detrimental to humans and animals, raise unemployment, and destroy biodiversity as humankind's ability to be self-sufficient. In contrast to this, subsistence as a perspective for the future means that humans regain control over their food production. Today we call this food sovereignty.

The consequences of this new policy for the poorest in the world

Peasants in the so-called Third World are being ruined by the same kind of agricultural policy (for instance by the so-called Green Revolution). Destitution drives them into the mega-cities where they end up in slums and cannot find paid jobs in one of the industries that would secure their existence. This development is part of a deliberate policy implemented by the World Bank, the IMF, the WTO and huge companies. What remains are large-scale farms that grow mono-cultures and produce the raw materials for multinational corporations.

Since the 1990s, neoliberal policies aimed at opening all the markets in the world. These not only ruined the peasantry in the poor countries, but also small industrial businesses. In contrast to the West, these small companies are not bolstered by a welfare state. Instead, multinational corporations prey upon their predicament by paying the lowest wages in the world wherever they erect new industrial plants in the textile sector, the IT-field and the automobile industry. The fact that up to 90% of the labourers in these Special-Economic-Zones and global market factories are young women shows that the reduction of wages for workers is essentially an issue of sex – today more than ever despite all the talk about gender mainstreaming.[1] Many people in poor countries are resisting the

---

1 It is precisely *because* of gender mainstreaming that this is happening, since gender mainstreaming pushes women into the market economy with the underlying pretence that it is about equality when in fact it is about disguised exploitation (see Hawthorne, 2004, pp. 87–91, <http://devnet.anu.edu.au/GenderPacific/pdfs/20_gen_mainstream_hawthorne.pdf>).

theft of their subsistence base – their water, their genetic and cultural diversity – by renouncing pesticides and artificial fertilisers, adhering to and rediscovering old forms of ecological agriculture, defending their traditions and consciously rejecting multinational corporations. People like Vandana Shiva in India, Farida Akhter in Bangladesh, as well as others in Africa, are proof that women are at the forefront of organising resistance and in preserving their subsistence base.

Why does the subsistence perspective entail structural elements that lead to a better economy and society?

To begin with, the subsistence perspective provides the material conditions which prevent people from falling completely victim to colonial exploitative conditions. Wherever they still have access to means of subsistence (i.e. land, water, woods, Commons, subsistence knowledge), and still live within a functioning community, they are less vulnerable to blackmail than wage workers who are often individualised and solely dependent on money.

It was and still is the strategy of Capital, however, to disconnect people from their subsistence base so that they are coerced into selling their labour and become mere consumers of goods. *War* and *debt* are the means by which they are *dispossessed by force*. The most recent examples of this are Iraq and Afghanistan, formerly wealthy countries which have been reduced to a pauper status by the USA's wars of conquest and become dependent on Western aid and the global market.

The subsistence perspective has already begun

For years my friends and I have emphasised that the alternative to capitalism is the subsistence perspective – and that it has already begun. Here a few examples:

The subsistence perspective is not an economic model but a *perspective*, an orientation for social ideas and actions. This does not mean that it is only wishful thinking. All over the world people have to first resist the destruction of their means of livelihood. Out of this resistance, initiatives have developed in poor as well as industrial countries to establish subsistence economic activities.

One example is Bangladesh where the new peasant movement *Nayakrishi Andolon* came into being in the 1990s. This movement helped many villages to declare themselves 'poison free zones' in which 'multinationals' are denied access. They use no artificial fertilisers, no high-yielding seeds, and no pesticides. They have revived old farming methods, such as water harvesting. Their yield is higher than with modern agricultural methods because, instead of monocultures for export, they produce a wide variety of goods for their own needs. In the course of this struggle, the former patriarchal relationship between the sexes was changed because the movement was primarily initiated by women. Each village shares a building to store communal seeds which the women conserve according to age-old methods. These villages are independent of Western companies. When I visited Dhaka some years ago, my friend Farida Akhter explained and showed me how women came together to establish a local market for peasants and weavers. Some communities are also proud to have abolished the dowry system, and to have declared themselves pesticide-free.

Examples of new subsistence endeavours also exist in industrial countries such as *Longo Maï* (a network of European cooperatives) and the Niederkaufungen commune near the city of Kassel, in sharing networks, in initiatives to establish parallel regional currencies as well as regional and local economies. The latter in particular prove that the economy can be organised differently than the growth-oriented, capitalist economy of accumulation we are familiar with.

Notable examples are the *community and inter-cultural gardens* that have been established in cities in the USA[2] as well as in

---

2 The most impressive example of community gardens was established by Grace Lee Boggs, called 'Detroit Summer', in the down-and-out city of Detroit after General Motors closed down most of its production there and thousands became unemployed, resulting in despair and a sharp rise in drug abuse and violence particularly among young men. Grace Lee Boggs and her husband James Boggs began to create open communal gardens

Germany.[3] The first such garden in Germany was initiated in Göttingen, primarily by refugee women from Bosnia, Eritrea, Ethiopia and other countries. Provided with land by the Protestant Church, these women worked together to grow fruit and vegetables as well as experimenting with growing produce from their own countries which they then shared and distributed amongst themselves. They did not produce for the capitalist market. They often organised feasts and celebrations in their communal gardens. The men built a baking oven so that each group could bake their own bread and share it with others. Today, more than 100 such communal and inter-cultural gardens exist in Germany and form a movement which is supported by its own charitable foundation.

This example is particularly worthy of note because a number of *subsistence principles* are applied here 'in one swoop', even if the term subsistence is not used:

- A portion of necessary foodstuffs are not bought but produced by hand;
- Production is carried out on a communal basis. New communities/neighbourhoods are established as a result;
- The soil is not private property but a Commons. A right of utilisation exists instead of property relationships;
- Political animosities can be overcome by community work. *Subsistence unifies, money divides!*
- Experiencing *one's own power* and *one's own ability* to provide for one's existence and not be dependent upon charity is a basic prerequisite for human dignity;
- Community gardeners experience that subsistence does not mean *scarcity* but rather *life in abundance*. Even on a tiny piece

in this dilapidated city in which youths began to work and learn how to produce their own food (Boggs, 2005).

3 Inter-cultural Garden Foundation Munich (Stiftung Interkulturelle Gärten München. Email: info@stiftung-interkultur.de). Elisabeth Meyer-Renschhausen visited and studied such gardens in various US cities such as New York (Meyer-Renschhausen, 2004).

of land, more can grow than is needed. This means you can always share what you produce;

- The community garden experience contradicts one of the major principles of capitalism, namely, that nature is stingy and that the economy began with the goal of overcoming scarcity;

- In these gardens, *new relationships between humans and nature, between the generations, between people of various cultural backgrounds, between men and women*, develop. That is why they are also excellent examples of successful integration;

- They offer a different idea of the *good life* than the one propagated by capitalism which is based on a supermarket-based wealth of money and goods;

- A different notion of the *good life* is the basis upon which people will comprehend the concept of economy differently, as *enrichment* not as *scarcity*.

This new concept of the *good life* meets an increasingly deep need felt by people, even in industrial countries. They are beginning to ask themselves why all their work is not bringing about the *good life* they are seeking.

Exchange of goods, international trade, technology and wage work

A subsistence economy is not a closed economy; it knows trade, even international trade. Goods marked for trade, however, are only those which have been produced in surplus of one's own needs. The importation of products such as apples, milk, vegetables, etc. which are produced within the country itself should be barred. This trade only serves profit-making and discriminates against local farmers who cannot sell their produce as it is undercut by foreign imports.

Technology also plays an important role. Once the economy in general is organised according to subsistence principles, different technologies have to be used. Technology is not a neutral element within the system. Capitalist structures (such as attrition and wastage) are built into industrial technology.

Wage work will also exist. Wage work will, however, lose its current character as the only work that creates value. It will be only one of many forms of work which contribute to maintaining human existence. As a consequence, housework, for instance, will no longer be considered unproductive and valueless. Hence, our concept of economic value has to be changed.

A subsistence economy must necessarily be ecological. It cannot deplete and destroy the resource base upon which it is built to such an extent that people, animals and plants will have no future on this planet. The much talked about concept of sustainability has not changed the destruction of nature. In a subsistence economy, one has to emphatically *say NO to capitalist-colonial production.* There is still the hope that both will be possible: a continuously growing industrial society and a healthy environment. The expectation is that this will be brought about by some sleight of hand on the part of a 'technological Deus Ex Machina', not by other social relations. I do not believe in this concept of a capitalist-technological 'sustainability'.

Conclusion

The subsistence perspective is, by necessity, based on ecological, social, political, cultural and economic grounds. The subsistence perspective is possible everywhere – in urban as well as rural areas, in poor as well as rich countries, and it can be established on diverse cultural and biological backgrounds. *The subsistence perspective has already begun in manifold ways.* In fact, it respects and maintains this diversity.

- This means first that people have to re-establish a different idea of the *good life* than that provided by Capital – that, instead of the production of goods and infinite increase of money, the immediate *production of life* should be placed at the centre of all social and economic activity. Subsistence work should be equally shared by men and women;

- The subsistence perspective has begun in countries of the North as well as the South. In our book *The Subsistence Perspective: Beyond the Globalised Economy* (1999) we reported on many examples in which people began to disengage themselves from the insanity, meagreness and indignity of carrying out meaningless work in paid employment, and of meaninglessly accumulating capital;

- The subsistence perspective is not only desirable, it is also necessary. This not only applies to countries and societies who have fallen victim to neoliberal pillaging (such as the countries of the South), but also to the centres of global capitalism. The crisis of today has made it more clear to us than ever that we can only achieve something similar to food sovereignty and a happy life in smaller, ecologically based economies;

- Subsistence means therefore 'freedom *in* necessity and not *from* necessity' and does not mean overcoming the realm of necessity as capitalists and Marxists understand it. This approach requires a different understanding of nature than the dominance-based model we are acquainted with;

- Most importantly, subsistence means that peace must be established between the sexes. However, as a prerequisite for this peace, patriarchal and capitalist rule must be overcome. It cannot be brought about by 'raising' women to a 'higher status' like that of men (i.e. equality through gender mainstreaming), but only by men and women's reorientation toward a different concept of the *good life*.

- Subsistence does not mean poverty and regression, but abundance and a new form of internationalism based on reciprocity, new communities and new social conditions.

10

Women and Development

Institute of Social Studies, Holland (1979–1981)

In 1975, the first UN Women's Conference took place in Mexico. Its purpose was to appraise the status of women in all of the countries in the world. The result was disappointing, as was to be expected. In none of the countries across the globe did women have equal political, economic, social and educational status with men. The assembly passed a 'Plan of Action' in which the governments were called upon to correct this shortcoming by the next UN Women's Conference. Yet most governments ignored the plan of action despite the growing women's movements in their countries.

Undeterred by this, some of the women understood how to turn the situation to their advantage to promote the women's issue. One of these women was *Mia Berden* from the Institute of Social Studies (ISS) in The Hague, Holland. Following the UN Women's Conference, the ISS 'allowed' her to organise a workshop with women from Africa, Asia and South America – from the so-called Third World. During this workshop, the women formulated a resolution in which they demanded that the next position of Senior Lecturer go to a woman who would establish a focus on *Women and Development* at the ISS.

Although Mia Berden was about to retire, she was a very active woman, a feminist. She made sure that the resolution was quickly accepted by the ISS where of the sixty colleagues, only two were women. Once the position was advertised, it became necessary to find eligible qualified candidates. My friend Gerrit Huizer who was a professor at the Derde Wereld Institut at the University of Nijmegen, recommended me. We had met each other during the 'Heksencollegen' which he organised at his university in 1977. I applied for the job even though it meant less pay and less status than my professorship at the Fachhochschule Köln (University of Applied Sciences, Cologne). What appealed to me however, was the fact that I would work with women from the 'Third World' and that this tied in with my research.

I was given the position and in February 1979 I began my work at ISS. The Fachhochschule Köln granted me a leave of absence, since I was unsure whether I wanted to remain in Holland. At that time, there were few women in Holland with a doctoral degree who had also acquired expertise in research on women in the 'Third World'. Moreover, ever since my attendance at the 'Heksencollegen' in 1977, I was known among Dutch feminists for my essay on the 'Method-ology of Women's Studies' which had been published in Dutch.

After I arrived at the ISS in The Hague, I soon realised that my position was not taken very seriously. The director, Louis Emmerij, invited me to dinner and told me I should take my time to become acquainted with my new colleagues and their programmes, to have a drink with them at the pub, and decide how and where I wanted to begin working.

The ISS was directed toward educating people from the 'Third World' who had already acquired a university degree and were working. Based on scholarships, the ISS offered them specific further qualification in expert fields such as 'rural development', 'adminis-tration', 'industrial development', 'communication', etc. At the end of their studies, they were awarded a Masters Degree in Development Studies. Other than the University of Sussex in England, no other university in the world offered a comparable course of study.

It was my job to develop an additional specialised Master's Degree programme for women in 'Development Studies'. Instead of following my director's suggestions, I immediately requested stipends for ten women students whom I would choose from India, Bangladesh or as refugees from Argentina and other 'Third World' countries living in Holland. I knew that my success at the ISS would be dependent upon gathering a committed group of students around me as soon as possible.

I also accepted young Dutch women into the programme who were interested in taking part in my courses. This was an absolutely unusual procedure for the ISS back then. But I admitted them and felt it was important for women of the South[1] and North to become acquainted with each other during their studies as a means of dissolving prejudices. The first students to take part in the 'Women and Development' programme were from India, Bangladesh, Ethiopia, South Africa, Argentina, Trinidad and Tobago, Holland and Belize.

From the beginning, I had to introduce various innovations to secure my programme. In my planning I attached great importance to having my students first develop their abilities to critically analyse the dominant scientific practice which, throughout the world, was characterised by the same positivist norms responsible for making science so sterile and irrelevant, especially with respect to social change.

That is why I began our 'Women and Development' programme with what we at the ISS called *Fieldwork in Holland*. By means of practical experience, all students from the South were to investigate whether Dutch women were really as emancipated as they had always believed. They had to organise themselves in small groups and make contact with feminist groups in Holland. They then worked with these women for a period of time, after which they wrote a report on their experiences. At the end of the semester, all groups participated in a workshop in which their reports were evaluated. The fact that

---

1 This had become the name given to countries that were formerly called 'Third World' or 'developing' countries. I use all three terms.

Dutch students participated in 'Fieldwork in Holland' proved to be very useful in that they often helped in establishing contacts. I also applied the methodological approach I had developed and practised in our project studies in Cologne in modified form.

For many of the women students from the South the 'Fieldwork in Holland' was a truly revelatory experience. Almost all of them had come to Holland with the idea that the women there were 'emancipated' and that they were all well-educated and had a profession. However, during the fieldwork they became acquainted with reality. Here are some of their stories:

One of the groups had made contact with a feminist organisation in Utrecht engaged in helping women practise self-examination. The method of self-examination of the female genitalia was deliberately chosen by the women's movement as a means of liberating women from being at the mercy of dominant gynaecological practice. Many women realised they did not know their own bodies. When this group came back from Utrecht they were surprised by, and enthusiastic about, self-examination. One woman from Bangladesh cried out "Why Not?" upon which they immediately founded a *Why-Not-Group* made up of women from Bangladesh, India, South Africa and Holland. The group existed for many years and the women remained close friends beyond their time at the ISS. They also brought out a newsletter called *Insisterhood* to keep each other informed.

One woman from the Philippines made contact with a group called 'Deliberately Unmarried Mothers' (Bewusst Ongetrowde Moeders) in Amsterdam and learned why women have children but do not want to marry. Upon her return she – a Catholic – was astonished to report on how she now understood why women in Holland needed a women's movement despite being educated and being employed:

I always thought Western values were good for Western societies and Eastern values were good for Eastern societies. Now I understand that Western values are not even good for Western society.

I have often quoted this wise sentence, spoken by my Philippine student Luzviminda (Luz) Tanganco. Neither she nor I would have been capable of such understanding through mere book knowledge. Another woman from Africa reported the following after her fieldwork:

I don't understand why Dutch women always talk of men. Whether they are single, married or divorced – they are always talking about men and 'love'. We don't do this back home and in this respect we are much more independent than Western women.

The ISS retained the 'Fieldwork in Holland' component as an important methodological innovation for many years after I had returned to Germany. It was not only important to quasi 're-invent' Women's Studies with respect to methodology but to do so with regard to the programme content as well. This was because no textbooks existed on the subject and there was no other example of university-based Women's Studies to model our programme on. This situation was aggravated by the fact that we also had no material to inform our women students on the status and history of the women's movements in the 'Third World' as well as our own countries. Our students also knew nothing of the history of the women's movements themselves. When, after the first year, I received reinforcement from Kumari Jayawardena, a colleague from Sri Lanka whose husband was Ambassador in Brussels, we decided that we would write the text-books ourselves and have them printed by the ISS's own printing press.[2]

---

2 In a very short time we produced a whole series of publications which our students used as textbooks, i.e. Maria Mies (1981) *Feminism in Europe: Liberal and Socialist Strategies 1789–1919*; Maria Mies and Rhoda Reddock (1982b) *National Liberation and Women's Liberation*; Kumari Jayawardena (1982) *Feminism and Nationalism in the Third World*; Maria Mies (1982c) *Fighting on Two Fronts: Women's Struggles and Research*.

This meant that not only our students but also I had to learn a lot very quickly. Our students not only learned from us as teachers but also from one another. At this time, I was also writing up the research I had done in India. Learning, teaching, organising workshops,[3] developing theories, writing – all of this was part of a single, very intensive, very creative and productive process, not only for myself but also for my students.

Here are a few things I learned from them:

1. *Raquia Dualeh* from Somalia wrote her Master's Thesis on female genital mutilation of Somalian women, something I had never heard of until then. It was one of the first papers to be written by an Indigenous woman on this misogynist practice.

2. *Rhoda Reddock* from Trinidad & Tobago, whose ancestors were slaves, wrote her Doctoral Thesis on 'Women and Slavery in Trinidad and Tobago' in which she proved that slavery was not just a 'pre-capitalist' means of production, but definitely a truly capitalist enterprise. Slave women – as well as men – were treated only as goods and traded according to the cost-benefit principle. This was why they were not allowed to have children, since it was cheaper for slave-holders to buy new slave women than to allow them to bear and raise their own children. "It is more profitable to purchase than to breed" was the slave-traders' guiding principle. If a slave woman became pregnant she was forced to have an abortion.

3. *Chhaya Datar* from India wrote her Master's Thesis on women who made *Bidis* in cottage industries. These are cigarettes made of just one rolled leaf of tobacco. The system resembled that of the lace industry in Narsapur.

---

3 One of these workshops took place immediately after Zimbabwe's liberation. It was called 'Women's Struggle and Research'. The Dutch government invited Sally Mugabe, Robert Mugabe's wife, to attend the workshop.

At this time I also began to write my most important theoretical work, *Patriarchy and Accumulation on a World Scale: Women in the International Division of Labour* (1986a). I wrote the book in English first because an English publisher – Zed Books – was going to publish it immediately. As was often the case in the women's movement, everything had to be done at once.

A few of our male colleagues supported us. Yet for many of them the tempo and intensity with which we moved forward was frightening. For our Women's Studies specialty, we not only laid claim to more research scholarships for students from the South but to more time and space. And we also wanted more money to fund a new research project on the women's movements in seven countries of the South. All of this meant competition to the established programmes.

The uneasiness of our colleagues also had other reasons. It was fuelled by the *feminist approach* on which I based our Women and Development programme and which my colleague Kumari Jayawardena later also shared. When our colleagues had problems with their wives, or when a wife even decided to leave (which happened in one case), I often heard: "Maria and her Women's Studies are to blame." But I did not even know the woman in question; I had never seen or spoken to her! My afflicted colleague's statement, however, shows how deeply unsettled men had become by our programme and our existence.

This unease was also due to the fact that our approach was formulated within a consistent feminist, anti-patriarchal, anti-capitalist and anti-colonial framework. Moreover, in accordance with our so-called Bielefelder approach, I had criticised classical Marxism. We were of the opinion that the 'women's question' (die Frauenfrage) encompassed *all* exploitive power relationships and therefore could not be viewed in isolation from them.

No wonder that my colleagues did not know in what theoretical category they should place me. The majority of my male colleagues knew too little of the old or new women's movement, of our goals, our history and our theories. In an intriguing contrast to their positivist belief in 'rationality' and 'objectivity', their reaction to feminist knowledge was 'from the gut'.

However, a few of our colleagues not only sympathised with our programme, but also considered it worthy of support, theoretically as well as politically. One of these men was Ken Post. Originally from England, he was a Trotskyist and had great solidarity with the women's programme from the very beginning. Yet he could not accept that this programme was not to be made available to men as well. He, too, had ambitions to work on our programme. Another sympathiser was Pieter Waterman.

According to the feminist view at the time, women needed to first establish clarity about themselves, their issues, their history and ideas for the future, apart from men and become familiar with their own theory and praxis. Experience had shown everywhere that in mixed groups, even if only two or three men were present among fifty women, men dominated the discussion. This is why at the ISS I insisted on restricting men from participating in the Women and Development programme, whether as students or as teachers. Ken Post was disappointed, but continued to support us, and I give him much credit for this.

Another colleague, Kurt Martin (formerly Mandelbaum) was the only one who had read the texts my friends and I had written on *domestic work and subsistence*. He had originally come from Germany, was Jewish and a Marxist who was forced to emigrate during the first years of the Nazi rule. When I met him he was very old and had retired, yet he had a phenomenal memory. He had known Rosa Luxemburg and Karl Liebknecht personally and in the 1920s, he had published a harsh critique of the ruling Social Democrats of the Weimar Republic. He gave me a copy of his old article which was republished in 1978 by Wagenbach publishers (Mandelbaum, 1978, pp. 17–18). Martin, who was called Mandelbaum then, denounced the German Social Democrats for continuing to emphasise the right of 'civilised nations' to maintain colonies after Germany had lost World War I. The Social Democrats argued that the nations of Europe needed colonies to develop their own productive forces while at the same time they would instil 'primitive peoples' – the colonies, that is – with the working class discipline necessary for their own development (see also Mies, 1986a/1988). I often debated with Kurt during lunch at the Institute's cafeteria. He criticised Rosa Luxemburg whose writings formed the basis of our subsistence approach; and he also criticised us. He said we – Rosa and the three of us subsistence feminists (Veronika Bennhold-Thomsen, Claudia von Werlhof and I) – had based our critique of Marx's labour-value concept from an historically correct point of view, but not from a theoretically correct one. I was glad that he expressed this to me so openly and clearly. This meant he took us seriously and that our theory interested him, as was not the case for many of the other men at that time. However, I did not understand why Kurt, who was a Marxist established in 'historical materialism', could argue from a purely theoretical standpoint I felt to be rather ahistorical as well as idealistic.

After about a year, it was decided in an Institute meeting to dissolve the 'Women and Development' programme as an independent course of study and, further, that Kumari Jayawardena and I should only offer a 'Women's Component' in other programmes. Our women students would be divided up among the other study courses. It became immediately clear to me that this would mean the end of our independent Women's Studies at the ISS. Clearly, this was not what I had come to Holland for. Right away I reported this to Kumari and my students, upon which they became angry and said that this would be unacceptable to them.

They painted a huge poster and hung it up in the foyer of the ISS. The poster proclaimed that, if the ISS dissolved the Women's Studies programme, the students would immediately make this public to the entire women's movement in Holland and make sure that the story would be published in all the newspapers. The students threatened that a major revolt would be the result, since by this time the Women's Studies programme was renowned as one of the most successful programmes at the ISS.

The Director, who was a pragmatist, invited the students one by one to meet with him. He asked them if Maria had incited them to the action. All of them said no. He could not understand how young women from such different developing countries could get together after just such a short time at the Institute and passionately fight to maintain a particular programme. Later he said to me, "Maria, I asked all of them, and all of them support your programme." He was afraid of a negative public reaction and as a consequence decided to drop the Institute's plans.

For the students involved who all came from various religious and cultural backgrounds, the action was not only successful because it showed that they could change something if they joined together. They had the far more decisive experience that religious and cultural differences are not a barrier to joint actions. Besides the protest poster they hung in the foyer, they also painted another beautiful poster that read:

CULTURE DIVIDES US!
STRUGGLE UNITES US!

This was the major lesson they – and I, too – learned during this action. I have never forgotten this sentence. And I consider it to be a particularly relevant one today in a time where the entire focus is on the various ethnic, cultural and religious 'identities' and divisions that supposedly cause conflicts and wars.

These 'politics of identity' later also spread to the women's movement and removed from the universities the kind of politics I represented and still represent. This switch in political orientation also affected the ISS after I left the Institute. In contrast, I have always emphasised that the problems we face do not revolve around our differences but our common experiences of exploitation and oppression under patriarchal, colonial and capitalist conditions. What later became the focus of much of feminist politics (especially postmodern ones), however, was whether a woman is heterosexual or lesbian, Christian or Muslim, black or white.

Nevertheless, my work at the ISS was very satisfying. Despite all the opposition, our 'Women and Development' programme became a worldwide success. The women from the South who received a Master's Degree from our programme were immediately offered good positions in their countries. This was because international organisations such as the World Bank put pressure on countries in the South in the early 1980s to do something against female discrimination. Our graduates not only had good chances of finding a position in their countries, they also were in a position to decide how their work was to be carried out. Where else in the world were there people who, in responsible positions in politics, administration, universities, employment, and labour, also knew what *women's liberation* actually meant?

The Women's Studies programme at the ISS later even became the most popular programme and drew women from all over the world. The methodological basis I had developed was retained for many years. One Dutch student from my first course was recruited by the ISS to introduce the course on 'Fieldwork in Holland' into the Women and Development programme.

I, too, was successful. Not only as a teacher but also as an author. I wrote various books at that time that were published in English, Spanish, Japanese and Korean. All of this was very satisfying. My work was my whole life. The only community I had come to know was an international community of students and colleagues. However, even though I worked in Holland I did not have much contact with its people, its country and landscape, beyond my circle of colleagues. Somehow I was living an island life in an international enclave.

I only saw my husband, to whom I had been married since 1976, during my semester breaks or when he came to Holland to visit me from India. Sometimes I roamed alone along the dunes or took walks on the beach and asked myself what I was doing here. At some point I realised that I was very lonely despite all my contacts and successes. What was more, the ISS was not even considering giving me the kind of permanent tenure as a professor I had enjoyed in Germany.

As a result, and although I regretted leaving the ISS's Women's Studies programme after having built it up as one of its kind in the world, I decided to return to Germany as soon as my contract ended in 1981 and take up my former position at the Fachhochschule Köln. Also, in 1982, my husband decided to leave his well-paid teaching position at the Goethe Institute in Hyderabad to come and live with me in Germany. We have been living together in Cologne ever since then.

11

Further Movements and Campaigns

When I returned to the Fachhochschule Köln (University of Applied Sciences, Cologne), it became impossible for me to reduce the scope of my teaching to mere sociological studies, as my job at the ISS in Holland had extended my horizon considerably. Back in Germany, I continued to actively participate in the women's movement, in its struggles, successes and failures, trials and tribulations. In doing so, it became clear to me that as women we pursued a logic, call it even a philosophy, that was in direct contrast to the linear logic of dominant epistemology. Indeed, readers looking at my life from an 'objective' standpoint might get the impression that I had been living a pretty chaotic life: jumping from one subject to the next according to my own whim and fancy.

For me, however, it is a different story; there is a 'red thread' running through my life which goes first in one direction and then in another depending on the situation. I may have followed this thread along by-ways steadily or even gone back to places I had thought I was already 'finished' with. And in the process, I began to realise that many issues had a deeper dimension than I was aware of at the beginning. Or certain issues would reappear in a different historical context, as for instance the question, "Maria, what do you think about religion?"; or the question of utopia and alternatives to our ruling system, or the whole complex of science and technology. Based on this experience of recurring issues, I formulated the following motto for myself:

NOTHING IS EVER FINISHED. Many feminists try to describe this different logic and system as a labyrinth or a meandering river. FROM ALL SIDES AT ONCE is the slogan feminists use worldwide to explain it.

Women against Genetic Engineering and Reproductive Technologies

When in 1984 feminists came together from around the world to start a campaign against genetic engineering and reproductive technologies I once again was struck by the diversity and variety of our movement.

The campaign began for me in 1984 at the Second International Interdisciplinary Congress on Women in Groningen (the Netherlands), where a few women reported on reproductive technologies and its 'successful' creation of life in a test-tube. Only a few years earlier in 1978, the first test-tube baby, Louise Brown, had been born in the UK. Renate Duelli Klein, Jalna Hanmer, Gena Corea, Robyn Rowland and others argued that this invention further expropriated women, specifically women's decision making with respect to procreation.

In vitro fertilisation (IVF) was celebrated as one of the greatest achievements of 'mankind' as it would allow infertile couples to have children. We recognised, however, that this technology would open the floodgates to the industrial and commercial production of human life. In industrial biotechnology, women are relegated to mere suppliers of raw material: egg cells and wombs (as 'surrogate mothers').

In Groningen, the US journalist Gena Corea even spoke of 'reproductive prostitution'. Women until then had sold or rented their vaginas as prostitutes to men. As 'surrogate mothers' they were now renting or selling their womb (Corea, 1984). She also reported that all the technological permutations had been first tested on cows. This was not because veterinarians wanted to help infertile cows become pregnant, but so that by means of these technologies cows would be made to increase their production of calves. It was all about a capitalist increase in productivity. With this technology, natural cycles could easily be disregarded. As Gena Corea put it: "First the cow then you" (Erst die Kuh, dann Du).

The horror and anger we all felt led to the spontaneous establishment of a new international network to fight the inventions produced by genetic and reproductive engineers. Most articles on this subject in the mainstream media voiced nothing but praise for the achievements of biotechnology. But we knew that there were many feminists working at women's health centres and universities around the world who were just as concerned about these new developments as we were. We could therefore count on sharing information from many parts of the world.

In Groningen, we also decided to organise a further international 'Emergency Conference' on the issue. It took place in Sweden in July 1985. In the meantime books by Gena Corea (1985) and Rita Arditti, Renate Duelli Klein and Shelley Minden (1984) were published on the subject. Many new women came to the Emergency Conference – the issue had immediately mobilised women from around the world. I gave a presentation called, "Why do we need all this?" I refused – and still refuse – to believe that a problem that has existed since the beginning of human history – involuntary childlessness – should be solved by technological innovations. Humans have always found *social* ways to creatively cope with infertility such as adoption, taking in related or unrelated children, through good neighbourly relations, to name just a few options. The desire to have one's own biological child reflects the kind of property thinking that exists in capitalist nuclear families. This 'desire to have a child' was vehemently supported by the new biotechnological and pharmaceutical industries who anticipated an increase in economic growth from it.

I felt our network had to take an unequivocal stand against the new technologies and that it was not enough just to observe their development. I therefore suggested we call it *Feminist International Network of Resistance to Reproductive and Genetic Engineering*

(FINRRAGE). An impossible name! Some women rejected this name at the conference not only because it was too long, but because it was too radical and we would never get any grants. We had a forceful debate on the goal of our international network. Some participants were not against genetic engineering *per se*. "I have a lot of fun playing around with these things" (meaning genes), a microbiologist said at the conference. Some lesbians hoped that reproductive technologies would allow them to fulfil their wish to have children without being dependent on men (seemingly not realising that they would then become dependent on patriarchal technologies). But Farida Akhter from Bangladesh, Jyotsna Gupta from India and I pointed out the already existing racist link between the methods of population control in the so-called Third World and those used in reproductive technologies. In countries such as India and Bangladesh women should have as few children as possible. In the white countries of the West they were to give birth to more children using these technologies. The pharmaceutical companies were expecting huge profits from both these 'deficits'. After a lot of discussion, we finally agreed on the long name: FINRRAGE it was! We also passed a resolution which was to be presented at the following international UN Women's Conference in July 1985 in Nairobi.

This resolution incorporated the demands of the campaign against genetic and reproductive engineering we had initiated in Germany earlier that year.[1] In April 1985, we organised an enormously successful International Congress *Women against Gene and*

---

1   We were not the first ones to address the issue of genetic and reproductive engineering. In Germany, *the Gene Archive* (Gen-Archiv) already existed which was founded by a medical doctor, Beate Zimmermann, together with other women. The Gene Archive did excellent work but did not reach a broad public until Beate Zimmerman held a lecture at our Congress on 'Old and New Eugenics'. As she said: "At that time there was an uncertainty about questioning scientific 'truths', but the societal consequences of genetic engineering seemed so clear that especially women became aware of the correlated issues and decided to address the subject in order to gain better understanding and monitor respective publications. This is how the Gene Archive more or less began." The Gene Archive's work became renowned across the country and many people – not only women – turned to it for information on the newest developments in gene technology.

Reproductive Technologies (Frauen gegen Gen- und Reproduktions-technik) in Bonn. We had invited women scientists and researchers not only from Germany, the UK and the USA but also from Japan, India and Bangladesh, to attend the conference.

The purpose of our Congress was to demonstrate that our resistance to these technologies was not only based on our concern as women and thus only directed against reproductive technologies, but that we also resisted genetic engineering of plants and animals. *We considered gene technology as such to be a fundamentally misguided scientific path.* I still think this today.

In order to make visible the interconnectedness of all living things – plants, animals, people – we placed a plant and a seahorse on the podium of Bonn University's auditorium. They stayed in their place as our representatives – and we spoke for them.

Our Congress in Bonn was a great success. Without having to advertise much, 2000 women gathered in Bonn and after the Congress, women's groups against gene and reproductive technologies sprang up all over Germany, triggering intense discussions amongst a wide range of people. It was particularly important that feminist theologians such as *Ina Praetorius* began questioning the ethics of reproductive technologies. No clear position had been taken on it by the official churches themselves. And the established political parties – Social, Christian and Liberal Democrats (SPD, CDU, FDP) – either remained silent or expressed support for genetic engineering

---

In 1987, the Gene Archive was raided by the Federal Criminal Authorities (Bundeskriminalamt, BKA) in a surprise operation; its archives were confiscated and its employees were arrested. The only reason given for this raid was that the Gene Archive's activity was supposed to be 'close to terrorism'. The BKA probably believed the raid would intimidate the Archive's employees into abandoning their work. The opposite happened. The totally haphazard raid on the Gene Archive in Essen not only made the Archive famous nationally and internationally, but also made the police's hysteria – grounded in the Federal Republic of Germany's fight against terrorism during these years – seem ludicrous. The BKA was forced to release the Archive's employees quickly and return the confiscated material (see Gen-Archiv, 1988). The Gene Archive continued its work and still exists today. Numerous students use the Archive in their research and their Master's and Doctoral Theses.

and reproductive technologies, relying in particular on 'science' as the source of all truth. The only party to side with us and clearly reject genetic engineering and reproductive technologies was The Greens Party. They also helped to finance our Congress in 1985.

But money was our least concern. All feminists back then knew that one could rely on sisterly solidarity. It was considered natural for conference participants from outside town to find a place to sleep in the home of a woman living in the area. Travel costs were paid wherever necessary, fees very rarely. Our meetings were understood to be political gatherings and not academic conferences. This understanding also influenced our meetings' methodology. It was all about first informing and mobilising one another, and second, about planning actions. It was not about competition among female scientists and researchers.

Both the German Congress and the FINRRAGE 'Emergency Conference' in Sweden in 1985 were successful because they gave the impetus for establishing many women's groups all over the world to fight developments in genetic engineering and reproductive medicine. The fact that we now had a network that received information from across the globe – which would otherwise have been impossible had we limited ourselves to relevant sources in Germany – clearly justified our endeavour to organise our campaign as *an international movement*. We were also correct in questioning the barriers between individual scientific disciplines so that biologists, medical doctors, sociologists, housewives, workers, unionists, political scientists, economists, psychologists, educators and theologians could cooperate on research and communicate with each other. This movement created something that had always been demanded but never achieved until then: *true interdisciplinary work on the basis of a common concern.*

The success of this movement was not only visible in Germany but even more so on the international level. As of 1985, our FINRRAGE network organised major annual international meetings in various countries where feminists were willing and able to organise such a meeting logistically and with enough expertise. Around this time FINRRAGE existed in over thirty-five countries. International FINRRAGE conferences took place in Spain, Australia, Brazil, and twice in Bangladesh (see www.finrrage.org).

The search for a new science

At these conferences, so many high-quality and original papers were presented that we decided to publish them in our own scientific journal *Reproductive and Genetic Engineering: Journal of International Feminist Analysis*. It was published by Pergamon Press in England and existed for many years. When, due to financial difficulties, Pergamon Press cancelled our contract (and went out of business), our journal ceased to exist.

As successful as our feminist resistance was, we could not overlook the fact that the scientific community, the mainstream media and even politicians – excluding The Greens Party – almost completely ignored it. These circles did not consider what we were doing as scientific and serious work. First, because we did not follow the rules of an allegedly 'objective' science, and second, because we were women. Everything women did at that time was considered biased in principle, emotionally laden and therefore not objective or scientifically based. Women working in universities were often faced with this general prejudice which even existed in the heads of many of those men who finally came to realise the dangers presented by gene technologies, and as a result established their own movement, such as the Gene-Ethic Network (Genethisches Netzwerk) in Berlin. It took many years before they were willing to consider reproductive technologies with the same seriousness as the issue of genetic engineering in agriculture.

Moreover, the raid on the Gene Archive in Essen in December 1987 made us all realise that our radical critique of genetic engineering and reproductive technologies was not only seen as undesirable but even considered 'dangerous'. One of the reasons for this was that many of us refused to take part in the numerous discussions on the 'pros and contras' of gene technologies which were organised at that time. Ours was a very clear and well-grounded position *against* these technologies. As the Gene Archive put it:

> Reducing the question of ethics to the sphere of application or non-application of scientific results spells the bankruptcy of ethics. This reactive form of ethics will always helplessly chase behind the work scientists produce, and try to limit its most harmful effects, as is the case with [Germany's] Parliamentary Ethics Commission on Reproductive Technologies (translated from Mies in Fässler, 1986b, pp. 214–215).

When the argument is accepted that technology can do everything, when there is no longer any need to question the natural sciences, and when there is the obligation to *do* whatever is possible *because it is doable*, then inevitably an instrument is needed to justify any further steps. Bio-Ethics was the name of this new instrument.

I learned a lot from these movements and by my participation in them. Although I am not a natural scientist or a medical doctor, I came to realise that these so-called life sciences would have a deep impact on every aspect of our lives – especially those of women – and change them fundamentally. I understood in particular that these 'life sciences' *had* to be problematic in principle because questions of ethics and of morality play absolutely no role in research but only become relevant to the industry *after* developing products that are 'ready to be put on the market'. Politics circumvent the issue by appointing ethics committees to decide whether a genetic innovation should be applied or not. The result is that the market, or rather economic interests, decide whether products are accepted or not. Scientists shirk their responsibility by researching and experimenting unrestrictedly, and then claiming that the decision to apply any new, genetically manipulated product or procedure, should be left to policy makers. Policy makers for their part hide in turn behind the authority of scientists and ethics commissions.

When Professor Starlinger, a geneticist at the University of Cologne, held a lecture at the Fachhochschule Köln (University of Applied Sciences, Cologne) on the promises and risks of genetic engineering, I asked him whether he could imagine himself at some point reacting like the nuclear physicist Robert Oppenheimer. After the first atomic bombs had been dropped over Hiroshima and Nagasaki, Oppenheimer said he wished they had never discovered nuclear fission. When I asked Mr Starlinger if he at some point might regret discovering the technique of gene splicing, he answered, "Well in order to regret it, we will have to have done it in the first place." This sentence clearly expressed to me the complete bankruptcy of dominant science.

But in contrast to the beginning of the women's movement, I realised here that this science not only excludes women and subjectivity, but that it *must* be without morality as a matter of principle, at least in its fundamental research, also because of its postulate of value neutrality. Morality and ethics are only allowed to play a role in the *application* of scientific research. The Gene Archive was correct in its assessment that ethics only legitimises whatever already exists. Prospective ethics has no role to play in fundamental research.

The better I understood the connections between industry, economics, biotechnology and politics, the more I began to realise the shared interests of large corporations and science. I began to understand that I would have to take a deeper look into the economic motivations behind biotechnology. Capitalist thinking not only determined the goals of genetic research but also those of science itself.

After I read an article written by Lori B. Andrews, "My Body, My Property" (1986), I understood that women had now to learn that their body – and all of its parts – are to be considered their property. They should learn to view their body parts solely according to economic criteria in order to sell them or rent them. In reply, I wrote the essay "From the individual to the dividual: in the supermarket of 'reproductive alternatives'" (1988).[2] This new deconstructive or analytical thought connected with the capitalist goal of profit maximisation, to free people – especially women – from sickness, poverty and childlessness. Ultimately, this thought cannot bring profit without violent invasion (into nature, the female body or a foreign country). *Violence* is therefore also necessarily connected with this 'science' (Mies, 1987c).

With this realisation, a very important dogma held by the old as well as the new women's movement collapsed for me: that women's emancipation and *self-determination* over our bodies would be established by particular *technological* innovations such as the pill or reproductive technologies, as Shulamith Firestone and others (e.g. Simone de Beauvoir) believed. In my essay, "Self-determination – The End of an Utopia?" (Selbstbestimmung – Das Ende einer Utopie? 1989), I critically addressed the assessment of modern technology as an instrument of women's emancipation.

Critique of technology

I learned that the Left, even Marx himself, expected all of human progress to be the outcome of technological innovations, to be precise, as the result of the development of productive forces. However, my experience – and that of many other women – taught me, especially through my research in India, that technological innovations did not fundamentally change the patriarchal man-woman relationship. On the contrary. Modern methods of prenatal diagnostics in India and also later in China resulted in the deliberate abortion of female foetuses. It was not until the Indian women's

---

2 It was first published in German under the title "Vom Individuum zum Dividuum, oder: Im Supermarkt der käuflichen Körperteile" (1987b).

movement protested this misogynist practice that it became public and was banned there. Today India and especially China suffer from an acute lack of women. And female foetuses continue to be aborted and are now even sold for the stem cell industry.

I continued being active in the movement against genetic engineering and reproductive technologies, especially against the *patenting* of all life forms after I had come to understand that the genetic manipulation of plants, animals and people was necessary to feed Capital's insatiable hunger for growth. Scientists develop the know-how and the reasons for making this technology necessary. At a conference, one young male geneticist countered my critique of the patenting of life in this manner, "If there are no patents for genetic innovations who would want to continue researching genetic engineering?"

Outraged about putting patents on all living things, I wrote the following song for a street action in Cologne:

Get yourself patented!
(Melody: Beethoven's Ninth Symphony)

1. Get yourself patented
   don't forget you're Capital.
   All your limbs and all your organs
   and of course your genes as well.
   Get yourself patented
   you're the only one of a kind
   Ere the multis cut you up
   have first choice and peace of mind.

2. Genes, genes and patents,
   it's the greatest, newest thing.
   The highest yield for your retirement,
   live the life of the mightiest king.
   Every creature great and small

Every plant and bird and tree
all things have a market value
all things are commodities.

3. Merck, Monsanto, Ciba Geigy
   Hoechst and Bayer play the game,
   on the prowl for fixing patents,
   on the run for money gain.
   Oh these grand and newest mothers
   give us food and heal our hurts.
   As long as money keeps growing
   we don't need our human hearts.

4. Isn't this life beautiful
   nothing happens naturally.
   Women don't bear children,
   no, they're made in a lab'ratory.
   Nature is no longer needed
   in this eternal vale of woe.
   Technology is our Mother
   and our Father Mr Capital.

5. What use is there living a life
   spent in eternal monotony.
   Look, your genes are quite immortal
   once they're freed of your body.
   Freedom for your genes to live
   yes, in a sperm bank happily.
   What great and exciting progress,
   thanks to global companies.

Maria Mies, Cologne, 1996
© Common Intellectual Property of People with Resistance
Genes (CIPPRG)

Children or no children?

Sometimes I was asked whether I, being so passionately committed to fighting genetic engineering and reproductive technologies, had ever wanted to have children. And my young niece Eva once asked my mother, "Why doesn't Aunt Maria have any children?" My mother answered, "Maria wants to be free."

Children or no children? For all women this is a very decisive and existential question. I am a woman. I can bear children. But I am also a political woman engaged in fighting the exploitation and oppression of women.

When in 1968 I began at the age of thirty-eight to study sociology in Cologne, I immediately became involved in the new women's movement. The campaign against §218 – the German law under which abortion was a criminal offence – was the first major campaign organised by the nascent women's movement demanding the freedom for all women to decide whether they wanted to have children or not. As in many other countries, tens of thousands of women took to the streets in Germany and called for the abolition of the abortion law. They organised demonstrations and shouted slogans like, MY BODY BELONGS TO ME! or CHILDREN OR NO CHILDREN IS SOMETHING WE ALONE DECIDE!

I took part in all of these demonstrations and shouted the same slogans. I shared the women's outrage over the way the churches, governments and economy used children as believers, soldiers and workers. No government, no church, no male had the right to decide whether a woman should have a child or not. But what about me? What was my answer to Eva's question?

First, I had never been directly confronted with having to decide whether I wanted children or not. Although I had been in love with men, I had always kept them at a distance. I wanted to remain free, as my mother said. But I would never have been able to have an abortion. I would never have been able to end a pregnancy. In fact, in German we describe a pregnant woman as one who 'is in good hope' (guter Hoffnung sein). An embryo is not a cancerous growth, neither is it a 'vegetable' or just a bunch of cells, as many gene and reproductive engineers claim. However, I would never condemn a woman for having a termination; no woman aborts a pregnancy lightly.

Had I become pregnant I would have gladly raised a child – by then I had the economic means to do so. Once reproductive technology appeared, there were many women who desperately wanted to have children and who were willing to allow 'technodocs' to fabricate a child for them. I would never have considered this an option. I did not need a child of 'my own flesh and blood' in order to feel like a real woman. I was and still am very satisfied with my life, even without a child 'of my own'. I love children and there is so much to be done to create a world in which children, women – and ultimately also men – will be able to live a *good life*. This was the reason – and is still the reason – for my battle against patriarchy and capitalism.

Successes and Conflicts

The Congress on *Women against Gene and Reproductive Technologies* organised in Bonn in 1985 was a huge success because it kicked off a broad and multi-facetted women's debate on the issue. It was also a financial success for us as the editors of the journal *beiträge zur feministischen theorie und praxis*. In preparation for the Congress we had published an issue called "Women between selection and elimination" (Frauen zwischen Auslese und Ausmerze, 14/1985). 'Selection' and 'elimination' were the terms used by the Nazis to eliminate people who supposedly threatened the 'purity' of the Arian race: those with hereditary disabilities, etc. Copies of the journal sold at the conference like fresh hot buns. There was no doubt about it: the women's campaign against genetic and reproductive engineering was a success story, nationally as well as internationally.

However, I do not want to conceal the fact that it also led to bitter conflicts among us women.

For the first time, the sale of our *beiträge* journal brought in a great deal of money. Until then, we as the editorial team had to advance the money to cover the cost of printing. We had all agreed to common rules: work on the journal was to be done on a voluntary basis. Only the woman working in the journal's office was to be paid a salary. The cost of rent was to be covered by the sale of the journal and by the membership fees from all the women members of the 'Association of Sociological Theory and Praxis for Women' (Verein für Sozialwissenschaftliche Forschung und Praxis für Frauen). The journal was the organ of this association. I also made the suggestion that we request all women members who had a regular income to make ongoing donations. Those who could afford to do that were primarily feminist professors working at universities.

This mixed financial plan had worked smoothly from 1978 until 1985. The woman who worked in the office was responsible for the bookkeeping, subscriptions and the journal's correspondence. She was also a member of the editorial team and took part in our discussions on planning the issues, selecting papers, and editing the texts. And in return, the whole group helped to mail out the issues. We rejected any differentiation between intellectual and organisa-tional/physical work. All of us were there to share all the work.

This went on perfectly well for eight years. We had practically no money. Although our publication had quickly become popular as the first journal in Germany to cover feminist theory and praxis, income from it was minimal. The success of our Congress against Gene and Reproductive Technologies in Bonn in 1985 was the turning point. A direct consequence of our sudden 'glut of money' was that the woman taking care of our office demanded a pay raise. She wanted to be paid a sum equivalent to the second highest tariff in the German civil service pay scale. We discussed this in the editorial team. The majority supported the new pay scale; I was against it. The majority argued that we – the team of editors – were *employers*. I could not accept this argument. I had nothing against the fact that the woman in our office wanted more money. What I rejected was the fact that our joint feminist project which so many women in Germany had worked on for many years with so much enthusiasm – all without any claim to being paid – was now to be divided up according to the capitalist manner into a class of 'employers' – meaning capitalists – and 'employees'.

Because an agreement was not possible I requested the issue to be addressed at the next general meeting of the 'Association for the Sociological Theory and Praxis for Women'. Furthermore, I wanted us to ask all the other donors as well because I was afraid our spontaneous windfall of money would not flow with the same intensity in the future. Again, a majority of the editorial team rejected this. They claimed the editorial group was 'autonomous' and capable of deciding financial issues by ourselves. Besides the 'class split', this new concept of autonomy was an additional shock for me.

The third shock was that a majority of the editors demanded that I, being outnumbered, bow to majority rule. And with that collapsed the entire political, grass-roots democratic concept I had understood to be the policy of our journal: dissolving the division of labour between intellectual and physical work; collective control over our finances; the principle of consensus. Instead we now had majority rule – and the cancellation of the journal's principle of democracy 'from the bottom up'. From a practical standpoint, we were now at a point where nothing separated us from the usual journal business of patriarchal capitalism.

News of our conflict spread to the rest of the women's movement in Germany. Few women knew my position, nor understood it. I had little interest in carrying the conflict out in public, especially because of the statements that were made about me, "Maria Mies, civil service employee and a professor, does not want to give an unemployed woman a raise in pay." The situation became increasingly unbearable.

Because the majority of the editorial group reduced the conflict to the sole issue of money and did not want to discuss my political objections, dialogue became impossible. I began to lose sleep and my creativity diminished. The journal was my most important feminist project, my 'dearest baby'. I saw no other alternative but to quit the editorial group, which I did in May 1986.

In March 2008, the *beiträge* ceased to exist. Heide Oestreich wrote in *die tageszeitung* on 22 February, 2008:

> No more *beiträge zur feministischen theorie und praxis*. After 30 years the autonomous feminist movement's oldest journal has made a quiet exit. It was the child of the women's movement. It carried out its conflicts. And now it has gone into retirement, like many of the protagonists of the women's movement.

The *beiträge*, however, did not just go into 'retirement' or cease its activity because of dwindling subscriptions. Rather, the editors had much earlier begun to uncritically accept the dominant, primarily academic feminist discourse – whether it was postmodern feminism or gender mainstreaming. Over the years my 'dearest baby' increasingly lost its initial movement-oriented radical stance.

I have often contemplated the relationship between success, conflict and defeat. I also noticed similar processes affecting other feminist projects and foundations, and ultimately also other social movements which had developed 'from below' out of disgust and outrage over unbearable social conditions. First, I thought that money was the culprit: corroding initially enthusiastic collaborative groups and substituting the originally successful egalitarian cooperation with competition, majority rule, the formation of a leading clique and finally a change from its original radical goal-setting. Later, I understood that although money was a very important aspect, it was not the only factor in reverting social initiatives or movements to familiar hierarchical structures. Besides competition for money and material things, it is primarily the desire for *visibility*, greater *publicity*, *reputation* and *prominence* on the part of individual group members that destroys the initial enthusiasm. Larger movements are also affected by the public media which plays a decisive role in the process of 'normalisation and acceptance' that initiatives and movements questioning the system undergo.

The fate of The Greens Party in Germany is an excellent example of this process: a party defining itself as a 'non-party' with the goal of retaining its radical egalitarian and ecological goals, once it entered parliament, ultimately turned into a 'normal', even opportunistic political party. The media, in particular television, almost completely focussed its attention on Petra Kelly and the 'wild sponti' Joschka Fischer. It also quickly set them apart, viewing them as the party's 'speakers' and informal leaders, resulting in major tensions within The Greens Party. The inner-party conflict was 'solved' by Petra Kelly's murder on the one hand, and by Joschka Fischer undergoing a process of normalisation.

The German women's movement in the 1980s shied away from taking part in this process of institutionalisation. We wanted to retain our radical, pacifist, anti-patriarchal, anti-capitalist goals as well as our grass-roots democratic organisational structure. At least many of us felt this way, myself included. Others who wished that the women's movement would develop more stability and continuity, made fun of what they called our 'mushroom culture': if one of the women stuck her head a little above the many others it was immediately felt to be an infraction against the movement's principle of equality and, before you knew it, that head was chopped off. Other countries call this 'The Tall Poppy Syndrome'.

I understood my conflict with the *beiträge* to be a result of this mushroom culture. The women's movement back then had a very mechanistic concept of equality. Because of this, we were not able to recognise the *unlimited diversity among women* worldwide as our strength and, as a consequence, we were incapable of using it in a positive sense for our movement. *Differences* were increasingly perceived as a threat. This trend intensified when, under the influence of the new French philosophy and 'French Feminism' (made in the USA!), the difference theory and constructivism[3] found their way into the German women's movement discourse.

---

3 According to this philosophy, the cause of all evil was not due to colonialism, class exploitation and patriarchy, but to the differences between people. It argues that human identity is constructed differently according to sex, culture, race, sexual orientation and education.

12

From the Women's Peace Movement to Ecofeminism

In the course of the new women's movement many women, including myself, had come to the understanding that the 'women's question' – or the relationship between women and men – was the most comprehensive and profound problem of our society. There was no societal question that did not touch this problem in some way. As a result, the women's movement had to address *all* important societal issues whether it liked it or not.

One of these problems concerned NATO's decision in 1983 to deploy nuclear cruise missiles in West Germany directed at 'the enemy to the east'. These cruise missiles were later followed by Pershing II missiles. A very powerful anti-nuclear peace movement developed in West Germany, in Europe and in fact in the entire Western world from this opposition to NATO's double-track-policy. The women's movement was an important part of this movement. In November 1981, three thousand feminists circled the Pentagon in the United States and wove a web around it, demonstrating that women and their worldwide 'network' were more capable of making peace than the US Defense Department with its nuclear weapons. In England, 30,000 camped in front of, and blocked the entrance to, the compound in which cruise missiles were stationed in Greenham Common.

In 1983, in Wiersdorf near Bitburg and in Wünschheim (Hunsrück), West German feminists organised a resistance camp in front of two central military cruise missile test bases for Europe. Each summer, women gathered there and planned actions at the bases and discussed the link between militarism and patriarchy, between day-to-day violence against women and war, between "love relationships and intermediate-range missiles" (as Helke Sanders called it), between patriarchy and capitalism, imperialism and nuclear war, between nuclear weapons and environmental destruction.

An Italian woman summarised our analysis in this way:

> Those who rule are once again tinkering with bringing our world to an end. Their lust for destruction is the epitome of the centuries-old male principle of power and violence, of a system that has been built on competition, struggle for achievement, oppression, power-seeking, exploitation of humans and nature, and ruthless and irresponsible technology. The system in itself is the real danger to women.
>
> We experience this destructive violence in a war machinery that not only takes the form of intermediate-range missiles, but also the form of rape, not only the form of shrapnel but also of beatings, not only the form of a destroyed environment, but also of subtle oppression (paternalism and men's exercise of power, discrimination). We are being forced to support this system by our service in offices, schools, factories, the health system and in families... (quoted from a leaflet distributed at the Hunsrück camp).

The knowledge that women all over the world were standing up against this destructive system gave us strength, courage and incredible creativity. The camp's call to action closed with the words, WE WOMEN CANNOT BE STOPPED!

I took part in the Hunsrück resistance camp in the summer of 1983 and I remember the wonderful atmosphere at this camp. At first I could not believe that we would actually succeed in entering the missile base to occupy it with our banners. The area was sealed off by a high and impenetrable fence, the gate was guarded by US soldiers. But on a date previously agreed on we suddenly found ourselves on the base. To this day I am not sure how we got there – whether through the fence or the gate. As if by some sleight of hand, we occupied the compound with our banners, shouted slogans and sang our songs. I particularly remember one song we had learned from the Greenham Common women, "You can't kill the spirit! She is like a mountain – old and strong – she goes on, and on, and on . . ." This song has stayed with me for many years.

These camps were not only places where women actively resisted the greatest military power in the world. They also functioned as an open-air university in which we listened to lectures on the dangers of nuclear technology, on the connection between militarism and violence against women, and where we discussed the destruction of our natural environment, of our base of existence. At the Hunsrück camp, the many reports from across the world taught me what *ecofeminism* meant.

I also took part in various activities organised by the women's peace movement, such as those by Zita Termeer. In one such event on 17 October, 1983, we planted an apple tree, a rosebush and a grapevine and sowed winter grain in front of the famous Cologne Cathedral. With this action we wanted to demonstrate that life does not come from missiles, nuclear reactors or from computers, but that humans, and especially women, continuously create life in cooperation with nature. The West German radio station WDR reported live on our action. Like many of the symbolic events organised by the peace movement, our activities also heightened people's awareness of the dangers of nuclear technology. However, they did not lead to a change in government policy or to the reversal of NATO's double-track policy.

On the contrary, the missiles were deployed in Germany under Chancellor Kohl's Christian Democratic government, and a number are still stationed near Büchel in the Eifel today.

The contradiction between our high goals on the one hand and our virtual powerlessness in the face of 'Realpolitik' on the other, led to intense controversy within the women's movement. In 1983, we published issue number eight of the *beiträge zur feministischen theorie und praxis*. It was called, "Against Which War – For Which Peace?" (Gegen welchen Krieg – Für welchen Frieden?) This issue contained most of the controversial points being discussed within the women's movement then. For example, Christina Thürmer-Rohr addressed the commonly held opinion that in wars, women were always only victims. She introduced the idea of women's *complicity* into the debate. In another essay, Theresa Wobbe highlighted the economic motivations behind the post-war East-West conflict and war-mongering. And Ulrike Schmauch, in her essay "Self-Critical Thoughts on Women's Peace Activities" (Selbstkritische Überlegungen zu Frauenfriedensaktionen), accused the women's movement of hiding behind women's alleged peacefulness and shying away from demanding that men:

> ... confront the issue of male violence as the basis of military structures and wars. They must finally shoulder their portion of critique and self-critique so that we as members of the women's movement may partially relinquish our female role as accusers and our fixation on male violence, as well as our one-sided responsibility and anger (Schmauch, 1983, p. 116).

Moreover, as a means of demonstrating women's power, there was serious debate about whether a general women's strike should be called which would include a stop to all housework. And Alice Schwarzer, the editor of the journal *EMMA*, suggested that women should enter the combat forces. She argued that unless women have access to the same instruments of violence, meaning weapons, they could not hope to be taken seriously by men.

I myself wrote an article on this issue and also addressed the contradiction that while we may reject all wars in our country, we at the same time supported the so-called Third World's wars of liberation – such as in Vietnam, Cambodia, Zimbabwe, Nicaragua and others. We considered women's participation in these wars as justified. In the article, I analysed the political and military role played by women, and questioned why women, called upon to leave their traditional roles to take up arms alongside men to fight for their country's liberation, after these wars, were – and are – expected to go back to their traditional roles as wives, mothers and housewives. Women continue to be stuck with 'reproduction' as in earlier times. A change in the *division of labour* between women and men has not taken place. Men, for instance, are still not really called upon to carry out housework. Nor do they do it in great numbers. An analysis of these historical contradictions led me to undertake a renewed critical examination of the theoretical basis of socialism with respect to women's issues. I came to the conclusion that not only *capitalism* but also real *existing socialism* – as presented to us by the German Democratic Republic (GDR) – had failed to do away with patriarchy, and in fact had established a *new socialist patriarchy*. Hence I began to question the dominant socialist theory of revolution. It was not enough to struggle for political power only. A totally different economy and relationship between the sexes had to be developed. And this was a task for men as much as for women (Mies, 1983c, p. 78). I refused to accept women's liberation as purely concerned with 'women's issues'. It was very clear to me that women *and* men had to work toward changing their relationship, and that men in particular still had not begun to do their 'homework', whether in capitalist or socialist countries.

In response to Alice Schwarzer's absurd demand for women to join the combat forces, we organised a protest demonstration on Cologne's

Neumarkt Square. Our slogan was, WOMEN IN THE ARMY? WE SAY NO! After her remarks on this issue in *EMMA* I could no longer take her seriously. What kind of liberation is it that allows women to be as stupid as men? War never was – and never will be – a solution for any social problem.

Many of the women of the autonomous women's movement thought the same as me. The following is a report on two of the women who were working with great dedication in the women's peace movement for a long time.

Zita Termeer

Even before the cruise missile policy became an issue, autonomous feminists were warning about the dangers of nuclear technology, even in its peaceful form. In 1978, the women's magazine *Courage* and the Cologne Women's Bookstore organised the conference "Women against Nuclear Technology and the Military". At this conference, Helen Caldicott, a paediatrician from Australia, spoke of the dangers in particular to children and infants posed by nuclear technology. Petra Kelly, an environmental activist who later became a founding member of The Greens Party, pointed out the connection between the allegedly peaceful and military use of nuclear technology.

Zita Termeer – at that time sixty years old and mother of six daughters – also took part in this conference. Zita was, and still is, someone I look up to. I admire the way she lived her life and how she fought for her independence against all odds, finally finding her place in the women's movement. She had read Holger Strom's documentation *Peacefully Into Catastrophe* (*Friedlich in die Katastrophe*, 1977). She was so shocked and upset by it that she wanted to do something about the nuclear threat. At the conference she told us she had a vision. She wanted to organise an anti-nuclear bus with other women and drive around the country to inform people of the dangers of nuclear technology in all its forms.

In the political atmosphere existing in the women's movement during that time, 'visions' like Zita's were not only discussed at conferences but acted upon. Women were enthusiastic about her idea and later, when the results from individual working groups were presented, one woman spontaneously stood up and said she would immediately go around and collect money so that Zita could begin. Three other women immediately said they wanted to collaborate on her anti-nuclear bus project.

Their first trip started at Easter in 1980. Equipped with a station-wagon donated by Zita's daughter, their goal was to reach the town of Gorleben where an international women's demonstration was to be held in protest of a planned disposal site for nuclear waste. The station-wagon was decorated with stickers and carried a big sun mounted on its top. On their way, the women stopped in cities and villages to inform people that none of the operators of nuclear reactors knew how to dispose of the poisonous nuclear waste capable of contaminating humans, animals and the entire environment for thousands of years, and that nuclear reactors can be used to produce nuclear bombs. Even today, no one has found a solution for getting rid of the nuclear reactors' highly radioactive waste.

In the course of time more women joined the project; in the end there were twenty-two. Eventually they drove in a minibus around the country to support all the local anti-nuclear groups involved in organising protest events in front of nuclear reactors or nuclear reprocessing plants somewhere. Zita and her women's anti-nuclear bus were a leading force in the anti-nuclear and peace movement of that time. She often appeared in the media. In an interview given in 2000 she wrote:

We drove our anti-nuclear bus to demonstrations and Easter Protest Marches. We collected signatures in support of the peace movement's 'Krefeld Appeal' which demanded that the Federal Government not allow intermediate-range missiles to be deployed [in Germany]. Resistance was so great that it could have been prevented (translated from Stolzenberg, 2000, p. 204).

What impressed me the most about Zita was the courage with which she carried out real public education throughout the country. She was neither a member of a party, a union or some other large organisation that would have protected her. She also did not belong to the group of most prominent anti-nuclear women activists who organised a sit-in at the Pershing II missile base in Mutlangen near Stuttgart. She was an ordinary housewife, mother and citizen.

I particularly admired how she dared to bring up women's issues in all of her activities, pointing out the connection between war, the nuclear arms race, militarism and violence against women. She writes how this led to controversial discussions again and again, even among both female and male friends in the peace movement. She, like many of us younger feminists, was often told, "Nuclear war threatens all of us, men and women alike. So why make it into a special women's issue?"

Ellen Diederich

Ellen Diederich was not only involved in all the major women's peace movements, but also in many other protest movements. In 1987, she participated in the major conference "Women against Nuclear Technology and the Military" mentioned above. Earlier in the 1980s, she had taken part in the huge women's peace march from Copenhagen to Paris in which nuclear-free zones and cities were demanded. In 1985, she was one of the organisers of the UN World Conference on Women in Nairobi which made women's work and peace central issues. Most importantly, she was offended by Alice Schwarzer who shared the mainstream press' opinion that women should join the army to make it 'more woman-friendly and humane'.

Alice Schwarzer became *the* icon of German feminism. The following are excerpts from the 'birthday greetings' written by Ellen Diederich to Alice Schwarzer published on the occasion of *EMMA*'s Thirtieth Anniversary in 2007.

Under the heading "To *EMMA* on its Thirtieth Anniversary" Ellen wrote:

> Alice Schwarzer to a great extent determines what feminism is today. She is the publicly respected icon of feminism, pinned with the Federal Cross of Merit and other medals of honour, highly esteemed by Roland Koch, Guido Westerwelle [leaders of the conservative Christian Democrats and Free Democratic parties, MM] and *Bild* tabloid magazine. The leading article of the anniversary issue carries the title, '*EMMA*, Alice and Angela. What we have achieved! A woman as the German Chancellor'. The *EMMA* editorial staff goes to Berlin and proudly pose with Chancellor Angela Merkel for a photograph (translated from Diederich, 2007).

On Schwarzer's call for women to join the combat forces, Ellen adds:

> The feminist movement has been split: some of the women support taking part in wars based on their definition of equality. What kind of rights we are to be made equal with, is not questioned. One of the vehement supporters of this is Alice Schwarzer. The founder and editor of *EMMA* titled its issue on this topic, 'Some of Our Best Soldiers Wear Lipstick'.
>
> Equality in the military means participation in war. Women as bomber pilots also drop bombs. What is a 'womanly' bomb drop? Do women pilots spray their bombs with perfume and tie a bow around them before they are dropped? Down below women and children run for their lives and we wave from above signalling,

'This bomb has been dropped by a woman! With best greetings from the rich countries where women have equality.' No, we cannot view this in the context of equality and careers for women. It is necessary to outlaw war as the greatest crime, to refuse to let men or women go to war and, instead, abolish war completely (translated from Diederich, 2007).

On 4 March, 1991, Ellen Diederich founded the Women's Peace Archive in Oberhausen. She understood that women's struggles against war and the destruction of the environment would not even be mentioned by future history writers if the testimonies of the women's peace movement are not collected and documented. The Women's Peace Archive still exists in Oberhausen – due to lack of money it is constantly in danger of being closed down.

In the winter of 1991, the autonomous feminists in Cologne organised regular Wednesday peace demonstrations against the first Gulf War. Our demonstration was not registered. The police left us in peace and even supported us. It was a very cold winter. We kept on marching until the insane US war over oil and American hegemony in the Gulf region stopped.

The 'Men-Question': Between Rambo and the Fairytale Prince

It took more than ten years before 'men's emancipation' became a public issue. This happened in 1994, when The Greens Party section of North Rhine-Westphalia organised a men's conference in Wuppertal with the goal of initiating a political discourse on men's emancipation. I was invited to give the keynote speech. In my address I emphasised that it was not enough to see individual men pushing prams through the park or helping their women do the housework. I said, "What we need is a broadly based political and economic men's movement in which men and women together fight the capitalist patriarchal system as one that is hostile to life. The first task in this process would be for men to publicly attack the militaristic image of manhood."

The applause after my speech was only moderate. In the following discussion, various men said I had spoken 'like a man'. This startled me at first but then I understood: many of those participating thought that men's emancipation meant they needed to take on the soft, so-called 'female' private virtues, meaning they should allow themselves to publicly express their feelings, and that they wanted to learn how to cry on the shoulders of other members of their own and opposite sex and talk about their relationship problems. They wanted to leave the economic and political field because it was the 'hard' and competition-driven domain of men. Was not this what many women and feminists demanded? Was not "the country needs different men" one of their slogans?

And here I was talking about the economy, politics, patriarchy, capitalism and the fight against it – which is precisely what they wanted to leave behind! I realised that many in the women's as well as the nascent men's movement were under a very serious misapprehension: the terms 'male – female' were understood as attributes connected to the biological sex in the dominant dualistic manner. In this context, emancipation means taking over the ascribed gender roles of the other sex, rather than questioning or even eliminating the entire dualistic, hierarchical system of dominance that characterises capitalist patriarchy.

This misconception has brought forth the majority of the problems in establishing programmes to promote *equality* between the sexes worldwide, and in particular it forms the basis of the discourse and policies of today's 'Gender Mainstreaming' (Mies, 2005b). After researching the old and current, bourgeois as well as socialist, women's movements and their goals, I realised that there is no point in just wanting to rise up to the status of men. Marxists had declared class conflict as the major conflict of society. Only after the class struggle had been won, they said, could remnants of the conflict between the sexes – which they called a 'secondary conflict' – be resolved by establishing legal 'equality'. The civil codes speak of equal rights for men and women. But we knew that patriarchy was much older than capitalism. Our hope, however, that the civil and/or socialist revolutions would resolve *die Frauenfrage* (women's question), has not been fulfilled despite all pretence to equal rights and anti-discrimination laws.

I and many other women still ask ourselves: why are women, if they are equal to men, still being exploited, oppressed, discriminated against, beaten, mishandled and raped?

Ecofeminism

When I was writing my first essay on "The Social Origins of the Division of Labour Between the Sexes" (Mies, 1983b), it had already become clear to me that the relationship between men and women in patriarchal-capitalist societies corresponds to the one humans generally have with nature. In both cases, the relationship is characterised by hierarchy, violence and dominance. In the course of our campaign against genetic engineering and reproductive technologies as well as other women's movements actions, many examples confirmed this insight. I remember a statement made by a Russian woman after the Chernobyl nuclear disaster in 1986. She said, "Men never think of life. They only want to conquer nature and the enemy" (in Mies and Shiva, 1993, p. 15). Other women from Sicily who were protesting the deployment of nuclear missiles in their country, made a more explicit connection between male violence against women, and violence against nature and foreign countries:

Our 'no' to war coincides with our struggle for liberation. Never have we seen so clearly the connection between nuclear escalation and the culture of the muscle men; between the violence of war and the violence of rape. Such in fact is the historical memory women have of war ... But it is also our daily experience in 'peace time', and in this respect women are perpetually at war … It is no coincidence that the gruesome game of war – in which the greater part of the male sex seems to delight – passes through the same stages as the traditional sexual relationship: aggression, conquest, possession, control. Of a woman or a land, it makes little difference (in Mies and Shiva, 1993, p. 15).

The Chernobyl catastrophe opened my eyes and those of many other women to these deeper correlations. I was particularly concerned about the fate of women with small children. During this time Marina Gambaroff published a volume of essays called *Chernobyl has changed our lives* (Tschernobyl hat unser Leben verändert, 1986). My essay in this book is called "Who Turned Nature into Our Enemy?" (Wer machte uns die Natur zur Feindin?):

Spring has finally come, everything is green and in blossom, the weather is warm again. But, not visible to the eye, prohibitive signs have been put up everywhere, 'Don't touch me! I'm contaminated.' We can only enjoy the trees, the grass, flowers and salad as voyeurs – as if the whole were a television pro-gramme. But we can no longer communicate with nature as living beings.

… Many women are experiencing this as an attack on their zest and courage for life, as if radioactivity has already seeped into their bodies.

… During fine weather they have to keep their children in the house and continuously wash them; they have to listen to their complaining and entertain them. Those 'responsible' for giving us this technology can easily decree, "Children are not allowed to play in sandboxes". It is not their task to take care of them (translated from Mies, 1986c in Gambaroff et al., 1986, p. 147).

Christel Neusüss, a friend of mine from Berlin who passed away far too early, was particularly appalled by the intellectual blindness of scientists and politicians who had no better idea than to continuously measure the radioactive fallout. "Look, they're measuring the fallout and then eating it!" she cried when politicians, with their wives at their sides, made public demonstrations of buying and eating salad to show how harmless it was.

The vehement protests of women, and in particular of mothers against nuclear technology and its industry were not shared by all feminists. After Claudia von Werlhof published her essay "We Will Not Sacrifice the Life of Our Children to Progress" in the same volume (Gambaroff et al., 1986, pp. 8–24), she was attacked by an *EMMA* writer who called her the 'Chernobyl Mother Beast'. The author accused Claudia of forgetting how much women's emancipation owed to the Enlightenment and technological progress, and that, by criticising technology, she was only following her animal mother instincts.

Later, while attending a conference on 'Chernobyl and the Consequences for Women and Nature', I learned that Japanese feminists had also split on the 'mother' issue. 'Leftist' feminists criticised that mothers had not protested against nuclear technology as *women* but explicitly as *mothers* and that they had organised their own demonstration.

The 'mother issue' made clear that many women, like Simone de Beauvoir before them, came to uncritically view technological progress as an instrument of women's liberation. Simone de Beauvoir's idea of emancipation is based on the understanding that women will continue to be excluded from the cultural achievements of the male world until they can control and master their 'wild' sexual cycles – meaning menstruation, conception, pregnancy, birth. In order to achieve control, de Beauvoir argued that technical methods and instruments are needed as well as a different relationship between a woman and her body, an instrumental one. She must divide herself into two parts: between a controlling and regulating head – the 'human' part – and the 'animal' part, her lower body. Over the past decades, the worship of such an instrumental approach has taken on increasingly alarming dimensions and dangerous forms not only among men, but also among women, especially younger women who are unable to accept their female bodies as a whole.

I began to examine the issue of technology and progress and still continue to do so today. Because of my critique of Simone de Beauvoir's instrumental concept of emancipation it was often claimed I was hostile to technology and progress. This critique intensified as soon as I became involved in the environment movement and began to denounce the Western *model of consumption* as the cause of poverty and environmental destruction worldwide. I published a brochure called, "Liberation from Consumption: Ways Toward an Ecological and Feminist Society" (Die Befreiung vom Konsum: Wege zu einer ökologischen und feministischen Gesellschaft). It was published by a consumer initiative in Bonn (Mies, 1987a). I find that the critique I formulated at that time has become even more relevant today.

"But I want my banana!"

I first presented my critique of consumption at the Cologne conference 'Women and Ecology' organised by Eva Quistorp with support from The Greens Party in 1986. In my speech I outlined the 'Contours of an Ecofeminist Society'. I showed that the Western industrialised nations' model of consumption cannot become a general model if we want to preserve nature for future generations and not exploit the 'Third World' any longer. We would have to reduce our own often damaging and unnecessary consumption. Why, for instance, do we need to import fruit from New Zealand, Chile and South Africa while we can grow good fruit in our own country? Why does everyone living in cities with excellent public transportation systems need a car? I had gotten rid of my car and felt liberated.

These and other statements set off a storm of protest among the conference participants. Many failed to see why women should be required to make yet another sacrifice. "But I want my banana!" a young woman cried out angrily and defiantly. "Like a three-year-old who doesn't want to hear a reasonable argument", I thought to myself. In any case, the sentence burned itself into my memory. It documents the actual dilemma feminists are faced with if their own emancipation is to be coupled with the demand for global justice and an ecological stewardship of nature. Many feel that having one's own car is an essential step towards their emancipation.

Angelika Birk and Irene Stoehr brought the dilemma to a head: in their speech they drew attention to the fundamental contradiction between the logic of emancipation familiar to us since the enlightenment, and the logic of ecology. The first – the logic of emancipation – is based on man's rule over nature, involving the destruction of nature as well as human nature through technology. In contrast, ecological logic is founded on the understanding that we humans, women and men, *are part of nature*. As a result we have to treat it gently and cooperate with it as we do with a living being (Birk and Stoehr, 1987).

The dominant definition of progress, even among women, is based on the logic of emancipation. This means that technological innovations are given the credit for most of the steps leading to women's emancipation, whereas no credit is given to any changes that have occurred in male-female relationships or in the relationship between humans and nature. One of the most popular examples of this is the discovery of the contraceptive pill.

When pondering this contradiction today, I think that even after all these years it has still not been solved. On the contrary, ever since The Greens Party joined the German government as coalition partners with the Socialist Democrats in the 1990s, the illusion seems to have spread that we can continue living in our industrial societies the way we have done until now, and still maintain a healthy and viable nature for generations to come. Faced with the undeniable fact that our earth is undergoing climate change, this illusionary bubble has meanwhile burst. Yet men as well as women have little of the passion left to change the world. Many have accommodated themselves to the way things are.

As already mentioned, in the various actions carried out by the international women's movement, a clear correlation between violence against women and violence against nature emerged. At the same time, a series of ecofeminist books were published in which not only critiques but also new perspectives for the future were outlined.[1] What I learned from these ecofeminist texts was that *everything is interconnected* and that the destruction of nature is as much a feminist issue as are war and peace. Many women felt overwhelmed by this comprehensive view of things. "Do we have to shoulder the whole world? Isn't it enough to keep to women's issues?" they asked. As far as I was concerned, this was not possible for me.

As always, the insights I gained were primarily derived from my practical activities in the various movements. I discovered that women were, and still are, the primary victims of wars and environmental catastrophes and that they are often also the first to offer sustained resistance. The brave women of Gorleben, Wackersdorf and Wyhl[2] have been shining examples of such resistance.

After all of these experiences, I wanted to write a book on 'ecofeminism', but such a book could not be limited to Germany and

---

1 In 1978, Susan Griffin published her book *Women and Nature: The Roaring in Her*. It was followed by a number of trailblazing books in which the domination by men over nature and women was criticised. What impressed me most was Carolyn Merchant's *The Death of Nature: Women, Ecology and the Scientific Revolution* (1980). In this book, Merchant analyses how the rise of modern science and technology could not have taken place if women and nature had not been dominated and exploited.

2 Gorleben was a site for dumping nuclear waste; Wackersdorf had been designated as the site of nuclear waste reprocessing but this was prevented by the anti-nuclear movement. In Whyl, a nuclear plant was to be built but this was stopped by a strong anti-nuclear movement in which women played an important role. The women in Whyl prevented the nuclear plant's construction by sitting in the holes dug out for the building's pillars. They simply sat there and knitted. The excavators could not do anything.

German women. It would have to at least include women's experiences from other countries, especially from 'Third World' countries. After the success of my book *Patriarchy and Accumulation on a World Scale* (Mies, 1986a), the publishers asked me whether I wanted to write a new book. When I met with Vandana Shiva at a World Bank and IMF conference in Berlin in 1988, I asked her if she wanted to co-author a book on ecofeminism. She agreed immediately.

I had met Vandana with her husband Jayanta Bandyopadhyay and their three-year-old son some years before when they visited me in Cologne. They were on their way back from the USA where Vandana had studied nuclear physics and written her dissertation on quantum theory. I gave her my book *Patriarchy and Accumulation on a World Scale* (1986a). As she wrote later, this book opened her eyes to the feminist perspective. Until then she had not been a feminist. She was also not an ecologist. She writes in our joint book *Ecofeminism*:

> In the 1970s, while studying to be a nuclear physicist, I came home rejoicing in a summer training course, feeling 'high' at being part of a privileged minority: the atomic energy establishment. But my sister, a medical doctor, brought me down to earth by revealing my ignorance of the risks of nuclear hazards. As nuclear experts we knew how nuclear reactions occur, but not how radiation affects living systems. The radiation badges and overalls were merely the ritual garb signifying membership of an exclusive club. This sudden exposure to my own ignorance as a budding nuclear physicist left me feeling shocked and cheated and led to my shifting to a study of theoretical physics (in Mies and Shiva, 1993, pp. 22–23).

She received a further shock ten years later when she was pregnant and the woman doctor told her she would have to have a Caesarean section. Having meanwhile become familiar with much of the ecofeminist critique, Vandana could not understand why this operation was necessary. The doctor told her she was too old to give birth 'naturally'. She was thirty. After contemplating the contradiction between 'expert and lay knowledge' she left the hospital delivery room and went to another 'ordinary' hospital where she gave birth to her baby without a Caesarean section and no complications.

Both experiences led her to critically examine dominant science, dominant economic and political practice, as well as the dominant relationship between men and women. Her critique was not only theoretical but was also expressed in her support of many new resistance movements against environmental destruction in India, against the deforestation of the Himalayas – the Chipko movement – and later also against the new economic policies of globalisation, liberalisation and privatisation. She understood herself to be an *activist scholar* and soon became renowned worldwide as a lecturer and author. In 1993, the year our book *Ecofeminism* was published, she received the alternative Nobel Prize.

Although we had quickly agreed on the content and purpose of our joint book, there were problems organising the practical aspects of our cooperation. For example, we had planned to spend two weeks together at Vandana's home in Dehra Dun in order to discuss and work out our book's concept and content. Our meeting never took place. When I arrived in Delhi at the arranged time, Vandana had already left for Orissa to take part in a meeting of peasants who were resisting globalisation policies. We met more or less accidentally at conferences in Europe or on the Indian sub-continent to which we had both been invited. Together with her husband, who was working in Kathmandu in Nepal, Vandana organised a conference on 'Women and Mountain Development' and invited many famous feminists from India, Sri Lanka and Pakistan. I, too, was invited.

At this conference we had more time to talk about our book. It also became clear that Vandana's new occupation with feminism was putting enormous strains on her marriage. Her husband was having great difficulty accepting his wife's new activity. Moreover, her lectures and publications were making her more renowned than him in India and throughout the world. It was not long before the two split up. Later, when we discussed this problem with other Indian feminists, I learned that most 'strong' Indian women who had made a name for themselves and had become more prominent than their men, suffered from the same problem in their marriages. After their divorce, Vandana was forced to fight a long and painful battle to retain custody of her son. She was personally confronted with all the traps of a patriarchal legal system. Again and again she was called to attend further court hearings to defend herself from her husband's accusations that she was not a good mother because she had enrolled her son in a boarding school. Courageously, Vandana did not give up until she received custody.

All of these personal problems had to be solved while we wrote our book. I realised that these are the conditions under which most women around the world still have to work and write. They cannot separate their private and personal lives from their political activities, even if they try. In my introduction to our book I emphasised that the *necessity to combine the personal and the political* is not a disadvantage but rather an enrichment, despite all the difficulties.

13

The International Struggle against Globalisation

Diverse Women for Diversity (DWD)

In November 1996, FAO (Food and Agriculture Organisation) held a World Food Summit in Rome in which plant genetic resources and food security were addressed. In preparation for this Summit, various critical groups and organisations met in Leipzig in June 1996, to agree on a shared strategy for Rome. The title of this preparatory conference was 'In Safe Hands: Communities Safeguard Biodiversity for Food Security'.

Vandana Shiva and I observed that in the discussion on 'food security', absolutely no mention was made of those who, since time immemorial, have been responsible for putting food on the table every single day. This pertained not only to the women involved in the preparation of meals but also to those in the direct production of food. In Africa, 80% of the food production is in the hands of women, in Asia it is 50–60% and in Latin America 30–40%. We decided that women's role in food security must no longer be ignored – neither on the part of the NGOs participating in Leipzig, nor by the FAO itself. In addition, Vandana had observed that the Biodiversity Protocol – accepted in 1992 at the Earth Summit in Rio de Janeiro – had still not been ratified by all member states and that the process had come to a halt. Neoliberal globalisation policies were increasingly undermining the Rio Consensus on protecting and maintaining the earth's bio-diversity. The industrial countries in particular were attempting to secure their control of the so-called Third World's biological diversity through TRIPS (Agreement on Trade-Related Aspects of Intellectual Property Rights which was a part of GATT – General Agreement on Trade and Tariffs). "We have to mobilise women to stop this development," we said.

We formulated the 'Leipzig Appeal for Women's Food Security' in which we made clear that the FAO's planned strategy for abolishing hunger in the world by 2020 through industrial agriculture and global free trade would bring about exactly the opposite, and that women and nature would be the victims of this strategy everywhere.

Our Appeal called for:

- localisation and regionalisation instead of globalisation;
- non-violence instead of aggressive domination;
- respect for the integrity of nature and her species;
- understanding humans as part of nature instead of as masters over nature;
- the protection of biological and cultural diversity in production and consumption;
- men and women to equally share responsibility for food security.

We wanted to create a network that was not only directed to women from the 'Third World' but to all women, so that true solidarity between women from the South and the North would develop. We realised that corporate-led globalisation and its dogma of free trade posed a dire threat to people's livelihood as well as our planet's biological and cultural diversity. We gave our network the name *Diverse Women for Diversity* (DWD).

Vandana and I signed the 'Leipzig Appeal' in June 1996.[1] We sent it to all our friends and acquaintances, as well as to all the

---

1 See DWD's original wording of the Leipzig Appeal in this volume, p. 320.

organisations known to us throughout the world, and requested their support. Between June and November 1996, the 'Leipzig Appeal' was publicised at various events organised by DWD: in September 1996, in San Francisco; in October 1996, at various discussions in the USA; and in November 1996, in Buenos Aires, Argentina.

By the time the Food Summit began in Rome in November 1996, approximately 1000 individuals – men and women – had signed the Appeal, which we submitted to the Summit's panel. The FAO reacted positively to our initiative by taking women's point of view into stronger consideration in its communiqués on agriculture and food security.

Women and food

The FAO's turnaround also came about through other initiatives organised by women. The *Women's Day on Food* at the FAO conference in November 1996 for example may have played such a role. The idea for the FAO Summit to dedicate one day to women alone came from my friend Farida Akhter from Bangladesh who as representative of the organisation UBINIG[2] was an official observer at the Summit and had also taken part in various preparatory NGO conferences. During one of these previous meetings she called me and said "The FAO summit has nothing organised for women. We have to change that." After some considerations we decided to apply for a whole day to be dedicated to 'Women and Food'. Farida submitted the application immediately and demanded that the largest space be reserved to accommodate 500 people.

The organisers of the NGO events were astonished at first, but in the end granted all of our demands. They were pleased to have at least one event organised from the point of view of women. Farida's application for the *Women's Day on Food* was submitted on behalf of our newly founded Diverse Women for Diversity network. As such it

---

2 UBINIG is the abbreviation of its Bengali name *Unnayan Bikalper Nitinirdharoni Gobeshona*. In English it means Policy Research for Development Alternatives.

was DWD's first public appearance. As was often the case, we had no money, no rich sponsors or official associations to support us. But we did have an idea and we had friends – men and women alike – throughout the world. And we knew that many women would take part in the *Women's Day on Food* once they knew it would be happening. As expected, the *Women's Day on Food* was a success. The main hall of Rome's abandoned air terminal was the site of the NGO panel discussions at the FAO summit.

One of the many novel and creative ideas I heard of at that time was that agriculture and food production is not limited to rural areas but can also take place in the city. *Monika Opole* from Uganda introduced her speech on 'Food as Culture' with the words, "I am a weed." She reported that her mother who was from the country, discovered edible plants everywhere in the city and collected and prepared them according to traditional recipes. Monika founded an initiative which collected these 'weeds' to extract and cultivate the seeds again. The group also collected old recipes and passed them on. She explained to us that her entire culture revolves around food – which prompted many women to tell of their own experiences. *Moëma Viezzer* reported on similar activities in Brazil.

These and other examples proved that 'food' is not just a matter of calories but is specifically about cultural relationships, about one's relationships to nature, to a group, to one's own body, to health and well-being. It is about a relationship between 'the wild' and 'culture', between the city and the country. The globalised free trade in plants and animals as raw material for multinational food corporations is not capable of maintaining this relationship, but only of destroying such a holistic approach to food. In the course of the *Women's Day on Food* we discovered what it means to respect and indeed celebrate cultural and biological diversity. Diversity is not only a prerequisite for life on this planet, it is also the source of our joys in life. DWD outlined all of this wonderfully well in various statements.

DWD became an international movement involved in fighting against corporate-led globalisation, liberalisation and privatisation. We were present at all major meetings, we organised our own conferences and workshops, and we published statements on each respective conference theme. As a consequence, many women who had previously never heard anything about globalisation were informed about this new capitalist strategy and were mobilised against it.

After the *Women's Day on Food*, a fourth meeting of the Convention on Biological Diversity was to be held in Bratislava in 1998, at which we wanted to celebrate the diversity of cultures, food and knowledge and make further preparations for the next WTO conference in Geneva. We wanted to send a clear message to those who think the world is just a marketplace and that the diversity of species and cultures are just raw materials for a global economy. We wanted to demonstrate to them that we believe we are members of a global family – and that all species and all men and women have the right to be protected and sustained, that we have the obligation to protect this right for all beings, including those who have been disinherited and excluded from the human community.

In Bratislava, we issued a statement that was read at the Convention on Biodiversity's plenary session. The Bratislava statement contains the core purpose of our international network. Here is an excerpt:

We are women from diverse regions and diverse movements committed to the continuation of the rich and abundant life on Earth. We come from different backgrounds and know our cultural and political history. We believe there are, and should be, limits to human use and appropriation of the Earth and its diverse living beings. We take responsibility for our use of the things of this Earth and demand that all others of our species do the same.

We are moral human beings. We know that we occupy a given time and given space and are responsible for how we live in that time and the condition in which we leave that space for the future. We do not accept distrust, greed, violence, and fear as ways of relating to each other or to other beings. We reject such ways of relating, whether they take the form of negative personal actions, unacceptable products, or structural alliances among transnational corporations and national governments that trade weapons, risk wars, and form free trade treaties and other schemes that roll back hard won social and environmental protections, appropriate and monopolise the living diversity of our planet, and threaten our democracies, our farms, our livelihoods, our cultures, and our communities.

We support Article 8 of this Convention because we recognise that communities have boundaries and rights ... We reject the patenting of life in any form and we avoid those technologies and products that threaten the food security, health and well-being of any living being ...

We recognise and celebrate the diversity and interrelatedness of species, cultures, and ways of knowing. We reject that which does not sustain the diversity of life and culture and so we reject the World Bank, the International Monetary Fund, the World Trade Organisation, the Multilateral Agreement on Investments, and other such agreements and collusions. And we support the Convention on Biological Diversity ...

(Statement by Diverse Women for Diversity to the Plenary of the Fourth Conference of the Parties to the Convention on Biological Diversity in Bratislava on 4 May, 1998).

After Bratislava, this DWD statement was read and made public at various international events: at a WTO meeting in Geneva in May 1998; in October 1998, in Montreal (Canada); at a conference on the TRIPS Agreement in Geneva (Switzerland) in 1998; at the famous WTO conference in Seattle (USA) in 1999; and at a conference on peace and justice in New Delhi (India) in 2001. On these occasions, we did not just reiterate our already formulated principles of biodiversity, but we also endeavoured to take a position on the problems and events that had meanwhile enveloped the whole world. New statements were therefore formulated and publicised for each respective event. Our *Seattle Statement*, for instance, dealt with neoliberalism, the WTO, and food sovereignty in the hands of communities, women and farmers. After 11 September, 2001, DWD organised a conference in New Delhi in which we condemned and rejected the US Government's policies and its planned wars against Islam.

What did Diverse Women for Diversity achieve?

The DWD network was conceived of as an international movement and a joint coalition of women from the South and North. The concern for biological and cultural diversity as the basis of life brought forth a new internationalism which was not inspired and held together by a central committee, worldwide hierarchy or formal structure. DWD was not an NGO, it was not an appendage to a political party, neither was it an association but rather a worldwide movement which sought to preserve the diversity of life, and resist a major global corporate trend towards establishing global monocultures and other monopolies.

The members of this network did not pursue a uniform political-ideological programme. We were all women, but many of us would not have defined themselves as feminists or ecofeminists. But in one way or another we all were against corporate global rule. This did not mean that we were all against capitalism and supported a form of socialism. Some women were Christian, others were humanists, yet others were social democrats or anarchists. Some were lesbians. In the statements we gave out we avoided emphasising our ideological-political differences. We were more interested in what we had in common.

Diverse Women for Diversity in particular considered itself to be part of a worldwide political protest movement against corporate-led globalisation. Those participating in the movement did not limit themselves to academic analyses but took part in the struggle on the streets, where they – as I – learned about the condition the world was in. Many understood themselves to be 'activist scholars' like Vandana and I, who fought within and beyond the universities.

In the South, many rural and urban women were already engaged in resisting the negative effects of global free trade and the WTO: they were fighting against the privatisation of water, the expropriation of communal property, the deprivation of biodiversity through Western pharmaceutical companies, the privatisation of public education and health systems, and in general against the destruction of their livelihoods. In contrast to many countries of the North, the countries of the South (with the exception of Australia and New Zealand), did not have a welfare state which would help victims of robber baron capitalism to absorb its negative effects. Many middle-class women in the North never felt the direct consequences of globalisation.

DWD's internationalism achieved something which major social movements of the past did not: a *horizontal understanding of solidarity*. Solidarity is often understood to be an activity in which those who have more – countries, communities, Northern organisations – support those who have less or nothing, particularly those people and communities from the South. This was – and still is – *vertical solidarity, from top to bottom*. Such an understanding of solidarity often leads to paternalism which in turn makes the recipients react with deep resentment. They do not want to be objects of charity. They insist on maintaining their dignity and independence.

DWD did not fall into this trap. First of all, it was not an aid organisation which had something to distribute. On the contrary, women from the North were more dependent on the solidarity of the women from the South than the other way round. The women from the South and their local experience in fighting to preserve their respective livelihoods, their courage, analyses and conclusions opened the eyes of many women and men of the North to the realities of glob-alisation. My Southern sisters have taught me an infinite amount of things. Their presence at protests against globalisation, the WTO, GATT, WEF, GATS, the G-7 summits, were an inestimable ex-pression of solidarity which gave us all the feeling that we were truly part of a major international movement, of a 'globalisation from below' as I called it later.

Despite the many things our movement achieved in demanding biological and cultural diversity, and despite the great interest DWD provoked in many men and women, I was not blind to the fact that DWD did not reach those people who had not already been sensitised to, or affected by, feminism or ecology issues. The major anti-globalisation forums and networks ignored DWD, even if they did include individual prominent members such as Vandana Shiva. One such example was the *Forum on Globalisation* which was established in the USA in the 1990s. Its initiators believed that the 'gender' aspect could be added to other theories. (The same applied to the NGO meeting 'Planet Diversity' organised in Bonn in May 2008 which hardly took notice of DWD.)

Like many ecofeminists, however, I rejected this additive approach. "Add 'women' and stir" was the sarcastic slogan coined by US feminist Charlotte Bunch in ridicule of the approach. Throwing in the 'women's question', like adding a new ingredient and stirring it around, still did not make the theoretical soup any better. To us, the 'women's question' fundamentally challenged the entire dominant – including the leftist – worldview, as much as the environment issue. As far as the environment is concerned, men and organisations of the left have meanwhile included the ecology into their programmes. But they have not yet done the same with regard to feminist issues. DWD's creative and transformatory potential could not develop completely because many feminists at universities and research institutes had meanwhile gone 'mainstream'. They did not understand why we were fighting the whole gamut of 'globalisation'. Many were beholden to neoliberal, postmodern changes in academia and had been granted research money and/or positions. The media also began to toe the mainstream line and it became increasingly difficult to place critical analyses of neoliberal economic policies in the print media, radio or television. At best, individual prominent women such as Vandana Shiva and Arundhati Roy were, and continue to be, given a say. Their critique of global free trade seems even to be welcome – a bit like adding salt to an otherwise tasteless soup.

Diverse Women for Diversity was not really capable of reaching all women. But it reached many women at the grass-roots level who were *fighting* for their survival and their livelihoods: for the control of water and their food supply, health care, the diversity of species and for their access to land, amongst other vital issues. DWD activities still continue in many countries including India.

14

Out of the Margin:
Against the Mainstream

'Out of the Margin – Into the Mainstream?'

While engaged in our campaign in the 1980s against genetic engineering and reproductive technologies, I had come to realise that the most important agents behind these new developments were not 'politics' and 'science' as such. Rather, the developments were motivated by the *economic interests* of the chemical, pharmaceutical and biotechnology industries which expected growth and profits from these technological innovations. I understood that I would have to examine *the economy and economics* more closely if I wanted to do something against these inhumane and nature-threatening developments.

In June 1993, feminists from Holland organised an international conference on women and the economy in Amsterdam. It was called 'Out of the Margin – into the Mainstream'. The organisers wanted to establish a *feminist* economy by positioning women's economic contributions at the centre of the 'mainstream' and away from the 'margin' where it had been relegated to. In order to give their efforts the appropriate weight, they invited a young American Nobel Prize Laureate for Economics, Gary Becker. In his speech, he explained to the women gathered why they had not been able to fully develop their 'human capital' potential. Armed with statistics and diagrams, he presented them with a graphic picture of how women experience a break in their biographies, arguing that through marriage and child-rearing, women were actually being deterred from developing careers in as streamlined a manner as men do.

This astonished me. Why was it necessary to fly in a male Nobel Prize Winner from the USA to provide us with this insight? It had already been acknowledged and documented years ago at the very beginning of our feminist campaign on housework in the 1970s and 1980s. I looked around me and saw that almost everyone in the room was enthusiastically applauding his speech. Only a few older women were looking as dumbfounded as I was. We later spoke with each other and came to the conclusion that the young women present obviously had no knowledge of our previous feminist struggles with regard to housework and capitalism. As a consequence, Gary Becker's information was actually new to them. This information was given added weight through the fact that a) he was a *man* and b) a Nobel Prize Laureate. It was particularly enraging for us older feminists to realise that our own insights and conclusions only become worthy of public acceptance – even among the female public – when presented by prominent males.

This fact can be observed on a daily basis – for instance with regard to current discussions on 'family' and 'child' policies. I also asked myself why a conference with this particular title was being held in 1993. How were we to understand the term 'mainstream'? Why was it necessary to take women out of their 'women's corner', out of the 'margins' or their 'niche' from where they had fought against patriarchy and capitalism, where they had hardly been taken notice of from a political and economic perspective? Why should women be included in the 'mainstream'? Only later did I understand that the strategy of bringing women into the 'mainstream' had something to do with the general change in the economic policies of the 1980s and 1990s. It

had to do with a shift away from the social welfare state in industrialised nations towards a neoliberal, corporate-led and solely profit-
oriented, global economic system. Women were – and still are – the
optimal, because cheapest, labourers for this system worldwide. And
this model – housewifisation – was now also to be applied to men, as
Claudia von Werlhof had already prophesised in the early 1980s (von
Werlhof, 1983).

The 'mainstream' is therefore nothing other than neoliberal robber
baron capitalism which, by means of its dogmas of free trade
(globalisation, liberalisation, privatisation), is directed at erasing all
regulations that earlier generations had set up to safeguard against
capitalist tendencies to exploit humans and nature.

The answers provided by most feminists to this new challenge did
not satisfy me. Many saw mainstreaming as a new chance for women
to get jobs. The majority of the women were not even aware that a
'shift' was occurring, because economics had never interested them
much. "I don't know anything about the economy" was a popular
statement many women were heard to make. Others, who did indeed
understand the economy and who were economists, believed that
women would build an entirely different economy based on the care-
taking and nurturing abilities ascribed to them. This economy would
not be ruled by unlimited growth and profit-making; and people –
children, the elderly, women and nature – would not be considered
mere material for exploitation.

I took part in various meetings organised by these feminist economists, but I was disturbed by the fact that they did not integrate a
critique of patriarchy and capitalism, and that their ideas for a new
economy were only focused on women. However, it was impossible
for me to imagine a new economy in which men no longer played a
role and one which was, in fact, a women's enclave. Starting from my
ecofeminist considerations, I realised that we would have to move
beyond current frameworks and create a different economy and
society based on new fundamental principles, based on a new world-

view, and, in particular, based on new relationships: between women and men, humans and nature, rural and urban areas, handwork and intellectual work, young and old, nature and culture and between the different countries on this earth. In short, we had to establish a *new economic and social paradigm*. From then on my slogan became: OUT OF THE MARGIN – AGAINST THE MAINSTREAM.

The 'University of the Street' – The Campaign Against the Multilateral Agreement on Investments (MAI) 1997–1998

I was not an economist. I had studied sociology and not political economy or business administration. However, according to Max Weber, you cannot understand a society without taking a look at its economic conditions. Moreover, through my examination of Marx's 'Critique of Political Economy', my feminist analysis of housework in capitalism, and my research in India, I had realised that the economy is the determinant factor in the formation of social conditions. But this realisation remained relatively abstract at first. It in no way made me a 'feminist economist' – at least not in the usual sense.

I only began to truly understand our dominant economy – real existing capitalism – when in 1997 together with other women and men I formed a small group in Cologne to fight the Multilateral Agreement on Investment (MAI). None of us had any idea what the MAI meant. A feminist friend of mine from Canada wrote to me in 1997, telling me that everyone in Canada was involved in the fight against the MAI. At the same time she sent me a pack of papers which included the draft of the MAI Agreement. At this time the OECD (Organisation for Economic Cooperation and Development) was negotiating the Agreement in Paris behind closed doors. The text was only available in English – a German version did not exist even though Germany was one of the negotiating parties to the Agreement.

When we read the English draft we understood that the MAI would introduce a totally new era of economic development in the world. Renato Ruggiero, the president of the WTO at that time, described the MAI in Singapore 1996 as the 'constitution of a single global economy'. The core aspect of the MAI included opening all national borders to international investment – basically giving foreign investors a blank cheque to do what they wanted in any country of their choice. The agreement called for the 'deregulation' or 'liberalisation' of environmental and labour laws and other regulations to allow major multinational companies free access to all areas of a country's economy. It was not until we began to analyse the wording in the MAI draft that we realised what the old and new neoliberalist free trade doctrine actually meant: it ultimately sought to abolish the welfare state as well as all state regulations of environment policies.

What upset us most about the Multilateral Agreement on Investments was the secrecy and lack of democracy and transparency with which it was being negotiated. Some in our group were unionists and social democrats. They in turn asked their union leaders what they were planning to undertake against the MAI. Their reaction was: no interest. We were faced with the same lack of interest when we took our issue to the print media, television and radio. Most of them knew nothing of the MAI and did not even want to know anything about it. In our edited collection *Licence to Plunder* (*Lizenz zum Plündern*) Claudia von Werlhof and I quoted statements from well-known politicians who expressed the same disinterest and ignorance (Mies and von Werlhof, 1998, p. 7).

It became clear to me that we would not be able to successfully mobilise major organisations to join our resistance. What were we to do, give up? Impossible.

In January 1998, I was invited to attend and speak at a conference in Berlin on the occasion of the anniversary of Rosa Luxemburg's death. This conference was organised by the *Junge Welt*, a Marxist-oriented national daily newspaper. I asked the organisers to grant me some time to inform the plenary on the MAI and its dangers. They refused. Here too, there was no interest. Undeterred, I then approached a few students from Berlin's Technical University who were also attending the Rosa Luxemburg conference. They immediately invited me to come to their university and talk about the MAI. I took the English version of the draft agreement with me and reported to the students gathered there what the Multilateral Agreement on Investments would ultimately mean for a new global economic policy. The students were outraged. They immediately suggested translating the draft into German and law students offered to help them edit it. This meeting kicked off an immediate Anti-MAI Campaign among German students which the Berlin students quickly helped to spread to other German universities.

In December 1998, the member countries of the OECD were to finally vote on the MAI, which would only come into effect if passed by unanimous vote – any dissenting vote on the part of one country would make it fail.

After returning from Berlin, our small 'Committee of Resistance to MAI' (Komittee Widerstand Gegen MAI) decided to organise an international conference to inform the public on the dangers of the Agreement and to mobilise their resistance against it. We invited women and men whom we were acquainted with from all over Germany and the world to speak at our conference, which was titled 'MAI – The Pinnacle of Globalisation' ('Das MAI – Der Gipfel der Globalisierung'). And many came as speakers: Martin Khor from Malaysia, Tony Clarke from Canada, Carla Boulboullé from Berlin, Claudia von Werlhof from Austria. Erik Wesselius from the Corporate Europe Observatory (CEO) came from Amsterdam. The conference was held at Bonn University (see also Hawthorne, 2002, pp. 345–349, for a discussion of the MAI).

As usual, we neither had money nor the time to organise the conference properly. But we wanted to stop the MAI at all costs. Together with students our committee mobilised as much as we could with the means available to us for this conference. Claudia von Werlhof and other women friends in Austria did the same – they quickly established the initiative: 'No-MAI-In-Innsbruck' ('MAI-frei Innsbruck').

When the conference began on 25 April, 1998, about 500 people were gathered in the University auditorium. In our opinion, the meeting was a great success. Yet despite intense media preparation prior to the conference, the German press did not show up, and the major daily newspapers hardly reported our conference. However, there was a great deal of interest on the part of those who had come to Bonn to learn about the MAI and its new economic policies. Because of this we decided to publish a reader on the conference and then a compilation of all the speeches and speakers' analyses as an edited collection *Licence to Plunder* (Mies and von Werlhof, 1998).

The Anti-MAI movement in Germany was the country's first campaign against globalisation. Despite all our efforts and certain successes, it remained a very modest campaign. The movement took on much more momentum in France, Canada and the USA. We were in constant contact with our international friends who sent us material on the movements in their countries. All of this took place without computer and internet. Instead we maintained contact by mail, telephone, fax and, when necessary, during various meetings.

During the final OECD negotiations in December 1998, France and Canada refused to sign the MAI. The French did not want to give up their cultural industry and place it under the control of trans-national corporations. "We don't want to have Mickey Mouse as our next Minister of Culture," the French said. As a result, the MAI failed!

For many this meant the end of the campaign against the Multilateral Agreement on Investments and its global economic policies. However, it remained clear to us that although the MAI might have been stopped at this point, it would pop up under a different name and a different place at some other time. After all we had learned from our international resistance to this new policy of free trade, it was obvious that the MAI represented only the first attempt to transform the dominant economic policies established since World War II in favour of more liberal policies for multinationals, and in favour of less democracy for citizens.

Seattle (1999)

Our friends from the USA, Canada, France, India, and Malaysia saw this in the same light. Martin Khor from Malaysia called upon all activists worldwide to prepare for the next 'Global Player' meeting, namely the WTO's Second Ministerial Conference[1] to be held in Seattle in November 1999. This meeting was already announced as the 'Millennium Round' in which an entire catalogue of regulations for the global economy and world trade was to be passed. These corresponded with the basic principles of the failed MAI agreement with the one difference that all countries of the world would be subject to it and not just the OECD member states.

To coordinate and prepare our resistance, Martin Khor called a meeting in the spring of 1999 in Geneva. He asked all of us whether we thought it would be possible to topple the 'Millennium Round' in the same way as the MAI. We were convinced that the French/Canadian rejection of the MAI was primarily due to our national as well as international resistance movements. Fuelled by this success, we said in Geneva that of course the WTO Millennium Round in Seattle would burst like a bubble. We formulated a statement and distributed it around the world. It was signed by the 'Members of International Civil Society Opposing a Millennium Round or a New

---

1 The WTO was founded in 1995. Located in Geneva, its responsibility is to guarantee countries' observance of the free trade agreements established during the eighth round, the so-called Uruguay-Round of GATT (General Agreement on Trade and Tariffs). The WTO is also responsible for extending and guaranteeing the free trade principles of GATT. It functions according to the unanimous vote principle and organises a ministerial conference of all member states every two years.

Round of Comprehensive Trade Negotiations' (Third World Network, 1999).

I prepared myself for a trip to Seattle. Diverse Women for Diversity had been invited to a meeting on the occasion of the WTO conference in Seattle in which we feminists wanted to make our resistance to the WTO and its globalisation policies public. Vandana Shiva was one of the most prominent opponents of the new free trade doctrine and had continuously criticised this policy from the perspective of the South and of women. I have learned an incredible amount from her on the true character of neoliberalism. In Seattle, we women from DWD organised our own protest meetings and took part in the major demonstrations. Due to the 'Millennium Round' statement, hundreds of thousands of people had become informed of what neoliberal globalisation meant to people and nature on a local as well as an international level. The statement also did its part in making sure that the WTO 'Millennium Round' in Seattle ended in a fiasco and that international opposition to global free trade grew to develop into a 'globalisation from below', as I called it (Mies, 2001).

In November 1999, a huge protest demonstration took place in Seattle. For all those who were there at this time it came as a complete surprise. There had not been as many people demonstrating in the USA since the Vietnam War. Protesters not only came from all over the world – from the South as well as the North – but also included numerous groups, organisations and interests: workers and environmentalists, unionists, socialists, young and old people, church representatives and anarchists, animal rights activists and feminists.

Vandana Shiva later wrote, "Seattle was a historic watershed" (Shiva, 1999). For the first time the self-claimed masters of the world were forced to experience that 'the people' from around the world rejected their policies and fought them. In the end, their acclaimed 'Millennium Round' turned into a catastrophe and broke down without producing results. The protest on the streets was extended into the conference halls. Particularly the member states from the

South realised they were being duped by the economic giants – the USA and the EU. They said, "We're not going to sign anything. This is not democracy" (Mies, 2001, p. 233).

I was truly surprised by our victory in Seattle. Later, I learned that this didn't just happen coincidentally, but was rather intelligently prepared by activists. Some had gone to universities and colleges across the USA to inform young people about what the WTO meant and how to organise creative and non-violent actions. Others had contacted the unions and environmentalists and succeeded in establishing an alliance between these groups.[2] For the first time the interests of environmentalists and workers had been brought together. And for the first time I experienced a new and practical form of internationalism which appeared to have overcome the barriers which had previously divided people. A general feeling of hope and confidence was widespread because of it.

At one of the closing events in a Seattle Church, a pastor said something like, "In the future, whenever global players come together anywhere in the world we will be there to confront them with our protest." He then listed the next global meetings: the World Economic Forum (WEF) in Davos in 2000, a meeting of the World Bank and the IMF in Washington and later in Prague. This was followed by a schedule of G8 meetings and the date of the next WTO Round.

---

2 According to police estimates, 50,000 people came to Seattle to protest against the WTO. According to the activists, there were between 50,000 and 100,000. The demonstration was led by American unionists. More than thirty buses with 5,000 unionists came from Canada. The American Federation of Labor (AFL-CIO) had called out the demonstration and been mobilising support for it since the summer. Tens of thousands of members from the American Steel Workers Union, the Teamsters (truck drivers union), the Longshoremen (dockers union) marched at the front of the demonstration. They were followed by a conglomerate of people and organisations. There were representatives from French and American Farmers' Groups who berated the WTO's agricultural policies. There were environmental organisations such as Friends of the Earth, the Sierra Club, Greenpeace, and many more who accused the WTO of pursuing policies that were a threat to health and the environment. Many groups were representatives from the South. It was an eclectic mix: Zapatistas from Chiapas marched next to American human rights groups and animal rights activists.

The character and success of Seattle's global 'opposition from below' inspired me so much that, upon my return to Cologne, I held lectures on Seattle everywhere and decided to write a new book. After all I had learned from this 'University of the Street' I knew what would be on my agenda for the next few years. It had not only been inspiring to me because of making contact with so many individuals from around the world, being able to demonstrate with them and express my creativity. It was inspiring because together we were able to make a real difference, we achieved something. Moreover, this 'globalisation from below' was a new and exciting experience. This 'University of the Street' taught me about how our economy truly functions. I would never have learned what I learned since 1997 until today, and beyond, in an economics course or from a textbook. Those participating in this international opposition to the WTO and free trade were not just activists travelling from one event to another as our critics claimed. We had to find answers to questions that had never been asked before in this way. Questions such as: how was it possible for the neoliberal shift to occur, why was the welfare state not able to stop it? Why do the people not stand up as a whole and oppose neoliberalism despite the fact that it brings only disadvantages to them? Why have politicians of all parties and unions accepted this 'new' economic policy without resistance, as if there were no alternative – like Margaret Thatcher's 1979 slogan, "There Is No Alternative" (TINA)? What is the connection between neoliberal globalisation and war? What does an alternative to this system look like?"

More work on spreading information about neoliberal policies and its consequences

When the NATO war against Yugoslavia began, followed by the wars in Afghanistan and Iraq, I began to become haunted by the question of why one war after the other was being launched by the world's greatest economic and military power at a time when the Cold War had just become history and the whole world was finally hoping for an era of peace? What did this militaristic boom have to do with globalisation? This and other issues were not only limited to the discussions we had within our own small group, but we published a Newsletter 'Against Corporate Rule and Neoliberal Policies' (*Infobriefe gegen Konzernherrschaft und Neoliberale Politik*).

During our anti-MAI campaign many people asked us where to get information on the developments, agreements and protest movements. As already mentioned, the media was almost completely silent about the issue, politicians as well. It seemed that globalisation and neoliberalism were not yet a public issue. We therefore decided to collect, translate and publish all the information we received from our friends across the world. This meant that men and women who thought the issue was important enough, volunteered their time to work on the project without the support of sponsors, offices and assistants, and without an association or NGO to back them. From time to time we also organised events on topical issues in Cologne.

The number of people who came to these events always amazed me. Obviously, they were looking for a public forum to discuss burning issues since all the other public places in Cologne had been shut down, were privatised or given a different purpose in the course of neoliberalised policies. Cologne's School of Adult Education (Volkshochschule) for instance had basically eliminated all critical and political courses from its programme. The Left was divided. Forced to apply neoliberal cost-cutting measures, universities for their part had degenerated into a place where one merely crammed in and amassed information.

I was able to observe this process of de-politicisation during one of my lecturing tours in the USA. In 1999, students at Cornell University complained to me that their school had become nothing else but a private corporation in which you could not study or discuss anything contradicting the dominant globalisation, liberalisation and privatisation trends. The universities in Germany had also become extensively de-politicised – to the extent that they were no longer the site of any open, critical and creative discourse on the central themes of our time, themes which applied to everyone, students included. It was not until the onset of the anti-globalisation movement that a few groups criticising neoliberal policies established themselves at universities. One of these was the Post-Autistic Economics movement.[3]

It was for this reason that we felt justified in our modest attempt to fill the lack of international information and discuss it in our *Newsletter* (*Infobriefe*). The fact that they have been a success and still exist to date has shown that we made the right decision.[4]

Attac and the Social Forums

The protest against neoliberal globalisation increased with every international meeting, and by the first years of the new millennium it developed into a truly new international social movement. The movement was able to promote the Seattle Agenda to such an extent that the media and politicians could no longer ignore it. However, many felt that our structure and goals were too indistinct and inadequate. We often heard people ask us, "We understand what you are against, but what are you actually for? What are your goals?"

This was the context in which, in 2000, Attac-Germany was founded. Attac is an international network fighting, among other things, for the taxation of cross-border finance transactions and for the regulation of financial markets by means of the 'Tobin Tax', a tax

---

3 The Post-Autistic Economics movement was founded by students of economics at the Sorbonne in Paris. They formulated a manifesto in which they claimed their professors were autistic because they only repeated what the textbooks said and never made reference to other dissident theories or to any topical issues, for instance the topic of the economy and the environment. They called themselves 'post-autistic' economists whose goal was to search for and distribute alternative economic theories. The movement was a success among French students and soon found imitators in England (Cambridge), and finally also in Germany.
4 The *Newsletter* was published four times a year. Besides addressing basic theoretical issues, it also took up topical economic and political problems.

named after its inventor, the economist James Tobin. Attac provided the global anti-globalisation movement with a fixed address and structure. However, Attac's first concept paper retracted most of the radicalism of the protest I had witnessed in the other countries' movements. The paper deliberately avoided describing Attac in terms of anti-globalisation, but rather as a network *critical* of globalisation.

Although our small 'Committee Resistance Against MAI' was not very satisfied with this weakened protest, we still decided to become one of the co-founding groups of the Cologne Attac chapter. Despite our ideological differences, we thought it was important for Germany to have a protest movement against neoliberalism and globalisation which would force the media, labour unions and politicians to take notice of it. However, we retained our autonomous status and continued to publish our *Newsletter* as well as organise our own events.

Feminist Attac

After attending the Amsterdam conference 'Out of the Margin – into the Mainstream' I no longer wanted to focus on women's issues only; rather I wanted to question the neoliberal global 'mainstream'. However, I could not ignore women: again and again the connection between neoliberal globalisation and women's oppression thrust itself upon me. And it was impossible for me to remain silent about it. Moreover, when I was in Seattle in 1999, I noticed that many young women were protesting. I observed the same when I attended the first major Attac conference in Berlin 2000. Many women attended the conference, but hardly any women were on the podium, and the issue of globalisation and women was not even mentioned by any of the speakers, although it was an obvious one.

This hardly seemed to bother the young women present. Some of us older feminists felt reminded of the beginnings of the German student protest movement, in particular of the German Socialist Students' Alliance (Sozialistischer Deutscher Studentenbund, SDS) where in 1969, tomatoes thrown by Helke Sanders in the faces of male comrades were to remind them that humanity is made up of two sexes, one that talks and the other that is silent and serves. During one of the breaks, a few older and younger women came together and decided to establish a women's network within Attac, and to present it as a new working committee to the participants at the end of the conference. Eva Quistorp submitted the request and it was accepted.

Despite this success I had a feeling of *déja vu*. Why is it, that at the start of every new movement involving many women, it is always necessary to bring attention to women's issues by a kind of 'coup d'état'? Why do men still not want to realise that there is a connection between the relationship between women and men and other social issues? Ultimately, Attac's coordinating group was pleased to include a women's network. Later it was retitled *Feminist Attac* according to the Austrian and international model.

I was one of the founding members of Feminist Attac, not least in the hope that we would be able to pass on our feminist critique of capitalist patriarchy to the younger generation and develop it further within the context of the anti-globalisation movement. It did not take long, however, before, sadly, my hopes were shattered, not only because Attac's coordinating group had difficulties dealing with women, but also because younger women found other issues more interesting than the analysis of capitalist patriarchy. They were more on a post-modernist trip and wanted to primarily carry out imaginative actions with other young men. They thought feminism entailed hating men which they rejected.

The Social Forums

Besides Attac there were other protest activities around the world and across Europe which increasingly focused on the various summit meetings organised by the 'global players'. One such summit was the annual meeting of the World Economic Forum (WEF) in Davos, Switzerland. The WEF brings together the economic, political, and cultural elites of the world to discuss future capitalist economic strategies once every year in January at the famous Swiss ski resort. And every year, globalisation protesters have drastically disturbed these meetings in various ways. In reaction, the Swiss government decided in 2000 to implement draconian measures such as police roadblocks and travel restrictions to effectively obstruct WEF protesters from coming to Davos. The major protest events were transferred to Zürich instead.

In preparation, women from the Protestant Church in Switzerland invited other women to attend a meeting in which they were critically informed of the consequences of globalisation, particularly with regard to women. This meeting was organised according to our tried-and-proven principle of combining praxis and theory. We put together flyers and designed a huge banner which we were going to try to smuggle into Davos by January 20, 2000. Although all 'suspicious-looking' persons were detained by the police, our rather conservative-looking Protestant women were able to easily enter Davos. They distributed the flyers in the churches and hung our banner on the market place.

Vandana Shiva, who was invited by the organisers as a critic of the WEF in a deliberate attempt to show how open they were to 'discussion' with dissenters, not only held a flaming speech against neoliberalism, but also went out into the street and continued her denouncement of the WEF there.

Despite these small successes, it became clear to the protesters in Davos that there was little sense in following the global players from one international meeting to another to protest wherever they were at any particular moment. Although the movement against neoliberalism had meanwhile reached millions of people and could no longer be ignored, it had also become impossible to come together at such global meetings to discuss the movement's further goals, strategies and steps. It was therefore decided that forums should be created, called *Social Forums*, which would organise their own events to address the local, national and international critique of neoliberal globalism, and to discuss and develop new perspectives and alternatives.

The first World Social Forum (WSF) took place in *Porto Allegre* (Brazil) in 2001. It was a huge success. In Porto Allegre the slogan was coined, ANOTHER WORLD IS POSSIBLE! This slogan went around the world.[5] It signalled that people no longer wanted to accept capitalist, neoliberal globalisation as the only alternative, in the way the operators of the economy would like them to do: as if it were a law of nature. In Porto Allegre, it was shown that this 'other world' was not only possible, it had already begun. The city's 'participatory budget', in which citizens decide the distribution and use of municipal finances themselves, soon became a model for many similar projects around the world. I was in Porto Allegre and at the World Social Forum in Mumbai, India, in 2004. Ever since the Attac meeting in Germany, it had become clear to me that, although there was minimal consensus among us, there were also grave differences that divided us. An example of this was the statement of principles formulated by Attac in which it distanced itself from those *opposing* globalisation. Attac principally considered and still considers itself to be only *critical* of globalisation. Others, however, adhered to their rejection of globalisation. I was one of them because I could not – and still cannot – conceive of a global economy that is genuinely democratic, participatory, anti-capitalist, environment- and people-friendly. It unavoidably becomes totalitarian as soon as a small power elite at the top is given the power to make decisions affecting the daily life of each individual in the world directly and deeply, without any possibility on the part of the individual to do something about regaining *sovereignty over his or her own life*. The policies implemented by the WTO, and the de facto global rule of multinational corporations already give an idea of the kind of totalitarianism and

---

5 The WSF also took place in Porto Allegre in the years 2002, 2003 and 2005. In 2004, it was held in Mumbai, India while in 2006 there were parallel WSF meetings in Africa, Asia and South America. In 2007 the WSF met in Nairobi, Kenya.

new wars awaiting us. I understand the outrage of all the many people in the world who rebel against these new economic policies. They understand that they have to regain sovereignty over their own lives: sovereignty over their work, livelihoods, water, access to land, infrastructures, culture, food, housing, seeds, forests, air, education, health, and over their own government policies and economy. They do not want to be ruled by a global bureaucracy such as the WTO in Geneva, nor do they want to be ruled from the executive suite of some multinational company.

The then German Chancellor Gerhard Schröder's coalition government convened its own expert commission on globalisation in 1999. Although the commission's report did include a detailed account of all the 'errors of current globalisation' (i.e. the increase in social polarisation between rich and poor countries, environmental destruction, lack of social standards), it concluded that globalisation was good and, most importantly, inevitable.[6] The necessary task at hand was to bring globalisation into a 'democratic form', for instance by 'introducing fixed labour and environment norms'. But how, I asked myself, was this to happen in a global economy ruled by multinational companies driven by competition and bent on globalisation/deregulation, liberalisation/privatisation and profit-making? A part of Attac also believed that globalisation could be 'humanised'.

Besides these fundamental differences in principles there were also structural problems within Attac, and later with regard to Attac's participation at the Social Forums which became a matter of great concern to me and others. One of the problems was a lack of transparency in decisions made on major issues and the fact that once again a group of leaders emerged who determined the course of action, controlled the press work, decided which working groups would be accepted within Attac, and – last but not least – determined

---

6 The report can be downloaded (in German) from the official Website: <http://www.bundestag.de/gremien/welt/glob_end/downloads.html> (last accessed: 17 December, 2009).

how the money was to be distributed. All this fatally reminded me of party structures. I had absolutely no interest in belonging to a party.

I now began to ask myself whether it made sense to travel the world over and take part in such major events, the success of which was increasingly becoming measured by the number of participants they attracted (the greater the masses, the greater the success, apparently …), and where there was no real opportunity to engage in discussions with each other because the sheer mass of people made this impossible.

I decided not to take part in such mass events any more. Instead, I wanted to continue my struggle at the local level, as I have always done. I realised that we will never have true democracy and sovereignty over our lives as long as we, the people, the grass roots, continued to accept the commercialisation of our lives, the transformation of all things into commodities with a market value, in such a misguided and resigned manner as is now being done.

THE WORLD IS NOT A COMMODITY! was one of the most important slogans generated by the anti-globalisation movement – a message that spread across the globe through the anti-globalisation world meetings. Undeterred, the 'Global Players' continued their agenda with even greater force than before by transforming the whole world, our entire lives, and life in general into commodities that serve profit only. This was not least reflected in the General Agreement on Trade in Services – GATS. Through GATS, an issue reappeared that has continued to be one of my big concerns ever since I began my first campaign for a battered women's shelter in Cologne: the exploitation of, and violence against, women. Women can be considered the archetypal, cost-free or worst-paid, service providers in the world.

Globalisation and Violence against Women

No end to violence

Since participating in the conference 'Out of the Margin' in Amsterdam in 1993, I had understood that the ruling political and economic elites were seeking to incorporate women more than they had before. It had become clear to me that this strategy would put a majority of the women of the world at a disadvantage, and that they would not be in a position to 'understand' or 'explain' these changes because the old theories, analyses and methods developed by the Left, with which they were familiar, had not prepared them to stop the triumphant advance of globalised Capital.

This insight came to me for the first time during a workshop in Thailand organised by the group 'Women for Women' in an attempt to address the problem of increasing violence against women. There was no end to the reports of violence against women presented at this workshop. Questioned when this violence began to increase and whether it had something to do with the global restructuring of the economy, the women from Thailand could give no answer. They viewed the increase of prostitution, rape, including the rape of young girls, and trafficking in women, as a timeless phenomenon of the traditional patriarchal relationship between men and women. Yet in this workshop, it was at least possible to draw attention to the connection between the new, neoliberal structures of the global economy and violence against women. The description of horror stories without analysis upset me greatly and also made me angry. I remember a particular case:

The organisers of the workshop, who were mostly lawyers, drove with me from Bangkok to Chiang Mai. They were trying to clear up a particular case: a fire had broken out at night in a brothel in Phuket. The prostitutes in this brothel burned to death because they had been chained and could not escape. The women from 'Women for Women' visited the families of one of the victims. They suspected that the daughter had been sold by her family to pay back a loan the peasants had received from a moneylender. Such contracts are indeed common, the women said to me. These contracts are characterised by the fact that these women's debt-bondage is not limited to a certain period of time and that they have no idea how much they earn or how much of what they earn is theirs. All they know is that their prostitution is helping their families.

When we entered the peasants' hut, the mother was present with another daughter, who was sitting on the bed. The father came in later. It soon became clear that the dead girl's parents did not want to talk. They particularly did not want to say whether they were in debt. The father left after a short time. What shocked me, however, was that the second daughter on the bed was looking through a pornography magazine. She was probably preparing herself for her 'career' as a prostitute in Bangkok or Phuket, too.

The entire region had been brought to its knees by the global agricultural market. The small subsistence peasants were now forced to grow tapioca for themselves, the local as well as export markets. The agricultural industry processed tapioca for pig fodder in particular, and as such it played a major role in the expansion of the meat industry in Europe. The peasants of Thailand had to go into debt, were often forced to sell their farms, and as a last resort sell their daughters into prostitution where they had to serve European and American men in Bangkok and the tourist paradises in the south of the country. Prostitution is therefore the last station in what the government, the UN and the World Bank call *development*.[7]

---

7 Sinith Sittirak from Thailand, one of my former students at the ISS, The Hague, makes a clear case of this in her book *The Daughters of Development: Women in a Changing Environment* (1998). She vividly describes how what we call 'development' is ultimately based on the brutal exploitation and debasement of women.

   In 2005, at a conference on 'Capitalism, Nature, Socialism' (CNS), a Peruvian social scientist, Ana Isla, who lives in exile in Canada, gave me an article in which she criticises the same procedures and methods of recent 'development' which, as in Thailand, also

Many years later, I was invited by the director of the Goethe Institute in Dhaka (Bangladesh) to give a talk. Here too, violence against young women had risen drastically. As in Thailand, the increase in violence had been primarily traced back to traditional patriarchal structures, but not to the economic changes in Bangladesh caused by the global capitalist free trade. Yet the connection was immediately obvious: Japanese, Korean, German and American textile firms had transferred their textile production to Bangladesh because the cheapest and most compliant workers were to be found there: young, inexperienced women, sometimes even children who without complaint sewed clothing for the Western market for a pittance, worked overtime and in shifts day and night.

My friend Farida Akhter had also told me that fires often broke out in these textile factories and that many women died because the stairs and emergency exits were always blocked by bolts of fabric. Together with Farida, I visited one such – Korean – factory in the so-called *Free Production Zone* (FPZ) outside of Dhaka. It was closed off like a prison. We had to pass at least five check points before we were able to see a manager. After finally meeting him face to face, he boasted that Bangladesh's high economic growth was completely due to the textile industry. Asked about the working conditions in the factory, he proudly told us that there was no child labour here, and that the women at least had some income from their work in the factory in comparison to the dire poverty existing in their villages where they could not earn a penny. The women were bussed from their villages to and from the factory, even for the night shift, which ended at two o'clock in the morning.

---

ultimately leads to women being forced into prostitution in South America. In contrast to Sinith Sittirak's analysis, Ana Isla however addresses the new, supposedly 'ecological' methods which even accelerate people's disconnection from their subsistence base, such as 'ecotourism' and the trade in 'air pollution rights' which she calls ozone trade, with which the Western industrial countries believe air pollution and global warming can be reduced (Isla, 2003, pp. 21–34). See also her essay in Ariel Salleh's book, *Eco-sufficiency and Global Justice* (2009).

Most of the violent attacks on women occurred at night when they returned from work.

The connection between the neoliberal restructuring of the global economy and an increase in violence against women was entirely obvious: women are the optimal flexible workers for a globalised economy. They are not organised in a union, do not know their rights, have to combine their family and work, and are therefore compliant and willing to accept less pay than men. We had already analysed these issues in the beginning of the 1980s in the context of the debate on housework. They are not only the cheapest production workers, they are also the cheapest service providers. And violence against them was another price they paid (see Mies, 1999).

Conference: Women against GATS and Privatisation Cologne, 2003

In the course of globalisation, particularly during the renegotiations for GATS in 2003, the question of women's labour in the globalised economy resurfaced as an urgent issue. The new agreement on services seemed to affect women much more than men. All over the world, they are the actual service providers: as secretaries, office assistants in all branches of work, as nurses and care workers, as waitresses in restaurants in hotels, as teachers in schools and nursery schools, as social workers, cleaning women, call-girls, prostitutes, and of course as housewives.

The term 'services' encompasses a sheer infinite list of activities which, according to the logic of free trade, are now commodities to be traded freely in the global market. Many of the service areas involved 'civil services', meaning public services such as the postal service, public transportation, health care, education, municipal services (i.e. water supply, sewage, etc.), and social services. Up to then, they had always been publicly administered. The GATS agreement threatened to ultimately privatise these government services.

And women would be much more negatively affected than men. However, women had no idea of these developments. We discussed this in our Feminist Attac group and decided to host an international conference in May 2003 called 'Women Stop GATS!'

This conference was held in the Fachhochschule Köln (University of Applied Sciences, Cologne). It was the first and only conference on the issue in Germany. More than 500 women, and also many men, came to Cologne to hear what the conference speakers had to say. Our goal was to show the consequences from GATS and other privatisation policies which are already visible throughout the world. We invited women from the South as well as the North to participate. This concept was very successful in that women from Germany, India, Bangladesh, England, Canada, Austria and Argentina were able to report on the effects from the privatisation of services from their own countries' perspective.

On hearing the reports, the participants were horrified and deeply concerned, and their feeling increased when *Naila Khan* from Bangladesh explained how neoliberal 'modernisation' of the health system made hospital care completely unaffordable for poor women, because the government had reduced its financial support of public hospitals and, as a result, an increasing number of private clinics for the rich were being established. *Bente Madeira* from England reported similar conditions. All of these accounts demonstrated that the effects of liberal economic policies are the same all over the world.

This became even more explicit when *Vandana Shiva* from India and *Maude Barlow* from Canada reported on the new policy of privatising water. What shocked people the most was Vandana's account of the Indian government's plans to sell the water from the Ganges, 'the holy Mother Ganga', to the huge French Suez power corporation and privatise it, meaning that people, and peasants in particular, would no longer have free access to water. Water was to become a profit-making commodity.

She then reported that women organised sustained opposition to the government's and the big multinational companies' privatisation policies everywhere until the government finally had to give in. Because of this opposition, the government also had to retract the privatisation of the Sheonath River in 2003. Vandana Shiva criticised the neoliberal logic of privatisation in this manner:

> There is a common argument used for privatisation, and it goes for health, it goes for education, it goes for energy, it goes for water. This basic argument is, 'Oh, there is all this cost in this, so there must be full cost recovery, and privatization is a way of making society pay the real cost.' That is their favourite phrase (Shiva, 'Women Stop GATS' Conference, Cologne, 9 May, 2003).

Vandana Shiva demonstrated that privatisation leads to an increase in multinationals' profits and power, and that all the earth's natural and existential resources are turned into 'raw material' and private property, and only accorded 'value' once they have been industrially processed. The Suez company for example defined the Ganges's water as 'raw water' which needed to be 'processed', 'civilised' and of course, sold. She also reported that the victims of this neoliberal policy were the earth itself, peasants and women in particular. Together with her colleagues, she visited the villages affected by the Ganges water project where women reported that over 100 women had committed suicide because their fields had dried up and they now had to walk extreme distances to get water. They were distraught and said, "The Ganga has always been our mother. Now she has become our grave. You know, the only benefit we have from the water is by jumping into it to die" (Shiva, 2003b).

In the same way that our first major women's conference against genetic engineering and reproductive technologies in 1985 had triggered many more events, our anti-GATS women's conference in 2003 also spawned many new activities against the privatisation of the service sector: of our water, healthcare system, education, energy supply; and against the entire transformation of life into a commodity. However, after this conference I was exhausted. I began to ask myself whether it made sense to continue organising major events like this.

Globalisation and War

Yet I could not turn my back on the issue of globalisation just like that. On the contrary, over the course of the next few years it became ever clearer to me, and to others, that the old/new global trade and economic system could only be maintained over time through further arms build-up and new wars. The NATO war in former Yugoslavia, in Bosnia and then Kosovo, made shatteringly clear to us that – with the end of the East-West conflict – a time had now come in which it was not only possible but considered *normal and desirable*, to propagate war around the world. The fact that The Greens Party agreed it was necessary for Germany to take part in this war was the greatest shock to us all. Many of us were even party voters and members of The Greens Party. The connection between the economy and the globalisation of war became particularly apparent after 11 September, 2001, when George Bush Jr first declared war on terrorism – and then Islam – as the greatest threat to mankind.

I began to collect material on the connection between 'war and economics' and over the next few years wrote a book that outlined the interrelationship between globalisation and war (*Krieg ohne Grenzen*, Mies 2004, with a chapter by Claudia von Werlhof). Working on this book opened my eyes in many ways to the link between globalisation and war. The fact that war and patriarchy are interconnected was something my friends and I had analysed many years ago. As I was in constant contact with Claudia von Werlhof, I was familiar with her findings that the modern capitalist-patriarchal economic system and our modern system of war together formed a single system: a global war system. This insight cut right to the heart of the matter.

Yet this insight was not one we were able to analyse in cool objectivity. Since 1999, devastating news on the NATO war against the former Yugoslavia reached us on a daily basis: news about waves of refugees, genocide and massacres. This was followed by the USA's wars against the Taliban in Afghanistan and against Saddam Hussein in Iraq as of 2003. All of these wars were ostensibly being carried out in defence of freedom and democracy (see Mies, 2003).

Yet none of these wars were legitimised by International Law, which did not stop the Federal Republic of Germany from directly participating in two of these wars and from still participating in one of them, the war in Afghanistan. For its part, the media joined in spreading the official war propaganda. It become conspicuously clear that the world had abandoned what was called the *Rule of Right* to fall back into an absolute *Rule of Might*, the kind of which we thought had been overcome long ago and which is characterised by the open and brutal rule of violence and despotism of the economically powerful over the weak. An era has dawned in which global wars continue to be fought on the outside as well as the inside. My Cassandra prophecy, epitomised in the title of my book *War Unlimited* (*Krieg ohne Grenzen*, 2004) has – unfortunately – not been refuted to date.

What upset me the most about these 'new wars' – to the point where I lost my previous optimism – was the realisation that these wars were not only just about gaining control over new resources, such as oil, but that the West was purportedly fighting a war against terrorism which in reality was directed at destroying the very ability of societies to be *self-sufficient and self-reliant*. They were literally being forced to open themselves up to 'free trade' and to American and European multinationals. Today, these countries are not only still war-torn, they have also become impoverished and are totally dependent on Western industrial countries. Moreover, war has broken out in the rich countries in the form of 'all against all' through the enforcement of a universal principle of competition. This not only heralds the end of the social welfare state and of solidarity, but it also means that the ability for people to imagine a 'different world' and to fight for it, is increasingly being undermined. War has become accepted as a normal affair.[8]

My work on my *War Unlimited* book, and the lectures I held across the country after it was published, affected me considerably. The issue of 'globalisation and war' literally went under my skin. Although I felt exhausted, I continued to give lectures across Europe and Germany in 2006. However, it became increasingly difficult for me to provide an inspiring and plausible alternative to this bankrupt and criminal system of war to my audience.

---

8 This 'war within' has meanwhile entered the hearts and minds of mostly young men and boys through computer games and other media that glorify violence.

15

The Search for a New Vision

Judging by appearances, it would seem that the prospects for a new vision are quite dismal – not only for the South but also for the wealthy North. What this means for our children and the next generation is that they will be confronted with an increasingly brutal competition for jobs, permanent stress, and a financially insecure old age. The elderly cannot generally look forward to living out their lives happily and contentedly in the circle of their loved ones, but can rather expect to vegetate in loneliness in senior citizen and nursing homes. Although the USA and Europe are still the main profiteers from globalisation, *depression* is raging in these countries as a now endemic disease. Many people, even very successful ones, are feeling helpless. Even the most critical, those who have valiantly fought for a different and better world, are finding it increasingly difficult not to give up. Before their eyes, major transnational corporations continue to follow their policies of globalisation, liberalisation and privatisation (GLP) and continue to transform everything into a commodity, despite the looming climate catastrophe, massive unemployment, increasing poverty and injustices in the South as well as the North. The fact that ever more people are carrying their rage onto the streets may irritate them a little, but it has done nothing to make them change their basic philosophy of permanent growth and accumulation.

In my lectures I am sometimes asked, "Where do you get your optimism from, your hope? What is your vision?" These are very good questions. Maybe I am generally an optimist because, as a child, I experienced that you do not really need a lot of 'things' to have a *happy life*. Maybe my optimism comes from all my good friends in the South who live in far worse material circumstances than I, and yet do not lose their hope, but rather gather their strength to go out and *do* something when they hear another catastrophe is looming, or when the brutalities carried out by the multinational-government alliances become unbearable. Dorothee Sölle once described the optimism among poor people in South America in this way, "The poor do not have time for pessimism. Pessimism is a luxury of the rich." Indeed, I often heard how many people in the USA complain, "We work and work. We invest and consume until we are old and grey. But when does the 'good life' come?"

Many people are at a great loss and cannot conceive of a new perspective for the future. Attac coined the following slogan, ANOTHER WORLD IS POSSIBLE. But what kind of world will it be?

On Pentecost/Whitsunday in 2002, *Dorothee Sölle*, my former colleague *Mechthild Höflich* and I organised one last Political Night Prayer in the Antonite Church in Cologne, on GATS. Our motto was:

ANOTHER WORLD IS NECESSARY!
ANOTHER WORLD IS POSSIBLE!
ANOTHER WORLD HAS ALREADY BEGUN!

These slogans may sound optimistic, but could they dissolve the lack of hope and perspective on the part of so many, especially the young? Has it not become necessary to ask ourselves *what kind* of world are we living in exactly? And what the 'good life' really is? I realised that the biggest difficulty in developing a new vision was because our ruling global capitalist system is in fact a *new religion*.

Capital as Religion

If we fail to bring about a new vision, our only alternative will be to completely surrender ourselves to violence and war, and accept the vision of unlimited goods production and capital accumulation. The god of this religion is called Capital; *patriarchal Capital* to be exact. This god is *invisible* (supposedly), *immortal, omniscient, omnipotent, omnipresent* and must grow eternally. He is considered the source of all life. This has never been as obvious as in our present age of corporate-guided neoliberal globalisation (see Mies, 2005a).

This god does not only have *churches* – banks and corporate headquarters – but also theologians and a *priesthood*. They are economists, scientists, technocrats and, above all, bankers. They do whatever is possible and whatever makes a profit. Like any religion, this one is based on a creed, the creed of unlimited increase of money and profits which everyone has to believe in, no matter whether our entire experience tells us that it is a big lie. The neoliberal creed can be summarised thus: 'Global free trade creates growth. Growth creates jobs and prosperity for all, the prerequisite for equality, freedom, democracy and peace'. The reason why many people still believe in this creed is because, among other things, the *real* worldwide effects of global free trade and actions of institutions such as the WTO, the World Bank and of the political leaders who serve the interests of corporations, have been hidden from them.

The vision of globalised capitalism centres on the idea that there really is no vision at all. This 'non-vision' needs to be observed as a pragmatic necessity, like the law of gravity. There Is No Alternative: TINA. Every religion has a dogma people must believe in. One of the priests of this religion summarised its dogmas in this manner, "Competition is ultimately the best method for creating jobs – even if the process is sometimes rough" (quoted in Mies and von Werlhof, 1998, p. 166).

It is therefore all about *believing* that without competition there is no investment, that without investment there are no jobs, without jobs there is no prosperity, no equality, no peace. Although daily experience shows us that these claims are not true, we are still asked to believe it. The motto is, *Credo quia absurdum* (I believe because it is absurd).

Every religion demands sacrifices

More than ten years of free trade policies have demonstrated that unlimited trade and the extreme growth in wealth for a few peoples and corporations is being paid for with the increasing bondage and poverty of a majority of the people on earth. Since the 1980s, the chasm between rich and poor countries has grown as never before; and the gap between rich and poor has grown within the richest countries of the world as well: the USA, England, Germany and France. UN organisations and even the World Bank have admitted that global free trade has caused this chasm to widen enormously.

In the so-called Third World, the gulf between the winners and losers of globalisation is of course much more dramatic. For many people in these countries, globalisation means that their *basic* existence is threatened. The major multinational corporations' invasion into their agricultural production has annihilated small farming through competition from the multinationals. The importation of agricultural surpluses from the USA and Europe at dumping prices has destroyed the existence of millions of peasants who were not able to find alternative jobs in industry.

The ecological and social consequences of globalisation have led to epidemic waves of suicides among farmers in India. These farmers first believed in the promises made to them by agribusiness, i.e. that genetically engineered cotton achieves higher yields. The cultivation of this cotton was an absolute catastrophe: many farmers went bankrupt and saw no other way out than taking their own lives. In

February, 2008, I read that even in India's wealthiest state of Punjab, masses of bankrupt farmers are committing suicide.

The victims of this new religion also include democracy, the environment, people's health, labour and social and human rights. Those who protested on the streets of Seattle, Prague, Washington, Nice, Melbourne and Davos were aware that globalisation, liberalisation, privatisation (GLP) not only widened the gap between the poor and the rich and powerful in countries, and between countries, but that labour, social and human rights which had been laboriously and slowly gained over hundreds of years, as well as the protection and preservation of creativity, were now to be subordinated to the unlimited chase for profits. Despite all these sacrifices, despite all these protests, the priests of this religion continue to carry out the destruction of the foundations for life on this earth. Their strategy seems to be: the dogs bark, but the caravan passes.

My question then is: where in this petrified TINA world is it possible for another social utopia to emerge if only shareholder value has any worth? Before another vision can develop, many people in many countries must first begin to stop believing in the promises of global capitalism. This loss of faith, and the development of a new vision and hope do not occur in academic debates carried out within the safe havens of universities and academic journals. This turn-around takes place on the streets, in protests against the allegedly so powerful global players.

Another World is Possible

I am often asked the question, "If you are against global free trade, what other economy and society do you suggest as an alternative?" The answer to this question starts wherever people begin to reject the TINA-syndrome and stop believing that there is no alternative.

Localisation instead of globalisation

ANOTHER WORLD IS POSSIBLE was the slogan of the first Social Forum in Porto Allegre, Brazil, 2001. The *Via Campesina*, an international network of peasants, formulated the following slogan:

> GLOBALISE RESISTANCE
> GLOBALISE HOPE

This is what it is all about: the worldwide protest movements against economic policies which place growth and profit above all else are the very beginning of hope that another world is possible.

What gave me hope throughout all the years spent opposing the corporations' power was the realisation that all over the world people were demanding to regain control over their immediate living conditions. They were no longer willing to accept having some bureaucrat in Brussels or Geneva, or some executive of a distant multinational corporation make decisions about their food, air, water, their health care system, their schools, environment and their public transportation in the name of monetary gain. This gave me the added insight that economic and political control over our immediate living conditions is only possible in *small economic units* in which people, like those in Porto Allegre, can truly participate in organising their public affairs democratically.

This perspective is not just an utopian idea but was, for instance, already being tried in England, where a movement developed out of the BSE ('mad cow disease') scandal. People wanted to know exactly what they were eating: they demanded *food sovereignty*. From May to July 2001, farmers' markets were organised in many cities where, next to information stands, local products were sold with the slogan, LOCAL FOOD FOR GLOBAL PROSPERITY. The Greens Party launched a broad campaign with the motto, PROTECT THE LOCAL, GLOBALLY. As an ecofeminist, I completely agree with this slogan.

What is happening to me?

During the first years of the twenty-first century I continued to give lectures on globalisation, war and subsistence throughout the world. I also published many articles and books. I was incredibly busy. But I increasingly felt that this manner of trying to change the world was exhausting me more and more. Although I was able to point to many examples where the subsistence perspective was successfully applied, I myself no longer had the energy to start a subsistence project of my own.

Since my retirement, I had rented a small apartment in the house of my deceased aunt in Steffeln, my mother's village in the Eifel. Whenever I had time, I would escape from the city and spend time there. I felt that the air, my walks through country and even just the sight of the area's beautiful volcanic hills, did me the world of good. Moreover, some of my brothers and sisters lived in the villages nearby with their families. All of this suited me. It was also fortunate that my cousin, Maria-Agnes, asked me if I wanted to take over and continue cultivating her mother's kitchen garden behind the house. Which I did with great pleasure. This garden has become a continuous source of joy, recreation, peace and sensuous enjoyment of life for me. In addition, through my gardening I gained ever new insights into what *subsistence* actually means.

In Steffeln, I was free to spend my day as I wished to. In the mornings, I sat at a small table in my apartment and wrote many manuscripts. My niece, Eva, typed them into her computer – I did not want to bring a laptop into my place of refuge. At midday, I went out into the garden and picked salad, vegetables and herbs I had sown in the spring. I bought potatoes from Hans, my cousin's husband who, together with his wife, continues to work his wife's family farm even after his retirement. It is a small, truly diversified farm with some cows, chickens, bees and fields where they grow grain, carrots and potatoes for their own consumption.

My immediate environment provided me with everything I needed to live with: the best and freshest possible quality milk and eggs, I got from Hans; vegetables, berries and fruit grew in my garden. Salt, sugar, oil, noodles, rice, tea and coffee I was able to buy from the small village grocery store across the street operated to this day by Edith, an eighty-year-old, full of energy and cheerfulness. What more did I need for a *good life*?

Lessons from my garden

1. *You have to work with nature,* as my mother always said. You have to know when it is time to sow, to weed and harvest. And you have to be there to help make things grow. You have to know and follow the rhythm of nature, otherwise nothing will thrive. You have to know when is the right time to do whatever is necessary. This is the first lesson I learned from my garden.

2. *You have to know what plants need.* An Indian farmer once explained his science of flourishing plants. He said plants need the same things a baby needs in her mother's tummy, that is "warmth, moisture and love." This was the second lesson from my garden: *warmth, moisture and love.*

3. *Diversity and carefulness is the basis of life, not monoculture.* Hans gave me cow manure in autumn to fertilise my garden, if I wanted it. I do not use artificial fertilisers as a matter of principle. I also do not use manure every year because the dark, volcanic soil in my aunt's garden is so fertile it does not need additional substances. From my childhood I knew that beans store nitrogen. As a result, I followed the principle of crop rotation. Where beans grew last year I planted red beets, swiss chard or onions. I ordered seeds from a company called 'Flail' (Dreschflegel) – founded by a group of friends who are dedicated to organic farming and in particular to reviving extinct plant varieties in order to maintain biological diversity. Hans installed a rainwater tank in my garden so that I would always have enough

water for my plants. Lesson number three: biological diversity is the key to success.

4. *Nature is not stingy.* My garden produced such an abundance of berries, vegetables, herbs, salads, zucchinis, swiss chard and especially beans, that I always had *too much*. When I went home to Cologne I had bags and baskets full of fruit from my garden. My husband and I had enough to eat from what I brought home. I usually also distributed some of the produce to the other families in our house. There was always too much. A garden the size of my aunt's kitchen garden was capable of feeding a large family all year round. Whatever was not eaten in the summer and autumn was preserved. My cousin taught me the old methods of preserving fruit and vegetables. I also bought a freezer in which I stored my garden produce. There was still too much. Lesson number four: nature produces abundance.

5. *You have to share.* I always had enough to share and distribute. Plants are not money. Money does not spoil and therefore can be hoarded. *Nature always produces more than can be immediately used. Nature is generous and teaches us to share.* This was the fifth lesson from my garden.

6. *A garden creates new relationships between people.* People often went by my garden and asked if I needed some more salad plants, or if I had snails in my garden and what did I do about them. My garden did not have a lot of snails and I did not use poison to get rid of them. I met new people across my garden fence, and people I had not known before became friends.

A garden is not just a place where you produce fruit and vegetables, but it is a place of encounter, a place where new, reciprocal, neighbourly, and generous interactions take place between people. This is lesson number six.

The 'good life' in the village?

The 'good life' mentioned above also includes good relationships. I am particularly close to my youngest sister Trudel. She lives with her family in my home village of Auel. Because I stopped having a car years ago, she regularly picks me up from the train station when I come to Steffeln and drives me back to the station when I go back to Cologne.

Although she has enough things to do with her children and grandchildren, the house and garden, she always finds time for me and we enjoy being together and exchanging news and thoughts on whatever seems to be on our minds: private issues, village topics, politics, church news and our large family. I also have a few close friends in the area who visit me regularly and with whom I can discuss political, feminist and subsistence issues. One of them is Agnes, a farmer from the neighbouring village of Schönfeld whom I mentioned in my book, *The Subsistence Perspective* (1999). The other is Tina, a worker, unionist and member of the SPD (Social Democratic Party) from Dahlem in the Eifel. Both are very strong women. They both stood up against the traditional norms of the Catholic Church and the conservative village community by being single mothers at a time when this was seen as a huge blemish. Both of them are feminists, politically active, and critical.

What I admire most is that they stayed in their villages and communities to fight from there for better conditions. I, however, went out 'into the world'. I do not think I would have been able to do what these women did. I would not have been able to hold out. It is important to remember that a village not only consists of neighbourly relationships but also of merciless social control, especially with respect to women. If one woman stepped out of line or had an 'illegitimate child', everyone knew. If someone was more popular than the others, he or she was not only admired, but other people became jealous and resentful which often led into real enmity. I would not have wanted to experience these troubles. I left.

I have not fully returned to the village, although I could have done so. I have often tried to explain my ideas about the ruling political practice to my family and all those I knew. I could see how neoliberal, industrialised agriculture was ruining our peasants, and I could not ignore the impact neoliberal capitalism had on our villages. If I had wanted to do something against this, I would have had to fully return to my village and stay there. I soon noticed that this would not be easy. I could not just return home and say, "Hi, here I am again after all these years. Now listen to what I have to say."

I was known as 'dat Kellisch Maria'. People knew I was a teacher or even that I had become a professor, but in the village I had no authority. I was known as a weekend guest and as a member of the Mies family. My efforts to explain my critical view of the effect of globalisation on our villages and region was usually met with responses such as, "Yes, you're quite right, but what are we little people to do?" I often had to think of Jesus's saying in the New Testament, "A prophet is not without honour except in his home-town." Even less so a prophetess!

It literally breaks my heart to experience how our self-sufficient villages have come to look like spruced-up suburban towns; how my own village, for instance, has only one farmer left and how most young people leave to find a meaningless job somewhere to earn money. On my walks, I see how monocultures are taking over our hilly landscape. Corn is cultivated as a monoculture, perhaps even the genetically engineered corn for biodiesel subsidised by the EU and Germany in particular.

The old tension, between homesickness and my yearning for far away places which has pulled me apart ever since my childhood days, has not been solved by these periodic returns to my mother's village: 'The village and the world' or 'The world and the village' remains a balancing act I have been trying to maintain for many years. It takes much strength to manage this tension, but I have learned a lot from being pulled in different directions. It has given me the power to live, and it has given me a zest for life. Despite everything.

16

My Body Says Stop

Despite attempts to create some of the 'good life' for myself in my village, I could not completely escape from the world. The global is just as much part of the local as the local is part of the global – in the positive as well as the negative.

Since working on my book *War Unlimited* (*Krieg ohne Grenzen*, 2004), in which I examined the correlation between globalisation and war, it was becoming increasingly difficult for me to take on a positive perspective. Especially since the observations I made in 2004 had become more and more a reality: unlimited warfare within and without, against humans, nature, and against life as such, and the transformation of all things into commodities to serve God Capital. Where was hope to be found in the face of the destruction of everything that lived? Working on this war book was too much: *I got sick.*

By the end of 2006, I was painfully reminded that I could not go on like this. I had begun to suffer from numerous epileptic attacks. No one in my family had ever had epilepsy. So what was the cause? There has never been a proper answer to this question.

In February 2007, I was sent to the Department of Epileptology at the University Hospital in Bonn for further examination. I was funnelled through the entire modern medical process. It was a nightmare. When I was told that there were a few white spots in my brain representing dead brain cells, I fell into a deep, dark hole.

Did this not mean dementia, Alzheimer's or something similar? It at least meant the end of my previous life, I thought. I was in despair. I was trembling and had to hold on to all sorts of things to stabilise myself. This was it; I could say good-bye to my independence. Outside, the weather was rainy and it was drizzling. I held on to the window handle and looked out into the rain.

And then I saw a bird. It was sitting on an ivy-covered tree looking at me. *"Life-bird or death-bird?"* I asked myself. My roommate came in and I showed her the bird. *"See there, that's our bird sitting on the tree!"* We both had to laugh.

In the middle of the night, I woke up with the thought, "White spots in my brain? What do they mean? Well, I'll just think with the other brain cells then, the ones that aren't white," I said to myself, "There are thousands of them still left."

It was not quite as easy as that, however. Here I was, directly experiencing the effects of the 'mystery of the world' on my body. My uncertainty remained. I remembered the Grimm 'Mother Hulda' fairytale in which the industrious and sweet-tempered stepdaughter accidentally dropped her spindle down the well, and her stepmother commanded her to jump after it and retrieve it. The golden girl, as she was called at the end of the story, fell into the well (or did she jump?). At the bottom, she found lots of things she had forgotten: an apple tree with ripe, golden apples needing to be picked; a baking oven full of bread loaves who all cried, "Take us out or else we'll burn!" The golden girl did whatever needed to be done, but, still uncertain, she (or rather, I), asked, "Am I the golden girl or the pitch girl?"[1] This was not yet clear.

I still trembled: my hands, head, legs. I also trembled within.

I composed the following poem for myself:

---

1 In the 'Mother Hulda' fairytale, the golden girl's stepsister who was lazy and bad-tempered, also jumped into the well, expecting to bring home gold like her sister. However, Mother Hulda rewarded her with pitch instead of gold. When she got home, she was covered head to foot with pitch that never washed off.

The old one sits on a stone,
wagging her head.
Trembling head, trembling stone.
Trembling life, heart and soul.
She holds tight to her stone, coloured red.
She shakes her head, "No, no, not like this,
Not this way!
I'm not yet dead.

It was Carnival in Cologne.[2] I knew I had to get out of the hospital. On Women's Carnival Night (Weiberfastnacht) I demanded to be discharged – I could continue my treatment as an out-patient. Saral picked me up and we drove to Cologne.

Back in our apartment, however, I noticed I was still trembling. I had become thin-skinned and very sensitive to noises. In the apartment above ours live two musicians with their little boys: eight-year-old Gabriel and five-year-old Tobias. At that time, Tobias was still in his terrible twos, and continuously ran back and forth like a tiger in a cage. He stomped with his feet and screamed and screamed. As soon as I heard him stomping and screaming, I automatically began to tremble again. You could hear everything through the thin ceilings of our old house. Up until then, I had never been disturbed by any noise. I love children. But now my body would immediately start shaking as soon as I heard Tobias scream and stomp. His anger transferred itself directly to me. I could no longer control my reactions. Once I yelled at him to stop screaming. He screamed even louder. I realised this was the wrong way to go.

So I opened our door and invited Tobias to come in. He came and immediately stopped screaming and stomping. He discovered the pistachios in my kitchen, broke them open with his fingers and ate

2 Carnival is a big event that takes place once a year in Cologne. Three days before the real Carnival (the Rose Monday Parade), women celebrate their own Carnival in which they make fun of men (called Weiberfastnacht, or Women's Shrovetide).

them. He and I then carefully placed the shells in a bowl of water. They swam on the surface, they were our boats. Then we created a convoy of ships.

He went into my large living and office room, looked around and discovered lots of things on my bookshelves, things from all over the world, things I had forgotten. There was a photograph of Farmer Hans with his two grandchildren, Katrin and Annemarie. There were stones and the bronze heads of two rivers in India, the Jamuna and Ganga. Tobias wanted to examine each of them carefully. I put them on my black couch table.

I had once received a postcard from my friend Elisabeth. On it was a picture of a pig followed by five little piglets. Tobias discovered the card on my table. He said, "A little pig? Where does it come from? And where is it going to? It looks like it's thrilled!" I was amazed – how did he know what 'thrilled' meant? I said, "That's Sophia the sow. She's looking for a farm for herself and her piglets."

This is how our pig story began.

How Sophia the Sow Finds a Farm

Tobias now often visits Maria. He wants to know how the sow story continues. Maria tells the story:

The sow is called Sophia. She has run away from a pig factory. Sophia is pregnant. She does not want her piglets to be born at the factory. She snorts and stomps with her hooves:

> I have to get out of here!
> I'm not going to stay another night!
> I've got to go!
> This is not a good place.
> They only fatten us here to kill us.
> My piglets are not going to be born here!
> No, No!
> Not here!
> Not like this, never!

The next day, Tobias's brother Gabriel comes too. Together with Maria, Tobias and Gabriel try to think of ways to help Sophia escape the pig factory. They gather ideas – Gabriel has the best ones.

Gabriel tells the story, "Woody, our pet dog, will help us get Sophia out!" The story develops into a real adventure. The pregnant sow Sophia escapes from the pig factory. Under an oak tree she gives birth to her five piglets, one after the other. Then they all run southwards to find Farmer Hans's farm ... Gabriel asks, "Is this a true story?" Maria says, "Yes, some of it is true, some of it is made up."

Maria continues, "I have to cut this story short, otherwise it will never come to an end. Let's do a short version." Gabriel answers, "We want to paint the story, too. Every story has to be painted. Let's get crayons. Do you have paper?"

Maria scrounges around. In a corner she finds numerous rolled-up calendars from the past few years. She takes them and puts them face-down on the floor so that the dates, conferences and schedules cannot be seen. Maria says, "I don't want to see this any longer. No more do I 'have to' do anything. Now, all we have here is a nice blank painting surface." They tape the sheets together into one panel. Then they continue developing their story. The story's goal: how do Sophia and her piglets reach Farmer Hans's farm in the Eifel? The children paint the story on to the paper. The whole thing gets longer and longer.

Maria continues spinning the tale, "Sofia and her piglets keep running towards the south. Tobias, Gabriel and Maria run behind them. They reach the Urft, a small river marking the beginning of the Eifel. The Urft is a fairy. Really, that's what the people call her. The Urft is a water fairy. The Urft fairy shows them the way. She tells them, 'Follow the banks of my river southwards and uphill'. She also tells them, 'Those who swim against the current reach their goal faster'. The Urft fairy continues, 'On the summit near Schmidtheim there is a watershed where the rivers and streams have to decide whether they want to flow south or north. You, too, have to decide where to go from there. If you want to reach Farmer Hans, you'll have to take the way to the south'."

Once in a while our tale gets interrupted. The boys' mother wants to know how things are going. She asks, "Isn't this too much for you? It's quite an art workshop here!" I answer, "No, this is fun for me and for the boys, too. Tobias especially doesn't want to stop drawing and spinning our tale. This is our therapy. His and mine."

The next day, Tobias appears again at my door, "We have to keep working on our pig story!" We both sit down on the floor and continue our tale while drawing. The story goes on and on, with side stories and detours which continuously sprout new stories like a meandering river – there is no limit to the children's and my imagination.

Instead of recounting all the other adventures Gabriel and Tobias made up, I would like to continue with the main story on Sophia the sow: followed by her piglets, she runs consistently southward as if guided by an inner compass. After climbing up to the watershed near Schmidtheim, she and her piglets run down its southern side and along the banks of the Kyll until they reach a brook to the right, the Oos. The Oos fairy. The Oos springs from a source near Steffeln which is the village Farmer Hans lives in. Sophia the sow runs ahead with her piglets. Tobias, Gabriel and Maria follow her. They run along the Oos to the west. The last part is all uphill again. Sophia is increasingly impatient. She has caught the scent of home.

Tobias is impatient as well. "When do we finally get to the farm?" He and Gabriel are running pretty fast. They finally catch a glimpse of Steffeln, the village. Maria is not so fast, she is a little older, you know. She sees the mountain, Steffelberg, and her heart becomes heavy.

She says, "This was the highest and most beautiful mountain in the entire Volcanic Eifel, the land of fire. They destroyed it with their excavators and lorries. They dug all the volcanic sand from the mountain to build the Autobahn from Cologne to Trier. Lots of big lorries now drive on the Autobahn carrying strawberries, tomatoes, cucumbers and other vegetables from the south of Spain to Cologne's supermarkets. The Autobahn was never finished, but the mountain has been destroyed. Where the mountain stood, there is now a big hole, a black hole: all the cars in the world, its skyscrapers, computers and mobile telephones, all of its tanks and aeroplanes cannot fill the hole in the Steffelberg."

Maria stands still and begins to brood, "This is how they've always done it: they build high-rise buildings, banks, planes, automobiles, tanks, computers and destroy Mother Earth, take whatever they can get, make war without end, drop bombs and missiles, and kill. They leave black holes behind them, on earth and in space. All in the service of their God, Capital!

Grain for bread doesn't grow on any of the fields on the Steffelberg any more, only corn to make bio-fuel for their cars to guzzle. They import food from all over the world so that the people in the industrialised countries do not have to starve. Only the others starve, the ones they steal from . . ."

Maria is very sad and tears run down her cheeks. She turns her back on all the black holes. She looks around and towards the east. There it is again – that broad horizon! One volcanic chain, and then another, and then another . . . Somewhat dazed, she stumbles down the Steffelberg.

But Sophia, her piglets and the two boys did not notice Maria's stop at the Black Hole. They continue to run past Steffelberg and into the village. And there to Farmer Hans's house. Together with his two grandchildren, Katrin and Annemarie, he is standing by the cowshed door to welcome them. Tobias calls, "This is just like in Maria's picture!" Farmer Hans smiles beneath his cap.

Sophia and her piglets have discovered the dungheap and are gleefully rolling around in it. Gabriel and Tobias discover the cows and their calves, the chickens and rooster, and the three cats running around, too. And then they see the tractor. They want to climb onto it immediately. Hans says, "You can go with me to our meadow to milk the cows tomorrow." Both boys shout with joy. Maria finally arrives, somewhat breathless but otherwise healthy and happy. "Those who spin the tale long enough finally reach the end!" she says.

But then she notices she has a stomach-ache and says, "I've got to go into the house right away. I have a belly full of stories that need to come out."[3]

---

3 This is only the short version. The long version is not finished. Whoever wishes, can spin the tale with us.

Epilogue: The Good Life

When Susan Hawthorne and Renate Klein asked me whether I would like to write an Epilogue to the story of my life and our times, I first hesitated. What could I write? Since I had finished my book in 2008, the world had not become a better place, quite on the contrary.

One crisis was followed by another: the hunger crisis, the oil crisis, the financial crisis in the United States, the breakdown of the major banks followed by a worldwide economic crisis, earthquakes, and other catastrophes everywhere, as well as an unlimited series of wars. All of a sudden poverty has become a reality for many, in the rich countries as well. Slowly, people have begun to realise that life cannot go on as they have known it until now. Already in 2003, Richard Heinberg had said so in his book *The Party Is Over: Oil, War and the Fate of Industrial Societies*. Many hoped that after the governments had spent billions of dollars and euros to save the global banks, things would return to 'normal', and some changes would be made that such a crisis would never happen again. But they saw themselves cheated. The banks continued with 'business as usual', the growth of money and capital remained their only goal. Regulations are far and few between.

Not only for the poor, but even for many of those who so far had benefited from the global capitalist system, life did not go on as 'smoothly' as before. Many committed suicide when they lost their jobs. In the rich countries, depression has become a common disease. In Japan, for example, more and more managers of big corporations suffer from burnout because of inhuman and constant stress. People call this 'karoshi'.[1] They are no longer able to work and support their families. The whole model of the 'good life' propagated by the rich industrialised countries – the supermarket model, as I call it – seems to be breaking down before our very eyes. This model so far has meant more and more money, more goods, more and more expensive cars, bigger and more luxurious houses, and supermarkets filled with goods from all over the world. People thought their children would also be able to enjoy this 'good life' forever, which is the main reason why they worked so hard, suffered much stress and tried to reach the standard of those 'on top'. 'Our children must have a better life', was – and is – the main justification for tolerating all one's sacrifices.

Apart from this, we have known for some time that our countries' lifestyle not only destroys nature, the basis for all life on our planet, Mother Earth. Many people from all over the world, including the USA, have begun to question this model of life in its entirety: its economy, its politics, its world view and what it holds to be the purpose of human life. One friend from the UK told me that people in the USA have expressed their disillusionment in the following way:

We work and work,
we produce and produce,
we invest and invest,
we consume and consume.
But when will the 'good life' come?

Those voicing these sentiments were not poor individuals from Africa and Asia. They were ordinary middle-class people from one of the richest countries in the world. Why were they not happy? Why did they not feel their life was a 'good life'? Was not their life the life everyone in the world was striving for? All the countries in the world, even those which have continued to follow the socialist path or have

---

1 The word 'karoshi' in Japanese means 'death by overwork'.

been called the Third World were aspiring to reach the West's standard of living. Why, therefore, are those privileged people not happy?

When I had began to ponder these questions, I realised that, in general, we in the rich world are not living happy lives; that for many, our life is indeed a miserable and meaningless one. A life without dignity and real joy. Most of the people in our countries will ask similar questions as above, "Where is the good life, and when will it come?"

I also realised, however, that it is easier to say what the bad life is than to define what a good one will be.

For years, I and many others have criticised the colonisation of nature, of women, and of the world's poor countries. I have talked and written about capitalist and patriarchal exploitation and the oppression of people, particularly of women. As an ecofeminist, I have long understood that the destruction of nature and of women is based on the same masculinist worldview. Namely, that the 'good life' is not possible without 'Man's' (sic) domination over nature and the whole universe. (Have a look at what scientists do today to explore the universe.) But then, what concepts do we have at hand to be able to define the good life differently? Many years ago, I and my friends had already formulated a new vision for what the good life could be: we called it the subsistence perspective.

What are, in summary, the main features of this new vision: its worldview, its economic, political, cultural and social features?

For me, subsistence means the good life for all creatures in this world and good relations with all: with nature in her fullness. She is not our enemy, she is our mother; we are all children of Mother Earth. Men are not the masters over nature. The good life means that we admire her beauty, her incredible diversity, abundance, wildness, power; her generosity, her creativity and her capacity to generate and recreate life. As women we share this creativity. We, too, can create life and make it grow. And we pass life on to our children. For me, and for most children, nature is a permanent source of joy. All good life starts with the experience of this joy, the joy of being alive.

Such a world view requires a new concept of economy, of society, of culture, and of politics and philosophy. This new philosophy of life will lead to better relations between 'us' and 'others'. Instead of selfishness, there will be generosity, instead of competition, there will be cooperation. Instead of private property, there will be communal use of the Commons (land, water, air, knowledge), friendly relations with neighbours and foreigners, cooperation instead of division into isolated, alienated individuals; speaking together, sharing joy and sadness. Subsistence means self-provisioning, mutuality, communality – no person is an island – sharing responsibility for the community and for the planet.

There is one thing I consider to be absolutely necessary in creating a new concept of the good life. It is the end of the alienation of work. Today, for too many people, work is seen as a burden only. The good life is supposed to come after work, in the evening, on the weekend, during the holidays, after successfully passing this or that exam, after getting a car, or a house, or at the end of one's working life, or in some sort of after-life. But as we know, if this remains our philosophy of the good life, it will never come. For me, therefore, the good life must begin here on earth: while we work, not after work. We must enjoy the work process, the sensuality of touching the creatures we care for, children, old people, animals, plants. Or the materials we handle while working, whether it is with wood, vegetables, earth, iron, clothes or thousands of other things which we can touch. And not to forget the things we cannot touch, such as music, art, writing, thinking, discussing ... Through this type of work, we also learn the necessary skills and competence to live practically in this world; we learn 'Lebenstüchtigkeit'. After all, we not only have a head, we are whole sensuous beings (like other animals). We want to know for whom we work. We want to share the burden of our work with others, as well as the result of our work. We do not want to do alienated work. Work is not only a burden but enjoyment, too. Today, having a good life means, above all, an end to permanent stress and the endless pressure to do more in an ever-shorter amount of time. What we all therefore need is to first reduce our pace – in German this is expressed as 'de-speeding' (Entschleunigung). This 'de-speeding' will not occur unless we are able to say: "Now it is enough. I do not need more to live a good life." The constant greed determining our life – not only that of bankers – is due to the fact that most of us never say, "Now it is enough." Enoughness is the secret of the good life. As Gandhi said: "There is enough for our needs, but not for our greed."

The good life will not drop from heaven. We will have to create it, through self-provisioning (subsistence), self-reliance, self-organisation, responsibility and care for others and nature. Such an economy and society will leave no room for today's myth of permanent growth, money and the unlimited accumulation of capital. As we all know, this creed of permanent growth leads to unlimited wars.

And what will the good life look like at the end of one's life? I hope and wish that everybody on earth will be able to look back on their life and say, as my mother did, "Wasn't that a good life! Now it is enough. I'll go." Some may ask whether this picture of the good life is not a bit too rosy. After all, people have to work, and work hard, some under inhumane conditions to earn enough money to be able to live. True. We have to work. The good life does not mean we can sit under a tree and wait until ripe fruit falls into our open mouths. We have to work if we want to live. And this work is often rather hard and exhausting. But the good life means that the burden of work is not separated from enjoyment, satisfaction, creativity and a sense of community, because humans must live and work together. As I said before: the good life does not come after work, but must be part and parcel of work. The unhappiness in our modern societies stems mostly from the lack of enjoyment, both in our work as well as in our 'free time'. This is why those cited above were not happy. They saw no sense, no enjoyment in their work. It was only taken on as a necessary burden to achieve a 'better life'.

As I was pondering these questions on the good life in February 2010, two events took place simultaneously which had a bearing on my own life:

1. the horrible earthquake in Chile on 28 February;
2. the cyclonic windstorm Xynthia which raged across Europe and Germany, and also across my village, Steffeln, where I had gone to finish my Epilogue.

These two events made clear that I had to give up my abstract search for a concept of the good life, for here Life itself was threatened.

One of my brothers, Hermann, lives in Chile. I tried to ring him to find out whether the earthquake had affected him and his family. My other sisters and brothers in Germany also tried to reach him, in vain. There was no connection. I rushed to the TV and switched on to CNN to hear more about the earthquake, where it had its worst impact, which areas or cities were destroyed. I saw only ghastly pictures of destruction, people in despair running about, searching for loved ones, horrified by the loss of all their belongings. The city of Concepción was totally destroyed. My brother lives further north in Quilpue, but I could not reach him. There were pictures of Santiago. Even there, there was no water, no electricity, no telephone and no cars since a number of bridges over the main highway connecting the north of Chile with the south had been destroyed. Life had come to a standstill.

While I was still preoccupied with Chile, running to and fro between the telephone and TV, I heard about the second catastrophe, this time in Germany itself. A violent windstorm – which they called Xynthia – was raging across Europe and also across our country. From my window, I could see how the windstorm shook the trees, driving rain and snow ahead. And then I saw on TV what devastation this horrible storm had caused all over Germany. First I was not very worried. We are used to such spring storms. In fact I love storms. And I thought, all right, I'll just sit down and do what I have wanted to do for a long time. To read a book by Erich Fromm, *Marx's Concept of Man* (1961). I began to read the chapter 'Economic and Philosophical Manuscripts' and had problems understanding Marx's language and sometimes also what he really meant. I put many question marks in the margins and asked myself, what would Marx think was a 'good life'? One thing was clear, for him the good life – which he called socialism – would come with the development of technology and productive forces. He expected it from 'Enlightenment' and 'Progress'.

At that very moment, the lights went off. Here I was, sitting in the dark. First I thought a fuse had blown, but that was not the case. I still was not worried. I knew about power failures from India, where they happen regularly. For such occasions my brother-in-law in Calcutta has three or four hurricane lamps. They provide enough light to do the necessary things, the things that have to be done.

But I had no hurricane lamp. In our modern countries, nobody has hurricane lamps. I looked around and saw three half-burnt out candles. I also found a matchbox still dry enough to make light. But with this poor light I could not continue reading my Marx. Obviously, one needs electricity to read Marx's 'Economic and Philosophical Manuscripts'.

I then began to realise that my room was getting cold. The heating had gone out. I went to the kitchen, but the kitchen oven was cold, too; my freezer, doorbell and coffee machine – nothing was working any more. Here I was, in the dark and getting cold. I couldn't even make a cup of tea or take a bath. Was this the good life I had written about some minutes ago? What still worked, however, was the telephone. I tried again to reach my brother in Chile. No luck. Nobody had been able to reach him yet, either by landline, cell phone or computer. There was no communication in this communication society. There was silence and darkness all over.

All of a sudden, I began to see the light.

When Mother Nature shrugs her shoulders or begins to laugh, there are earthquakes in this or that corner of the world. (Or are these earthquakes a consequence of the experiments the Pentagon is carrying out as the 'ultimate weapon of war', as Rosalie Bertell suspects in her 2002 book *Planet Earth: The Latest Weapon of War*?) When such catastrophes happen, all of modern science and technology fall into a heap. None of the computers and other high-tech machines can work without electricity. No calculations and simulations can help to understand what has happened, let alone stop the disaster. Some people may be able to compensate for the lack of electricity with diesel generators. But for ordinary people this is not a solution because generators are too expensive and troublesome for home use. As a result, nothing works any more.

But what still worked was our concern for our brother, for the people in Concepción, and our love for all creatures affected by the catastrophe. Eventually, after many more attempts, a friend of my brother finally was able to reach Hermann in Chile. All right, I do agree that for such occasions some technology is necessary. But how much of it do we need? And what kind? I think that love, concern and friendly relations are definitely more important than technology.

The next day I wanted to return to Cologne. I usually take the train and my sister brings me to the railway station. But she rang me up and said, "You can't return to Cologne. The trains are not running. The rails are blocked by fallen trees. Nobody knows how long it will take for the trains to run again." I realised this could end up becoming a long stay in my village. 'Unintended De-Speeding', I thought. Not bad.

But what about food? People have to eat. And they need warmth. Basic needs! My heater was cold and there was no food left in my freezer. Then my cousin, Maria Agnes, rang me. As I mentioned earlier in this book, she and her husband live just across the street. She said, "If it's too cold, why don't you come over. We still have an old stove which can be fired with wood. And if you have nothing to eat – we still have bread. You know, some days ago I baked eighteen loaves of bread in our old baking oven. We won't starve. And, can you imagine, when the electricity failed, I wrote a poem" (Maria Agnes is a poet). "The title is 'Trapped in the prison of progress'. It's not quite done, but I'll give it to you when it's finished."

We both laughed. Wasn't that the epitome of all I had talked and written about for many years? My critique of our modern, industrialised society and the need for a new subsistence perspective? Are we not all 'trapped in the prison of progress'? Is there no longer any alternative to this modern 'free' world? Are we 'Westerners' really the model for the future for all people in the world? We no longer even have the survival tools and subsistence skills people used to have in the past to survive natural disasters and recreate life.

"Now we are beginning to understand how dependent we have become on all new technologies," Maria Agnes said. We asked ourselves what this power failure may mean for other people, particularly if the electricity stays out for several days or even a week. "What will those big farmers do with their modern cow factories with up to 1000 cows? How will they milk the cows if their milking machines are not functioning? My God, how will the poor creatures cope? They'll go mad and moan horribly. And of course, you cannot milk 1000 cows by hand. But Hans, my husband, can still milk his six cows."

We continued to imagine the consequences of Xynthia: what will those people who no longer have a kitchen garden do? Even out here in the country we have allowed ourselves to become totally dependent on the big supermarkets. Will the food begin to rot in their huge freezers? Will everything have to be thrown into the garbage? What will people eat? And what use will big tractors be to farmers, most of whom bought them on credit? Imagine what will happen when electricity not only fails, but becomes scarce or too expensive! None of the big farmers will survive such power and oil crises, no matter how much money the European Union ministers of agriculture may give them as subsidies. Even they will have to realise that you cannot feed a whole country with imported food. Would big farmers – and perhaps also managers of the industrial food factories – commit suicide as people did in Japan and the USA?

We stopped thinking about the consequences of a longer power outage. However, as I was 'trapped' in my village, I had to get some food. The next morning I went to Edith. Edith lives just across the street. At 84, she still runs her little country grocery shop. She is not only a very competent storekeeper, but has a tremendous amount of humour as well. Apart from her grandchildren and great-grand-children, her shop is her life. This is where everybody in the village meets. In this little shop you can find everything you need, from soap, butter, cheese, bread, newspapers, matchboxes to beer, wine, pencils and writing pads, and of course, sweets for the kids. Edith's shop also functions as the village 'newspaper'. All the local news, including people's death and sicknesses, their marriages, as well as news about relatives is exchanged here. People also talk 'big politics' in Edith's shop. They express their anger over, and contempt of, our politicians, political parties, the war in Afghanistan and Germany's insane participation in this criminal war.

On this morning the main theme was, of course, Xynthia, the violent windstorm, as well as the earthquake in Chile. Everyone in Edith's shop began to tell how they had survived the power outage. Local village people, tourists, and newcomers who had only recently settled down in the village, began to talk to each other. Everybody laughed about their own strategies to keep warm and have some light. They boasted about their new (old) subsistence technologies and their need to become more self-sufficient. "Do you still have an old kitchen oven? Do you still have a chimney in the house? Perhaps we have to begin to raise chickens again, or pigs, or hold cows, like Hans." Everybody laughed. "Are you crazy? We've turned all our pig sties into apartments for tourists. We can't go back to the Middle Ages.

Impossible! If there's no food here, we'll just go to the supermarket and get something to eat, because they get it from all over the world." "But how will they transport the tomatoes from Spain to Steffeln? Or keep them fresh?"

Edith interjected. "My two fridges have a limited capacity. Without electricity, I have to throw everything away. We don't even have a dung heap here in the village, except for the one Hans has. But I do have two kitchen ovens: a new electric one and an old one, fired by wood. I have an alternative." Others asked how long it would take until the trains from Trier to Cologne would run again. Many of the men work in Cologne and have to commute from Steffeln to Cologne on a daily basis. The distance is ninety kilometres each way.

People suddenly began to understand the connection between the earthquake in Chile, and the violent windstorm Xynthia in Germany. Of course, not in all its complexity, but emotionally. Then the discussion turned to the damage the storm had done to our forests. So many of our old birch trees and oaks had been blown over like match sticks. "How long will it take for these trees to grow again to such heights and be as thick as the old ones?" "At least a hundred years. We'll be dead by then!"

I was surprised about the concern everyone had for the consequences from the destruction of nature and the catastrophe in Chile. In spite of their fear of having to go 'back' to the old days, they began to understand that things could no longer go on as before. Some realised they had to recover or re-invent some old or new subsistence tools and skills. A little old woman standing among the customers said, "Yes, yes. Everything will come back again." What a wise sentence, I thought. One thing surprised me most. In spite of all the bad news we exchanged, there was no pessimism. People even laughed when they talked about alternatives to the disastrous situation. "Well, it's easy for us to laugh. Soon things will be all right again here. But what about the people in Chile? How long will it take for them until their lives become normal again?"

"But what is 'normal' in this crazy world?" I asked myself. Before the good life can come, we must protect and preserve Life itself on this planet, our Mother Earth.

When will the good life come? And where will it start?

Perhaps here, in Edith's grocery shop.

Maria Mies
Cologne, April 2010

Leipzig Appeal for Women's Food Security

Food Security in Women's Hands: Food Sovereignty for All
No to Novel Food and No to Patents on Life

For thousands of years, women have produced their own food and guaranteed food security for their children and communities. Even today, 80% of the work in local food production in Africa is done by women. In Asia, 50–60% and in Latin America, 30–40%. And everywhere in the world, women are responsible for food security at the household level. In patriarchal society, however, this work has been devalued.

All societies have survived historically because they provide food security for their people. This policy, however, has been subverted by the globalisation, trade liberalisation, industrialisation and commercialisation of all agricultural products under the auspices of the World Trade Organisation (WTO) and the World Bank/IMF.

In November 1996, the UN's Food and Agriculture Organisation will hold a World Food Summit in Rome. Its goal is to achieve 'universal food security' by the year 2020, eradicating hunger and malnutrition. However, the technical preparatory papers show that this objective is to be met through a continuation and extension of industrialisation and the worldwide trade of food. Food will be produced where labour is cheapest and environmental protections weakest. Poor communities will be forced to produce luxury products for export to rich countries and classes. These trends are already in effect, with devastating results: large-scale disappearance of peasants, the end of food self-sufficiency, reliance on monoculture, genetic manipulation of food, loss of biodiversity and ecological sustainability. The impoverished rural people who are displaced through this world agriculture policy end up as marginal members of society in overcrowded, mega-cities without work, hope or food. Although it is known that this policy is the cause of poverty and malnutrition, it is still proposed as a remedy for these very ills. The most vulnerable groups affected by these policies are poor rural women and children.

This policy also threatens food and safety in the North, where the family farm has been rapidly replaced by chemical-intensive agribusiness. Consumers have become virtual hostages to a handful of transnational food processing, and trading corporations. At the consumption end of the globalised food chain, women as housewives can no longer guarantee that they can give their families wholesome and healthy food.

In Peru, Chile and other countries of the South, women are fighting against this monopolistic policy, building their own communal food and health systems. Women in indigenous societies fight against land alienation, women in export-oriented agriculture oppose hazardous chemicals. They are supported by groups in the North who call for boycotts of these export products: flowers, vegetables, shrimps. Many groups in the North and the South reject genetic manipulation of food. We are told that this bio-technology is necessary to feed a growing world population. However, 60% of cereals are fed to animals in industrial farming systems. More and more land in the South is not used for nourishing local people, but for the production of luxury items for export.

The commercial interests connected with this technology are particularly apparent in the promotion of patenting of life forms – plants, animals and humans – under the protection of Trade Related Intellectual Property Rights (TRIPs). In the South, the patenting of life-forms is opposed because it is, in many cases, based on simple piracy: theft of indigenous biodiversity and local knowledge. In the North, many people oppose patents on life forms for ethical reasons.

On the consumer side, a majority of Europeans oppose genetically manipulated foods. Yet the European Union promotes such 'novel food', even refusing to label it, thus denying consumers their human and civil right to determine what they eat. Consumption in this so-called 'free market' becomes a matter of coercion.

Worldwide, women are resisting the policies which destroy the basis of their livelihood and food sovereignty. They also create alternatives to guarantee food security for their communities based on different principles and methods than those governing the dominant, profit-oriented global economy.

They are:

- localisation and regionalisation instead of globalisation
- non-violence instead of aggressive domination
- equity and reciprocity instead of competition
- respect for the integrity of nature and her species
- understanding humans as part of nature instead of as masters over nature
- protection of biodiversity in production and consumption

Food Security for all is not possible within a global market system based on the dogma of free trade, permanent growth, comparative advantage, competition and profit maximisation.

On the other hand, Food Security can be achieved if people within their local and regional economies feel responsible, both as producers and as consumers, for the ecological conditions of food production, distribution and consumption, and for the preservation of cultural and biological diversity where self-sufficiency is the main economic goal.

Our Food Security is too vital an issue to be left in the hands of a few transnational corporations with their profit motives, or up to national governments that increasingly lose control over food security decisions, or to a few – mostly male – national delegates at UN conferences who take decisions affecting all our lives.

Food Security must remain in women's hands everywhere!
And men must share the necessary work, be it paid or unpaid.
We have a right to know what we eat!
No to Novel Food and No to Patents on Life
We will resist those who force us to produce and consume in ways
*   that destroy nature and ourselves!*

Leipzig, 20 June, 1996
Maria Mies, Vandana Shiva

Bibliography

Andrews, Lori B. (1986) "My Body, My Property" *The Hastings Center Report* 28, pp. 28–37.

Arditti, Rita, Renate Duelli Klein and Shelley Minden (Eds) (1984) *Test-Tube Women: What Future for Motherhood?* Pandora Press, London (translated as *Retortenmütter*, Rowohlt Verlag, Reinbek bei Hamburg, 1985).

Aust, Stefan (1985/1997) *Der Baader Meinhof Komplex.* Hoffmann und Campe, Hamburg.

beiträge zur feministischen theorie und praxis (1978) "Erste Orientierung" (Where to from here: Taking stock) 1/1978.

beiträge zur feministischen theorie und praxis (1983) "Gegen welchen Krieg – Für welchen Frieden" (Against which war – For which peace?) 8/1983.

beiträge zur feministischen theorie und praxis (1985) "Frauen zwischen Auslese und Ausmerze" (Women between selection and elimination) 14/1985.

Bennholdt-Thomsen, Veronika (1981) "Subsistence Production and Extended Reproduction" in Kate Young et al. (Eds) *Marriage and the Market.* CSE-Books, London.

Bennholdt-Thomsen, Veronika, Maria Mies and Claudia von Werlhof (1983) *Frauen, die letzte Kolonie: Zur Hausfrauisierung der Arbeit.* Rowohlt Verlag, Reinbek bei Hamburg and Rotpunktverlag, Zurich (1992).

Bennholdt-Thomsen, Veronika and Maria Mies (1997) *Eine Kuh für Hillary: Die Subsistenzperspektive.* Frauenoffensive, Munich.

Bertell, Rosalie (2002) *Planet Earth: The Latest Weapon of War.* Quartet Books, London.

Birk, Angelika/Irene Stoehr (1987) "Der Fortschritt entlässt seine Töchter" in Die GRÜNEN im Bundestag/AK Frauenpolitik (Eds) *Frauen und Ökologie. Gegen den Machbarkeitswahn.* Kölner Volksblatt Verlag, Cologne.

Boggs, Grace Lee (2005) 'Living for Change'. Lecture held during the Workshop 'Self-Organisation Processes – Self-Sufficiency as a Mutual Undertaking' 21–23 October, Cologne, Germany.

Bornemann, Michael (1841) *Beitrag zur Geschichte der Ardennen,* Part I. Druck und Kommissions DEBIT der Fr. Lintz'schen Buchhandlung, Trier.

Briffault, Robert (1927) *The Mothers: The Matriarchal Theory of Social Origins.* George Allen & Unwin, London.

Brunner, Otto (1966) "Das 'ganze Haus' und die alteuropäische Ökonomik" *Familie und Gesellschaft.* Tübingen, pp. 23–56.

Bühler, George (1886) *Sacred Books of the East: Laws of Manu* (Volume XXV) <http://www.sacred-texts.com/hin/manu.htm> (accessed 15 July, 2009).

Burckhardt, Lucius (1987) *Falt-Plan für die Fahrt nach Tahiti.* Kassel University Press, Kassel.

Butenschön, Rainer and Eckart Spoo (Eds) *Töten-Plündern-Herrschen. Wege zu neuen Kriegen.* VSA-Verlag, Hamburg.

Chattopadhyaya, Debiprasad (1959) *A Study in Ancient Indian Materialism.* People's Publishing House, New Delhi.

Corea, Gena (1984) "Wie durch die neuen Reproduktionstechnologien das Bordell-Modell auf die menschliche Reproduktion angewandt werden kann" *beiträge zur feministischen theorie und praxis* 12/1984.

Corea, Gena (1985) *The Mother Machine. Reproductive Technologies from Artificial Insemination to Artificial Wombs.* Harper & Row, New York.

Dalla Costa, Maria (1972) *Die Macht der Frauen und der Umsturz der Gesellschaft.* Merve Verlag, Berlin.

Diederich, Ellen (2007) "Emma zum Dreißigsten" *Ossietzky* 3/2007; <http://www.sopos.org/aufsaetze/45eaba1d0e10b/1.phtml> (accessed 29 December, 2009).

Engels, Friedrich (1884) *The Origins of the Family, Private Property and the State.* Marx and Engels Internet Archive <http://www.marxists.org/

archive/marx/works/1884/origin-family/index.htm> (accessed 9 April, 2010).

Frauenhaus Köln (1980) *Nachrichten aus dem Ghetto Liebe*. Verlag Jugend und Politik, Frankfurt.

Freire, Paulo (1970/2000) *Pedagogy of the Oppressed*. Continuum Publishing Company, New York, London.

Friedan, Betty (1963) *The Feminine Mystique*. Dell Publishing Company, New York.

Fromm, Erich (1961) *Marx's Concept of Man*. Frederick Unger Publishing, New York.

Galtung, Johan (1975) *Strukturelle Gewalt – Beiträge zur Friedens- und Konfliktforschung*. Verlag Rowohlt, Reinbek bei Hamburg.

Gambaroff, Marina et al., (1986) *Tschernobyl hat unser Leben verändert. Vom Ausstieg der Frauen*. Verlag Rowohlt, Reinbek bei Hamburg.

Gehendges, Friedrich (Ed) *Eiflia Illustrata*, Vol. II (1982). Translated from Latin into German by Georg Bärsch. Verlag Zeller, Osnabrück (reprint).

Gen-Archiv (1988) "Police Raid on Gene Archive – News from West Germany" *Reproductive and Genetic Engineering: Journal of International Feminist Analysis* Volume 1, No 1. pp. 103–105. <http://www.finrrage.org/pdf_files/RepTech%20General/Police_Raid _on_Gene_Archive_West_Germany.pdf> (accessed 24 May, 2010).

Griffin, Susan (1978) *Women and Nature: The Roaring in Her*. Harper & Row, New York.

Hardin, Garrett (1968) "The Tragedy of the Commons" *Science* 162, pp. 1243–1248.

Hawthorne, Susan (2002) *Wild Politics: Feminism, Globalisation and Bio/diversity*. Spinifex Press, North Melbourne.

Hawthorne, Susan (2004) "The Political Uses of Obscurantism: Gender, Mainstreaming and Intersectionality" *Development Bulletin*, 89, pp. 87–91 <http://devnet.anu.edu.au/GenderPacific/pdfs/20_gen _mainstream_hawthorne.pdf>

Hegel, Friedrich (1807) *Phenomenology of Spirit*. Translated by A. V. Miller with analysis of the text and foreword by J. N. Findlay. Clarendon Press, Oxford (1977).

Hegel, Friedrich (1837) *Lectures on the Philosophy of History.* Marxists Internet Archive <http://www.marxists.org/reference/archive/hegel/works/hi/hiconten.htm> (accessed 9 April, 2010).

Heinberg, Richard (2003) *The Party Is Over: Oil, War and the Fate of Industrial Societies.* New Society Publishers, Gabriola Island, British Columbia.

Höffner, Josef Cardinal (1969) *Ehe und Familie im Licht des Glaubens.* Cologne Archdiocese, Cologne.

Huizer, Gerrit (1973) "The A-Social Role of Social Scientists in Under-developed Countries: Some Ethical Considerations" *Sociologus,* Volume 23, No. 2, pp. 165–177.

Isla, Ana (2003) "Women and Biodiversity as Capital Accumulation: An Eco-Feminist View" *Socialist Studies Bulletin* 69, pp. 21–34.

Isla, Ana (2009) "Who Pays for the Kyoto Protocol?" in Salleh, Ariel (Ed) *Eco-sufficiency and Global Justice: Women Write Political Ecology.* Spinifex Press, North Melbourne; Pluto Press, London, pp. 199–217.

Jayawardena, Kumari (1982/1986) *Feminism and Nationalism in the Third World.* Institute of Social Studies, The Hague; Zed Books, London.

Karve, Iravati (1953) *Kinship Organisation in India.* Asia Publishing House, Bombay, Delhi, Madras, Lucknow, London, New York.

Luxemburg, Rosa (1913/1951) *Accumulation of Capital.* (W. Stark, Ed). Routledge and Kegan Paul, London.

Mandelbaum, Kurt (1978) "Sozialdemokratie und Imperialismus" in Mandelbaum, Kurt *Sozialdemokratie und Leninismus, Zwei Aufsätze.* Wagenbach, Berlin.

Marx, Karl (1845a) *The German Ideology.* <http://www.marxists.org/archive/marx/works/1845/german-ideology/ch01a.htm>

Marx, Karl (1845b/1977) "Theses on Feuerbach" in *Selections of Karl Marx and Frederic Engels. Selected Works in Three Volumes.* Fortu-printing, Moscow.

Marx, Karl and Friedrich Engels (1846) *Marx Engels Complete Works* Volume 6. The Marx/Engels Internet Archive, <http://www.marxists.org/archive/marx/works/1846/02/20.htm> (accessed 28 July, 2009).

Marx, Karl (1848) *Manifesto of the Communist Party.* Marx and Engels Internet Archive <http://www.marxists.org/archive/marx/works/1848/communist-manifesto/ch01.htm> (accessed 9 April, 2010).

Marx, Karl (1852) *The Eighteenth Brumaire of Louis Bonaparte*. The Marx/Engels Internet Archive <http://www.marxists.org/archive/marx/works/1846/02/20.htm> (accessed 28 July, 2009).

Merchant, Carolyn (1980) *The Death of Nature: Women, Ecology and the Scientific Revolution*. Harper & Row, San Francisco.

Meyer-Renschhausen, Elisabeth (2004) *Unter dem Müll der Acker. Community Gardens in New York City*. Ulrike Helmer Verlag, Sulzbach/Taunus.

Mies, Maria (1967/1968) "Why German?" *Bulletin* Volume XXVIII, Parts III and IV, Deccan College Research Institute, Pune.

Mies, Maria (1973) *Indische Frauen zwischen Unterdrückung und Befreiung*. Anton Hain Verlag, Meisenheim; EVA-Verlag, Hamburg (republished 1986).

Mies, Maria (1978) "Methodische Postulate zur Frauenforschung – dargestellt am Problem der Gewalt gegen Frauen" *beiträge zur feministischen theorie und praxis* 1/1978.

Mies, Maria (1980) *Indian Women and Patriarchy*. Concept Publishers, New Delhi.

Mies, Maria (1981) *Feminism in Europe: Liberal and Socialist Strategies 1789–1919*. Institute of Social Studies, The Hague.

Mies, Maria (1982a) *The Lace Makers of Narsapur: Indian Housewives Produce for the World Market*. Zed Books, London.

Mies, Maria and Rhoda Reddock (1982b) *National Liberation and Women's Liberation*. Institute of Social Studies, The Hague.

Mies, Maria (1982c) *Fighting on Two Fronts. Women's Struggles and Research*. Institute of Social Studies, The Hague.

Mies, Maria (1983a) "Towards a Methodology for Feminist Research" in Gloria Bowles and Renate Duelli Klein (Eds) *Theories of Women's Studies*. Routledge & Kegan Paul, London, pp. 117–139.

Mies, Maria (1983b) "Die gesellschaftlichen Ursprünge der geschlechtlichen Arbeitsteilung" in Claudia von Werlhof/Maria Mies/Veronika Bennholdt-Thomsen (Eds) *Frauen die Letzte Kolonie. Zur Hausfrauisierung der Arbeit*. Verlag Rowohlt, Reinbek bei Hamburg and Rotpunktverlag, Zurich (1992).

Mies, Maria (1983c) "Frauenbefreiung und nationaler Befreiungskampf – Geht das zusammen?" *beiträge zur feministischen theorie und praxis* 8/1983.

Mies, Maria (1984) *Indian Women in Subsistence and Agricultural Labour*, World Employment Programme (WEP), Working Paper No. 34, International Labour Office, Geneva.

Mies, Maria (1986a/1999) *Patriarchy and Accumulation on a World Scale: Women in the International Division of Labour*. Zed Books, London; Spinifex Press, North Melbourne; *Patriarchat und Kapital: Frauen in der internationalen Arbeitsteilung*. Rotpunktverlag, Zurich (1988).

Mies, Maria (1986b) 'Frauenforschung: Wissenschaft und Verantwortlichkeit'. Lecture held on 19 November 1986 in Fässler, Hildegard (Ed). *Das Tabu der Gewalt*. University of Innsbruck, pp. 214–215.

Mies, Maria (1986c) "Wer machte uns die Natur zur Feindin?" in Marina Gambaroff et al., (1986) *Tschernobyl hat unser Leben verändert. Vom Ausstieg der Frauen*. Verlag Rowohlt, Reinbek bei Hamburg.

Mies, Maria (1987a) "Die Befreiung vom Konsum: Wege zu einer ökologischen und feministischen Gesellschaft" *die Verbraucherinitiative*, Bonn.

Mies, Maria (1987b) "Vom Individuum zum Dividuum, oder im Supermarkt der käuflichen Körperteile" *tageszeitung*, Berlin, 1 August, 1987.

Mies, Maria (1987c) "Wissenschaft – Ethik – Gewalt" *tageszeitung*, Berlin, 1 August, 1987.

Mies, Maria, Veronika Bennholdt-Thomsen and Claudia von Werlhof (1988) *Women: The Last Colony*. Zed Books, London.

Mies, Maria (1988) "From the individual to the dividual: In the supermarket of 'reproductive alternatives'" *Reproductive and Genetic Engineering: Journal of International Feminist Analysis* Volume 1, No. 3, pp. 225–237 <http://www.finrrage.org/pdf_files/RepTech%20 General/In_the_Supermarket_of_Reproductive_Alternatives.pdf> (accessed 29 December, 2009).

Mies, Maria (1989) "Selbstbestimmung – Das Ende einer Utopie?" in Paula Bradish et al. (Eds) *Frauen gegen Gen- und Reproduktionstechnologien*. Frauenoffensive, Munich.

Mies, Maria and Vandana Shiva (1993) *Ecofeminism.* Zed Books, London; Spinifex Press, North Melbourne; *Ökofeminismus, Praxis und Theorie.* Rotpunktverlag, Zurich (1995).

Mies, Maria and Claudia von Werlhof (Eds) (1998) *Lizenz zum Plündern. Das Multilaterale Abkommen über Investitionen MAI – Globalisierung der Konzernherrschaft – und was wir dagegen tun können.* EVA Taschenbücher, Hamburg.

Mies, Maria (1999) "Globalisierung der Wirtschaft und Gewalt gegen Frauen" in *Frauenfrust, Frauenlust, Beiträge zu einer Ökonomie aus feministischer Sicht.* Bundesverband der KAB (Ed), Ketteler Verlag, Bornheim.

Mies, Maria and Veronika Bennholdt-Thomsen (1999) *The Subsistence Perspective: Beyond the Globalised Economy.* Zed Books, London; Spinifex Press, North Melbourne.

Mies, Maria (2001) *Globalisierung von unten. Der Kampf gegen die Herrschaft der Konzerne.* EVA, Hamburg.

Mies, Maria (2003) "Von der Lizenz zum Plündern zur Lizenz zum Töten" in Rainer Butenschön and Eckart Spoo (Eds) *Töten – Plündern – Herrschen. Wege zu neuen Kriegen.* VSA-Verlag, Hamburg.

Mies, Maria (2004) *Krieg ohne Grenzen. Die neue Kolonialisierung der Welt.* Papyrossa Verlag, Cologne.

Mies, Maria (2005a) "Globalisierung und religiöser Fundamentalismus" *Infobrief* No. 18: Gott und die Globalisierung. Netzwerk gegen Konzernherrschaft und neoliberale Politik, Cologne.

Mies, Maria (2005b) "Der Bluff mit dem Gender-Mainstreaming" *Infobrief* No. 21. Netzwerk gegen Konzernherrschaft und neoliberale Politik, Cologne.

Mies, Maria (2006) "A Global Feminist Perspective on Research" in Sharlene Nagy Hesse-Biber (Ed) *Handbook of Feminist Research: Theory and Praxis.* Sage Publications, London.

Nietzsche, Friedrich (translated by Walter Kaufmann, 1974) *The Gay Science.* Random House, New York.

Oestreich, Heide (2008) "Keine *beiträge zur feministischen theorie und praxis* mehr" *die tageszeitung*, 22 February, 2008.

Politisches Nachtgebet (1969) *Teufelskreis Entwicklungshilfe*, 2 February, 1969, Antoniterkirche, Cologne (pamphlet).

Politisches Nachtgebet (1971) *Die Emanzipation der Frauen*, 5 January, 1971, Antoniterkirche, Cologne (pamphlet).

Politisches Nachtgebet (1972) *Bangladesch: Ende oder Anfang?*, 11 and 12 January, 1972, Antoniterkirche, Cologne (pamphlet).

Roy, Arundhati (2010) "Walking with the Comrades" *Outlook Magazine*, 29 March, 2010. <http://www.outlookindia.com/printarticle.aspx?264738> (accessed 8 May, 2010).

Schmauch, Ulrike (1983) "Selbstkritische Überlegungen zu Frauen-friedensaktionen" *beiträge zur feministischen theorie und praxis* 8/1983, pp. 116–118.

Shapiro, Norman R. (1998) *One Hundred and One Poems by Paul Verlaine: A Bilingual Edition*. University of Chicago Press, Chicago.

Shiva, Vandana (1999) "The Historic Significance of Seattle" 12 December, 1999. Co-globalizing gaia's children, <http://www.ratical.org/co-globalize/HSoS.html> (accessed 6 December, 2009).

Shiva, Vandana (2003a) Speech given at 'Women Stop GATS' Conference, Cologne, 9 May, 2003 <http://www.nadir.org/nadir/initiativ/agp/gender/antipat/vshiva.htm> (accessed 17 December, 2009).

Shiva, Vandana (2003b) "Multis privatisieren Indiens Flüsse" *Infobrief* No. 13, Cologne.

Sittirak, Sinith (1998) *The Daughters of Development: Women in a Changing Environment*. Zed Books, London; Spinifex Press, North Melbourne.

Sölle, Dorothee (1967) *Christ the Representative: An Essay in Theology After the 'Death of God'*. SCM Press, London.

Sölle, Dorothee and Fulbert Steffensky (1969). *Politisches Nachtgebet in Köln*. Kreuzverlag, Stuttgart.

Sölle, Dorothee (1999) *Gegenwind, Erinnerungen*. Piperverlag, Munich.

Stolzenberg, Margit (Ed) (2000) *Elf europäische Frauen im Interview*. Trafo Verlag, Berlin.

Strom, Holger (1977) *Friedlich in die Katastrophe. Eine Dokumentation über Atomkraftwerke* (self-published).

Third World Network (1999) "Members of International Civil Society Opposing a Millenium Round or a New Round of Comprehensive

Trade Negotiations" <http://www.twnside.org.sg/title/wtomr-cn.htm> (accessed 6 December, 2009).

von Werlhof, Claudia (1991) "Kaputt durch Naturschutz" in Claudia von Werlhof *Männliche Natur und künstliches Geschlecht. Texte zur Erkenntniskrise der Moderne.* Wiener Frauenverlag, Wien.

von Werlhof, Claudia (1983/1992) "Der Proletarier ist tot. Lang lebe die Hausfrau" in Claudia von Werlhof/Maria Mies/Veronika Bennholdt-Thomsen (Eds) *Frauen, die letzte Kolonie. Zur Hausfrauisierung von Arbeit.* Rowohlt Verlag, Reinbek bei Hamburg (1983) and Rotpunktverlag, Zurich (1992).

von Werlhof, Claudia (2004) "Vom Wirtschaftskrieg zur Kriegswirtschaft: die Waffen der 'Neuen Welt Ordnung.'" Beitrag in Maria Mies *Krieg ohne Grenzen*, PapyRossa, Cologne.

Index

If you would like to know more about Spinifex Press,
write for a free catalogue or visit our home page.

SPINIFEX PRESS
PO Box 212,
North Melbourne,
Victoria 3051, Australia
http://www.spinifexpress.com.au